This book is due on the last date stamped below.
Failure to return books on the date due may result
in assessment of overdue fees.

FINES	.50 per day	

RETURN PASSAGES

Return Passages

Great American Travel Writing
1780–1910

Larzer Ziff

YALE UNIVERSITY PRESS

NEW HAVEN AND LONDON

Designed by Rebecca Gibb. Set in Linotype Centennial type by Keystone Typesetting, Inc., Orwigsburg, Pennsylvania. Printed in the United States of America by Sheridan Books, Chelsea, Michigan.

Library of Congress Cataloging-in-Publication Data
Ziff, Larzer, 1927–
Return passages : great American travel writing, 1780–1910 :
American travel writing from exploration to art / Larzer Ziff.
p.   cm.
Includes bibliographical references and index.
ISBN 0-300-08236-3 (cloth : alk. paper)
1. Travelers' writings, American—History and criticism. 2. American prose literature—19th century—History and criticism. 3. Voyages and travels—Historiography. 4. Americans—Travel—Historiography. 5. Travel in literature. I. Title.
PS366.T73 Z54 2001
818'.30949104—dc21
00-032099

A catalogue record for this book is available from the British Library.

The paper in this book meets the guidelines for permanence and durability of the Committee on Production Guidelines for Book Longevity of the Council on Library Resources.

10 9 8 7 6 5 4 3 2

For Ruth
Born Cosmopolite

Travelling. This makes men wiser, but less happy. When men of sober age travel, they gather knolege which they may apply usefully for their country, but they are subject ever after to recollections mixed with regret, their affections are weakened by being extended over more objects, & they learn new habits which cannot be gratified when they return home.

Thomas Jefferson: Paris, 1787

There comes a time when one set of customs, wherever it may be found, grows to seem to you about as provincial as another; and then I suppose it may be said of you that you have become a cosmopolite. You have formed the habit of comparing, of looking for points of difference and of resemblance, for present and absent advantage, for the virtues that go with certain defects, and the defects that go with certain virtues.

Henry James: Paris, 1878

Contents

———◆———

Acknowledgments

Amy K. Presser and John Tofanelli of the Johns Hopkins University Libraries assisted in the gathering of illustrations; Theo Davis solved a vexing research problem; Jean McGarry was a sympathetic and encouraging reader; Sharon Cameron gave me the benefit of her extensive knowledge of Henry James; and Linda Ziff followed the book's development with her customary insistence upon clarity and impatience with superficiality.

RETURN PASSAGES

Introduction

In January 1783, as the American Revolution was drawing to the official conclusion that would be reached by the signing of the Treaty of Paris in that year, the Connecticut State Assembly received a "Memorial" from a native son who offered a brief—three long sentences—but extraordinary account of himself before making his petition. John Ledyard explained that in 1774 he had sailed to England on a New York merchant ship, hoping there to "mend his fortune" but while in Bristol was apprehended by "a kind of Police" and compelled either to ship himself for the coast of Guinea (the notorious locale of the infamous slave trade and a region of deadly fevers) or enter into the British army. Young, inexperienced, and destitute, he said, he chose the army as the lesser of the evils, but when ordered to Boston in 1775 asked for and was granted another posting because he was a New Englander and would not fight against his countrymen. Stationed at Plymouth in the following year, he saw the ships preparing for Captain Cook's third voyage to the Pacific come into the harbor and seized the opportunity to free himself from the prospect of returning to America as her enemy. Prompted "by curiosity & disinterested enterprise"[1] he enlisted on the expedition. When he returned from the South Seas (the voyage had departed in July 1776— Ledyard thus setting forth in the month the colonies declared independence—and dropped anchor back in Deptford in October 1779), Ledyard petitioned the Admiralty for discharge. This was denied and in 1782 he was sent on a tour of duty to America "where he remained on board a British frigate many months before he could meet with an opportunity to renounce the service & return to his country." It seems apparent that just as he had sought to avoid service in America during the years of combat so when hostilities were ended he welcomed the opportunity to return there and effect his escape from the service.

After giving this concise, third-person account of himself, every detail of which arouses far more curiosity than it satisfies, Ledyard went on to assure the assemblymen that despite his service in the English navy he was a loyal American both politically and culturally, that, indeed, if he had acquired "any merit by his conduct, his travel, or his writings, they are all due to his country." By "due to" he implied both that the merit was derived from and should be assigned to his native land. Most evidently he intended this claim to prepare the assemblymen to act favorably on the requests that followed, but this consideration need not impugn either its sincerity or its truthfulness. American colonials of Ledyard's time were British subjects and when in England were also, if they chose, Englishmen, in speech, manners, and outlook; in, that is, their character as well as their characteristics. One has only to consider, for example, the ease with which Benjamin West of Pennsylvania or John Singleton Copley of Massachusetts settled into London society; or Benjamin Franklin's plan, before he read the premonitory signals of the coming revolution, to live in England in his retirement; or the strange career of the American-born Israel Potter, whose struggle against anomie during decades of residence in England was so to attract Herman Melville that he rewrote Potter's life as a novel. Americans could elect not to be American or, as those who did so choose might have contended, not to become provincial but remain English. Indeed, Lieutenant John Gore, who also sailed on Cook's third voyage, was American born yet, as Ledyard knew, thoroughly English. It was more difficult, in fact, to remain American than to become English under the conditions of service on an English vessel with its demand for assimilation in so many areas of daily life. Ledyard's sense that his conduct and achievements were American did not, then, derive simply from the accident of his birthplace. He had elected to maintain that identity, and as his later career was to indicate, for him this meant, among other things, the maintenance of an outlook that did not confuse social distinctions of class or military distinctions of rank with differences in natural worth.

Pointing out that his desertion from the British frigate, an "abrupt departure" as he phrased it, had left him without means, Ledyard's petition closed with two requests. First, generally and somewhat vaguely he asked that the governor and legislature offer some employment that would enable him to be of service to his country in that time of war while providing him with sufficient funds to move in the circle to which he felt he belonged. Nothing seems to have come of this request.

But more particularly and far more momentously:

> He also humbly intreats the honourable Assembly to take into consideration a history of the memorialists last voyage round the world which he proposes to publish in a manner which he thinks will not only be meritorious in himself but may be essentially usefull to America in general but particularly to the northern States by opening a most valuable trade across the north pacific Ocean to China & the east Indies—and that the memorialist may have the exclusive right of publishing this said Journal or history in this State for such a term as shall be thot fit.

No copyright law existed in any of the newly united states but the committee appointed by the assembly to study the matter promptly reported that it appeared reasonable and just that Ledyard should have exclusive rights to his work for a reasonable term. Moreover, "as it appears that several Gentlemen of Genius & reputation are also about to make similar Applications" they took the opportunity to propose an "Act for the encouragement of Literature and Genius," wishing, as the preamble declared, to encourage men of learning and genius to do honor to their country and service to mankind.[2] Passed within the same month as his petition, the act granted Ledyard and all future authors the sole privilege of printing and vending their works for fourteen years, renewable for another fourteen, and set forth penalties for violators. It became the model for the copyright legislation passed in other states as well as the federal copyright law of 1790.

Thus protected, Ledyard sold the manuscript of *A Journal of Captain Cook's Last Voyage to the Pacific Ocean and in Quest of a North-West Passage*[3] to the Hartford printer and bookseller, Nathaniel Patten, for twenty guineas. It appeared in two parts in June and July of 1783 and was immediately popular because the public appetite for news of the voyage on which the celebrated Cook had been killed and supposedly cannibalized was large. The official, two-volume account based on the journals of Cook and Captain James King, who succeeded to the command of the voyage after Cook's immediate successor, Clerke, also died, was not published until the following year. Indeed so popular was Ledyard's *Journal* that he was also commonly thought to be the author of the only other widely read account to precede the authorized version. Published anonymously in London in 1781 with a title similar to Ledyard's, this was *Journal of Captain Cook's Last Voyage to the Pacific Ocean on Discovery Performed in the Years 1776, 1777, 1778, 1779.*

Since somewhat more than twenty percent of the Ledyard *Journal* repeated verbatim material in the earlier, anonymous London *Journal,* there was ground for a belief in identical authorship. But one could also read in the London *Journal* that on the homeward voyage "the Commodore called all hands aft, and ordered them to deliver up their journals and every writing, remark, or memorandum that any of them had made of any particular respecting the voyage, on pain of the severest punishment"[4] and suspect that the author was an Englishman whose anonymity was intended as protection against the "punishment" that might follow from his publishing in advance of the authorized version.

4

Moreover, most of what Ledyard reprinted verbatim from the London *Journal* consisted of navigational data, details of longitude and latitude, especially during the homeward voyage, information accessible to officers who could consult the logbook but not to members of the rank and file such as he. Still, it was not until the twentieth century that Ledyard's authorship of the London work was definitively disproved and that of Lieutenant John Rickman established.[5]

The amusing fact is, then, that more than a fifth of the first American book to benefit from copyright legislation was taken verbatim from a previous work, was, that is, in violation of the spirit of the copyright its author sought for himself[6] and, in the event, established for all who followed as well. Yet plagiarism seems too harsh a word to apply to Ledyard's use of the Rickman work because in the main he copied objective data, not subjective narration. He gave his own account of the voyage, no one else's.

Other accounts of Cook's third voyage appeared after the authorized one of 1784 as public—to be succeeded eventually by academic—interest remained high. (Indeed, yet another firsthand recollection of the voyage was printed for the first time as recently as 1982.[7]) Ledyard's is certainly not to be distinguished from them on the basis of its greater accuracy nor of the scientific use to which his observations can be put. As Marshall Sahlins, the distinguished scholar of the anthropology of Cook's encounters in the Pacific, bluntly notes, "Ledyard is not the most reliable of the Cook chroniclers."[8] Yet his book rewards more attention and deserves more credit than it has received because of both the intrinsic appeal of his narrative and the extrinsic fact of its qualifying as the first American travel book. "First," to be sure, is open to many definitions. Explorers' accounts of America from the sixteenth century forward, for example, can be called "American" travel books, and in the colonial period Americans wrote although did not at that time publish descriptions of their travels.[9] Still, in addition to the literal fact of its being the first travel account by an American to be published in the new nation, Ledyard's narrative stands out because he deliberately brought to his experiences, especially his encounters with native peoples who had never before been made the subjects of written discourse, a self-consciously American attitude. This Americanness was defined both in contrast to the English culture it resembled and in comparison with the Pacific-island cultures from which it so apparently differed.

Perhaps an even more vital element in the claim that can be made for the singularity of Ledyard's book concerns his motive for seeking the copyright. In his memorial to the assembly he referred to the "merit" that might possibly be attributed not only to himself but to his writings, and he further talked of his want of money. The two were put together when he sought exclusive rights to the vending of his work. Ledyard, that is, regarded his writing as an important source of income and thus pioneered the field of professional authorship in America, blazing the trail with a travel narrative.

Beginning with the writings of John Ledyard, this book traces the history of distinguished American travel writing from the end of the Revolution to the outbreak of the First World War. It follows the evolution of this popular and critically undervalued genre through its major stages from description of the exotic and reports of discovery by those who traveled to explore the unknown and then wrote of their travels, to those who wrote for a living and traveled principally in order to acquire material for their consciously literary narratives. In the great travel books that mark these stages, however, exploration and artistry are never mutually exclusive. Discoveries depicted by an astute traveler invoke emotional as well as intellectual responses, and familiar scenes when passed through the sensibility of an accomplished writer become matters of thought as well as occasions for feeling.

The history of travel's relationship to writing extends so far back into antiquity that as one pursues it the two blur into one another. To travel is to survey; "theory" is derived from the Greek word for viewing a sight the way a traveler (in Greek a "theor") does. Until the rise of the local university in eighteenth-century Europe, travel was the principal means for the education of a gentleman, and such travel implied keeping a journal in which what one learned along the route was recorded.[10]

6

Most obviously the new knowledge a traveler sets down in writing is of other places and other peoples. But together with such knowledge travel also promotes a deepened self-knowledge and this, too, forms part of the travel narrative. Away from the familiar surroundings that formed and sustain his sense of himself, the traveler becomes radically aware of where he ends and all else begins; his individuality is, as it were, thrust upon him, and as a result the written account of what he sees and does serves inevitably to affirm the self he has discovered in the process of moving among strangers.[11] Although the consistent popularity of travel narratives from antiquity to the present certainly stems from their bringing the foreign, the exotic, and the fabulous home to sedentary readers, the power of great travel writing resides as well in the author's capacity to present his heightened self-awareness in a manner that serves to move readers to question the unexamined familiarities of their own lives.

In seventeenth- and eighteenth-century America the popular appeal of travel narratives was increased by the prevalence of religious, moral, and even political prejudices against fiction as at best a waste of time and at worst sinful lying. Accounts of adventures in faraway places fed the appetite for sensation and the capacity for wonder that fiction met, and yet were exempted from the prohibitions against fiction because they were "true" and so educational. Moreover, the original settlers had arrived with expectations formed from their reading of the accounts of earlier travelers to North America and themselves added to this literature in letters they sent to the homeland. If America is a nation of immigrants, it may further be noted that the consumption and the production of travel literature were never far apart in the immigrant experience.

As successive American-born generations appeared and a distinctly different American society emerged, its members, defensively conscious of their want of national traditions yet aggressively proud of their new ways, maintained a particularly strong interest in measuring those ways against the manner in which other societies met the problems of living the daily life. They could not satisfy this by popping across a border but they could by following the travel reports of their fellow Americans.

Estimating the book market in early nineteenth-century America, the head of Harper & Brothers, America's largest publishing firm, said, "Travels sell about the best of anything we get hold of. . . . They don't always go with a rush, like a novel by a celebrated author, but they sell longer, and in the end pay better."[12] Other publishers agreed, and travelers found that even though their journeys had been undertaken for reasons of business or health their accounts found print with relative ease.

But that the travel narrative could maintain its popularity into the twentieth-century era of scientific investigation led so eminent a thinker as Claude Lévi-Strauss to express bewilderment at the appeal it continued to exert. What was important to him was the object of travel—in his case the anthropological study of a primitive culture—and "The fact that so much effort and expenditure has to be wasted on reaching the object of our studies bestows no value on that aspect of our profession, and should be seen rather as its negative side." He viewed the modern travel book as a string of uninformative personal anecdotes interspersed with "scraps of hackneyed information which have appeared in every textbook during the past fifty years."[13]

The kind of travel narrative to which Lévi-Strauss made such objection, one that seeks primarily to entertain rather than inform, emerged in the late eighteenth century in intentional contrast to the rise of science. As explorers acquired increasingly precise ways of identifying the geographical location, classifying the fauna and flora, and constructing the ethnographic portraits of the lands and peoples they encountered, and their narratives bent more and more in that direction and away from subjectivity, a counternarrative arose that emphasized traveling as an art rather than a science. The picturesque traveler wrote solely for the entertainment of readers. "Earlier travelers, to be certain, had described natural settings," one student of the subject has written, "but always with the objective of joining instruction with pleasure, and never with the picturesque aim of arousing in their readers an emotional response to the beauties of a particular geographical location."[14] Now no matter how familiar, even hackneyed, the sight or situation encountered, the challenge for the picturesque traveler was to reinvent it through a feeling literary response. Laurence Sterne's *Sentimental Journey Through France and Italy* (1769) provided the supreme model, and the members of the countless army of his successors are the eminently eligible targets of Lévi-Strauss's rancor.

Yet the disengagement of picturesque from scientific writing has never been complete, as Lévi-Strauss himself recognized when he wrote of his own travels in the very work in which he scorned travel writing. At an early period in the history of the disengagement, John Ledyard in his *Journal* mingled subjectivity and objectivity as well. When he embarked on the Cook voyage it is unlikely that he would have subscribed to the proposition that to travel is to write, but it is certain that once he began writing the *Journal* the two coalesced. His premature death while traveling in Africa precluded further publications, but he kept journals, in great part now lost, when he traveled, and even considered a plan of aiding his memory by tatooing notes on his skin should he be deprived of writing materials in the more primitive regions he visited. This scheme of carrying his account on his body may well serve as a metaphor of the indivisibility of Ledyard the traveler and Ledyard the writer.

The five writers at the center of this history are John Ledyard (1752–1789), John Lloyd Stephens (1805–1852), Bayard Taylor (1825–1878), Mark Twain (1835–1910), and Henry James (1843–1916). As one moves from the earlier to the later of them one is struck by how the American background of each informed his impression of other peoples, and how both historically from writer to writer and biographically within the career of each writer America increasingly became the object of his critical scrutiny in consequence of the lessons travel abroad had taught. In their works travel's capacity to compel personal self-definition leads to cultural self-awareness, a reevaluation of what in American life may be exceptional and what common, what worthy and what reprehensible.

Unlike the four who succeed him in these pages, John Ledyard produced only one book in his lifetime, the account of Cook's third voyage, but his subsequent travels can be followed in both his journals and letters and those of his contemporaries. His strong sense of what it was to be an American—intensified by his impressment into the British service at the time of the Revolution—shaped his attitude toward the fixed class structures of the societies he observed in his subsequent travels as well as his reactions to primitive peoples in the Pacific. Moreover, his distinctly democratic outlook was conspicuous in his person as well as in his writings. At a time when the cultural independence of the United States was uncertain at best, acquaintances such as Thomas Jefferson and Sir Joseph Banks saw in him a model of the national character, proof that the new nation did indeed breed a new kind of person. They gave amazed support to his fantastic plan to walk around the world, and in the interim Banks sponsored his African exploration while Jefferson awaited its completion in the hope that Ledyard would then undertake the transcontinental crossing of North America about which the two had often spoken. More than a decade after Ledyard's death his ideas remained with Jefferson when he commissioned the Lewis and Clark expedition.

A memory of Ledyard stirs in the pages of John Lloyd Stephens, New York attorney and man of business in the Jacksonian era, whose first travels to Europe and the Middle East initially followed well-worn tourist routes. But before they ended Stephens impatiently left the beaten track to make a daring trek to Arabia Petraea. His books about these travels were not only immensely popular—the first, published in 1837, sold 20,000 copies in the first three months—but won the admiration of literary contemporaries, Poe and Melville among them, and he succeeded to Ledyard's title of the "American traveler."

This, however, was only the beginning. With the proceeds from his first two books of travel Stephens financed his search for ruins in Central America and Mexico, hoping to discover in the New World monuments that would rival those he had visited in the Old World and, if he succeeded, then to bring back specimens for display in New York in emulation of the exhibitions of ancient Greek and Egyptian relics he had seen in the museums of London and Paris. His motive was patriotic as well as personal. In parallel with political independence from Europe, civilization in the Western Hemisphere would then have an independent genealogy.

Stephens's results were sensational. Today he is recognized as the discoverer of Mayan civilization and the father of Mayan archaeology, but no less remarkable are the books he wrote about his travels in the lands of the Maya. Stephens approached his travels and reported upon his discoveries as would a man of letters rather than a modern scientist. His lively narratives mingle personal incidents with the revolutionary political events then transpiring in the regions he traversed, and shrewd observation of the existing social scene with animated descriptions (aided by excellent pictorial illustrations) of the ruins that were uncovered. Their literary quality is a fitting match for the archaeological importance of the findings, such as the uncovering of Tulum and Chichen Itza, that they describe. In scope, wealth of incident, and significance of detail, Stephens's narratives remain unsurpassed by the books of travel of any other American.

Between the explorations and discoveries of Ledyard and Stephens in the early part of the nineteenth century and the accomplished travel literature of Twain and James in the latter decades stand the writings of Bayard Taylor. As an impecunious nineteen-year-old he had procured a ten-dollar steerage passage to Europe in order to visit the great sites with which his youthful reading in the Romantic poets had filled his imagination, hoping some day to join their ranks. The scant funds he managed to pull together were acquired by contracting to provide travel letters to journals back home, and upon his return he used those letters as the basis of a book about his tour. The sites he had visited were conventional enough, the stuff of many another travel book, but Taylor's somewhat awkward effort differed from others in two consequential ways.

First, he was unabashedly enthusiastic about his experiences, finding in place after place a confirmation of the literature he so reveringly carried about in his memory. Free of the sophistication, feigned or otherwise, of other travel reports on well-worn European sites, his youthful ardor was engaging.

And second, with very little money he had worked out a way of following an itinerary hitherto available only to the affluent, and his book revealed how this was done. Quite unintentionally, Taylor thus opened Europe to Americans of modest means, especially the young, and, to his chagrin as he grew older, he could never quite shake his reputation as the man who had traveled Europe on the cheap and shown others how to do it.

Throughout his career Taylor regarded himself as a poet and his other writings as secondary if also necessary for the material support of his vocation. But the success of his first travel book led to his being commissioned to undertake other travels in order to report on them, and he drifted into travel writing as a livelihood, becoming, in effect, the first person who kept traveling solely because of the books that could be written about the journeys. California on horseback, the Nubian desert by camel caravan, Japan with Perry's warships, the Arctic Circle on a reindeer sleigh: unusual routes and unusual modes of following them became Taylor's stock-in-trade. He had invented travel writing as a profession.

Although his volumes have now lost a considerable part of the great appeal they exerted in their day, Bayard Taylor is, nevertheless, the central figure in the history of American travel writing. Coming after those who traveled for a range of reasons—exploration, education, health, recreation—and then wrote about it, Taylor led professional authors such as Twain and James to consider travel writing not only as a profitable source of income but as a legitimate literary activity.

Taylor's work is important also because he brings to the fore the entwined issues of racism and imperialism that are never far from the surface of other travel writings. He has no doubt about the racial inferiority of Africans and Asians and the inevitability of white colonial dominance, and in travel literature such opinions do not appear so much as explicit contentions as they do as observed facts, objective reports by one who has been there and seen *them* as the reader has not. They are, that is, given as descriptions of the world that is out there rather than as personal opinions, and while Taylor most clearly exemplifies this potential of travel writing, in varying degrees Stephens, Twain (until late in his career), and James also release it. In his democratic idealism Ledyard alone appears exempt.

Twain's first book was a travel book and during his lifetime none of his works of fiction sold so well as it did; indeed from his day to this no travel book by an American has surpassed *The Innocents Abroad* (1869) in popularity. When in need of funds Twain fell back upon the genre time and again, producing within his massive, shaggy volumes narratives of a quality equal to all but a few of his works of fiction. A self-proclaimed tourist when others, even tourists, preferred to think of themselves as "travelers," he drew a great part of the humor in his books from a display of his unabashed touristic "innocence" and his delighted observation of the follies of his fellow tourists as they went about acquiring "culture" for the credit it would gain them back home rather than for any value it had in itself. Although he did not absolve his own bumbling visits to opera houses and art galleries from the same crude ambition, a core of horse sense lies at the center of this humorous and at times unconscious uncouthness, one that strips hallowed sites of the traditions that surround them and compels the reader to see them with unclouded eyes.

To follow Twain in his later travel writing into the African and Asian worlds of color is, at the same time, to go back with him along the path of memory to the South of his boyhood and his shocked awareness that it too was a land of colored people, although his consciousness then denied them the distinction he now felt on a street in Ceylon or at a terminus in India. *Following the Equator* (1897) contains the kind of satire on white pretensions to racial superiority that one finds elsewhere in Twain's writings, but here also, as nowhere else in his work, are deeply moving personal recollections of his own complacent participation in the shamefulness of racial discrimination. His fusion of adult experiences abroad with the memories they invoked of a boyhood spent in a slaveholding family is, in its understated eloquence, unmatched by his other writings on American racial injustice.

Henry James's travels began in his infancy—he was not yet one year old when he was first taken to Europe—and continued throughout his adult life. His travel reports likewise began in the infancy of his professional career and continued to his maturity and the recognition he received as a modern master. At the midpoint of his career, speaking in explanation of his characteristic subject matter, James asserted that while a European writer did not have to deal with America at all if he chose not to do so, an American writer had no choice but to deal with Europe if he wished to be complete. Midway into the twentieth century this pattern reversed itself, and European writers began to regard it as necessary that they come to terms with America. But to James's day, Washington Irving, James Fenimore Cooper, Henry Wadsworth Longfellow, James Russell Lowell, and William Dean Howells, to mention a prominent few, bore out his assertion. The conscious struggle of American writers to create a national literature demanded of them that they confront a world beyond the national boundaries. They did so in poetry, fiction, and literary criticism, and they did so also in travel writing. In thus completing themselves, to use James's term, they were also working to complete America.

James's great novels of Americans abroad respond to the obligation to complete the American self (of both author and reader) through the experience of Europe, and to a large extent his travel writings are engaged in the same task. But they go about this end differently. Unlike the novels, the travel accounts place James himself on a steamer down the Thames, a French railway car, or an Italian footpath, and, unlike the author of the novels, in them he advances a conscious and often self-proclaimed American outlook. Quite surprisingly for those who have read only his fiction, as he travels he is frequently impatient with the pieties of European tradition and for all his admiration of that civilization exhibits a distrust of idealizing the past for its own sake that seems a product of the self-reliant Emersonian America of his youth. It is not so much a different Henry James one sees when his travel writings are considered in themselves as it is a more personal, and, at many points, more personable Henry James.

In the last and greatest of his travel books, *The American Scene* (1907), the writer who had decades before "chosen" Europe, as he himself worded it, returned after twenty years to bring memories of a younger America as well as a sensibility finely tuned by Europe to a consideration of the land of his birth. The book is the keystone in his completion of himself as well as a biting recognition of America's compulsive incompleteness.

Twain also brought to his two books of travel into the American hinterland, *Roughing It* (1872) and *Life on the Mississippi* (1883), an awareness shaped by his travels abroad. In them he may have been remembering with relish the adventures of his young and unfinished self in a land that was also invigoratingly young and unfinished, but the memories were those of a mature writer who had since toured Europe and the Middle East. His vision of America was a re-vision of America.

If, then, the history of the genre of American travel writing is tied to the authorial search for a completeness that the young nation alone could not furnish, it might be conjectured that as America aged and accumulated its own history so a sense of adequacy in the face of foreign cultures would also grow. Strikingly, travel writing reveals that the reverse occurred. A child of revolutionary days such as Ledyard faced other societies with an unarrogant confidence in the democratic ideals of his homeland that compensated for its shortcomings. Whatever America had to learn from other societies was not so important as what those societies were yet to learn from America's great experiment in republicanism. Stephens was more concerned with cultural artifacts than Ledyard and so more aware of national shortcomings, but he saw international trade as the source of not only economic but cultural growth. Bred in the political and financial marketplaces of New York City he had an informed and highly cheerful confidence in the capacity of American politics and American commerce to construct a great society although his travels emphasized to him the need to abolish slavery, an institution that was not only inhumanly unjust but obstructed the influence that America would otherwise assert abroad. As one proceeds to Taylor and then Twain and James, however, one more and more sees in the mirrors held up by foreign societies the lineaments of America's failings. Racism replaces slavery in belying the nation's proclaimed ideals; the pleasures of living the everyday life are more apparent among those who accept tradition with all its attendant prejudices and restrictions on social advancement than among money-minded, upwardly mobile Americans; and beauty, the heir of time, seems forever to elude a people who in their constant uprootings destroy the sites to which beauty attaches itself. The history of travel writing becomes also an animated index of cultural self-awareness.

Ledyard in the Aleutians in the 1770s fixed his gaze eastward and contemplated a transcontinental journey that would enclose his open-ended homeland; Stephens in the jungles of Chiapas was exhilarated by discoveries that he felt would give America a monumental past of its own; Taylor in travels that culminated with the Perry expedition to Japan saw himself as pursuing America's path to empire; and Twain in following the equator pondered the lesson of racial difference that had to be mastered by his fellow Americans if their society was ever to become civilized in a more meaningful sense than that applied to the production and acquisition of works of art. Like James they traveled toward an ever-receding horizon of completion, writing back to a curious people at home even as they themselves moved forward. And, indeed, what is significant travel writing if it is not simultaneously a movement forward past domestic boundaries and a meditation backward on the limits that have been transcended?

CHAPTER I

John Ledyard

A Journal of Captain Cook's Last Voyage to the Pacific Ocean and in
Quest of a North-West Passage (1783)
John Ledyard's Journey Through Russia and Siberia, 1787–1788
(Posthumous)

When John Ledyard's sea-captain father died in 1762 the eleven-year-old boy was sent from Groton, Connecticut, his birthplace, to live with his grandfather in Hartford. Put to the study of law in his teens he found it dull, and his grandfather, a friend of Eleazer Wheelock, founder and president of Dartmouth College, thereupon arranged to send young Ledyard there with the intent of his becoming a missionary to the Indians. Such an academic pursuit combined the dual ends of Dartmouth, which Wheelock saw as both a classical seminary and a school for Indians. In the spring of 1772, Ledyard arrived at Hanover, New Hampshire, by horse and buggy, bringing with him, among other things, costumes for theatricals he intended to produce. But a year later, with the Connecticut River in spring thaw, he took his permanent leave of the college in an even more dramatic fashion, launching a dugout canoe he had constructed and paddling 140 miles down the river to reappear at the doorstep of his astonished family in Hartford. Years after, a cousin

17

who knew him well said that Ledyard in his brief year at Dartmouth had "absented himself without permission of the college govt. and made a tour among the six nations of Indians on the borders of canada."[1] While this contention cannot be verified absolutely, several factors appear to confirm it: when with Cook off the northwest coast of America, Ledyard was to speculate with some acuteness on the common origin of Aleuts and northeastern Indians, claiming firsthand knowledge of the latter when gaining his initial glimpses of the former; the dugout canoe he fashioned seems to derive from direct observation of Indian practice; and in later years his uncle wrote that at Hanover "he acquired a tincture of the language and manners of the Natives of the forrest."[2] Certain it is that while his plan to become a missionary was abandoned the interest in native peoples that formed an essential part of this scheme remained dormant within him to be awakened by the Cook voyage and thereafter become a powerful motive for further travel.

Still restless, Ledyard within months of beaching his canoe at Hartford embarked on a trading vessel to the Barbary Coast commanded by a friend of his father's and when they touched at Gibraltar, to Captain Deshon's consternation, enlisted in the British army. The alarmed Captain reasoned with Ledyard, expostulated with his commanding officer, and managed to detach him from the army, but the fact that Ledyard had so volunteered not only indicates an addiction to changed scenes but also suggests an unstated sense of desperation at his financial and social prospects. As Melville's Ishmael—who uncannily resembles Ledyard in disposition and philosophy—later observed in *Moby-Dick,* enlistment was a grimly cheerful acknowledgment that one had reached the end of one's means. So when within a year Ledyard once again sailed from America, this time aboard a merchant ship bound for Falmouth, and was in England compelled to enlist in the British army, although the impressment must have been as unwelcome as readers of his Memorial were later invited to believe, the promise of adventure may not have been.

Not the least of the remarkable qualities that contributed to the greatness of Captain James Cook to whom Ledyard made application was his acute judgment of men. He chose those who were to serve together in close quarters under hardship, uncertainty, and danger with amazing discernment as the monumental success of his voyages indicates. Two of his more celebrated subordinates, George Vancouver and William Bligh, did, to be sure, acquire notorious reputations for their later mismanagement of their crews, but both were extraordinarily skillful navigators and marine surveyors who had a permanent effect on the mapping of the Pacific. It was a source of personal pride as well as a matter of public distinction to be known as one who sailed with Cook not just because of the discoveries in which he participated but also because of the remarkable company in which that placed him. "We are perhaps somewhat partial to one another," one of them reflected, "for it is an article of faith with every one of us that there never was such a collection of fine lads take us for all in all, got together as there was in the *Resolution* & *Discovery*."[3]

That the twenty-three-year-old soldier who applied to Cook in person was enrolled by him and assigned the position of corporal of marines, suggests a worthiness in Ledyard beyond the ordinary. Cook referred to him as an "intelligent man," and this quality combined with a vivid imagination that seemed, at times, extravagant but never vainglorious continued to attract other of the great men with whom he later came in contact: John Paul Jones, Thomas Jefferson, Sir Joseph Banks, the Marquis de Lafayette, Thomas Paine, and a score of scientists, diplomats, and men of letters eminent in their day though lesser known in this. Almost without exception they are on record as having been captivated by his intelligence, his verve, and his lack of vanity. If he struck them as unrealistic in the daring of his plans he also gave them the feeling that he just might be capable of accomplishing the impossible travel—across Siberia, or North America, or Africa—that he proposed. He seemed the perfect democrat, at ease with those who in his world were still to be regarded as his betters yet free of presumption, self-assured yet not self-important, possessed of an urbanity acquired more from contact with the gentlemen of the primitive world than those of the city, and, most importantly, able to accept rebuffs, to undergo in order to go.

Almost all of Ledyard's *Journal* of the Cook voyage makes interesting reading; only at the end when the ships are homeward bound and Ledyard copies the details of the track they pursued with no narrative intervention does his book lapse into tedium. A great many of the events about which he writes have been more reliably reported by others, yet his narrative stands out in the freshness with which he approached those events, most notably encounters with alien cultures. Sinclair Hitchings is certainly right when he observes of the *Journal,* "We shall remember him more in years to come, I suspect, for his passionate interest in primitive peoples, his writings about them, and his remarkable understanding of them," than for a comprehensive account of the voyage. "What makes it worth reading are Ledyard's comments on the native peoples he saw and talked to."[4]

But while this is so, further emphasis should be given to the reasons for it. One of "the people," as those below commissioned officers in the British navy were termed, Ledyard had little or no access to the kind of information that contributed to a global view of the aims and accomplishments of the voyage, or even to accurate information on the charted location of where he was at any given date. What he could and did have opportunity to observe and ponder, however, was the way the natives he visited perceived of reality. Although this was a subject for conjecture in the officers' reports, Ledyard's ground-level viewpoint, the terms on which he mingled with the island commoners, was as superior to that of the officers, who confined their dealings to island royalty, as the officers' bird's-eye view of the voyage as a whole was to his. In Tahiti, Lieutenant Rickman reported, "there was hardly a sailor on board that had not made a very near connection with one or another of the women of this island, . . . " adding in candor "nor indeed many officers that were proof against the allurements of the better sort, who were no less amorous and artful, though more reserved, than those of the inferior order."[5] He thus assured the British public that even in matters of sexual pleasure the protocols of class and rank had been observed. Unconfined to the "better" and "more reserved" order Ledyard wrote on the meeting of cultures from the viewpoint of the ship's

JOHN LEDYARD

people and, to the best of his ability, from the viewpoint of the islands' peoples as well. His, for example, is the first attempt to see the death of Cook from the natives' point of view.[6]

That none of the other people wrote an account of the voyage is not surprising in view of the ragged state of learning, indeed of widespread illiteracy, among those who sailed before the mast. More than a half century later, Herman Melville was to have the authenticity of the manuscript of his first work, *Typee* (1846), challenged by his English publisher on the ground that a common sailor, as he claimed to be, was not capable of writing a book. What Ledyard as well as Melville could reply was that it was not unbelievable that a simple American sailor possessed the capacity since he came from a country that extended common schooling to all classes, nor was it unusual that he had an uncommon curiosity about primitive cultures since he came from a land where such cultures were under pressure of annihilation from European expansion.

The major purpose of Cook's third voyage was to search for the Northwest Passage that would obviate the need to pursue the lengthy, costly, and hazardous voyages by way of the southern capes. Although not made public, the Admiralty's offer of a reward of £20,000 to those who made the discovery is what lured Cook to sail round the world once again. The announced reason for the voyage, however, a manifestly thin one in view of the fact that two ships, the *Resolution* and the *Discovery*, were involved, was the need to return Omai to his home. This Society Islander had been brought to England on Cook's previous voyage and was there lionized, meeting the king, dining with Dr. Samuel Johnson, and having his portrait painted by Reynolds. He was widely regarded as proof of the fashionable belief in the innate nobility of savages.

Outward-bound the two-ship expedition proceeded around the Cape of Good Hope in late 1776 to Australia and New Zealand, and then satisfying itself that a southern continent did not exist turned northward in the following spring, discovering the Cook Islands and revisiting other groups known from earlier voyages.[7] In the summer of 1777 Omai

21

was delivered home, the visitors indulging themselves in the fabled pleasures of Tahiti, and then in January 1778, bound for the Pacific northwest, they stumbled upon what proved to be the expedition's major geographical discovery, the Hawaiian Islands, named by Cook the Sandwich Islands after the First Lord of the Admiralty. On March 7th of that year the North American coastline was reached, the expedition came in contact with Aleut and Eskimo cultures, and a friendly meeting was held with Russians who occupied a trading post on Unalaska. Then in November 1778 the voyagers returned to Hawaii, where Cook was killed in the following February, after which his successors led the ships north to make yet another cast at finding the Northwest Passage and while there to acquire from traders in Siberia necessary European supplies, such as shoes, before the long homeward journey. There they also purchased furs, primarily for their own use, but when they touched at mainland China—where for the first time since their departure they met English-speaking traders and received news of the European world—they were offered such astoundingly high prices they then sold them. They returned thence to England by way of Good Hope.

The element of their interchanges with the diverse islanders that drew the greatest attention of all who reported on them was the way in which Cook dealt with the natives' incessant thievery. Amiable and generous in their trading exchanges, the natives also spirited away anything that was not closely guarded with a proclivity that seemed unstoppable. No degree of remonstrance before the fact was efficacious and Cook as a consequence took severe punitive measures after the fact. He had the ears of known thieves cropped, permitted his men to maim with boat hooks any who approached too closely uninvited, and, in cases of major loss, burned huts and canoes and threatened to continue the firestorm if missing items were not returned. On occasion he even resorted to holding hostage the island royalty who had unsuspectingly accepted his offers of hospitality until their subjects returned what was missed. Although his subordinates recognized that the success of their enterprise crucially depended upon Cook's ability to acquire food, water, and wood as they proceeded on their lengthy passage, and that to do this he had to retain an adequate supply of trading goods and essential equipment such as navigational instruments, they nevertheless expressed consternation at the harshness with which he punished the theft of such objects. The natives appeared to them to be admirable, nature's noblemen indeed. Lieutenant Rickman, for example, insisted that no appellation could be worse applied to them than that of savages "for a more civilized people does not exist under the sun," and he likened an island king to a European gentleman.[8] He suspected the natives regarded theft as a sign of cunning rather than of dishonesty and felt the punishments inflicted were wanton acts of cruelty that provoked rather than prevented further vexatious, if not openly hostile, behavior. And young Midshipman Gilbert told his journal that the harshness must have proceeded from fits of anger not premeditation as he tried to explain to himself why the admired "Capt Cook punished in a manner rather unbecoming of an European."[9]

While the officers dealt with community leaders, Ledyard on shore mingled with the commoners and his account of Cook's punitive policies is not so much concerned with the measures themselves—their injustice or unseemliness—as it is with his perception of the natives' reaction to them. At his worst he writes of this in an all-too-theatrical fashion, as when speaking of the punishment of a Tonga chief whom he admired, he exclaims "How often Phenow, have I felt for thee, the embarrassments of these involuntary offences against a people thou didst as well love and wouldst as soon have befriended when thou wast accused and stood condemned as when not" (p. 29). But fortunately both this kind of sentimentalizing and the inflated second-person address in which it is clothed are rare. Characteristically Ledyard offered straightforward analyses with the assurance of one who had been on the ground and knew the islanders through everyday associations rather than command-level negotiations. His island encounters confirmed him in the admiration for primitive cultures he had developed in his year on the Canadian border. (He frequently applied the term "Indians" to Pacific natives, as did almost all others.) But the closer he drew to the natives and the more clearly he perceived what they and he shared in

Poulaho, a Tongan king, as depicted by J. Webber, the expedition artist. He is possibly the very king whom Ledyard called "Phenow," and whose treatment at Cook's hands he deplored (James Cook and James King, *A Voyage to the Pacific Ocean, 1786;* Amherst College Archives and Special Collections).

common for all their cultural differences the more keenly was he aware of the differences. Romanticizing island culture as exemplary of the original state of all societies and so seeing the islanders as "truly civilized," others were in such praising also patronizing, reducing the differences to those between a simple child and a knowledgeable if also somewhat tainted adult. The implication was that at any point of opposition the adult should have his way.

But Ledyard was far more respectful of the strength and irreducibil-
ity of cultural difference. In opposition to theories of the primitive as a
representation of the civil harmony that prevailed in original society he
speculated that civilization is original and the savage state a decline
from it. Customs found among the "civilized and wise," he argued,
"measured on a philosophic scale, are uncorrupted, while those that we
find existing in parts remote from civilization and knowledge, though
they have a resemblance which plainly intimates from whence they
came, are yet debased, mutilated" (p. 76). Idiosyncratic as the theory
might be, it stems from a practical respect for the power of cultural
difference. Accordingly, his comments on Cook's severe punitive measures are not concerned with whether they are just or gentlemanly from
a civilized standpoint but rather with the way they are read by the
natives. Cook "would perhaps have done better," he writes of measures
taken at Tongatapu, "to have considered that the full exertion of extreme power is an argument of extreme weakness, and nature seemed
to inform the insulted natives of the truth of this maxim by the manifestation of their subsequent resentments" (p. 37).

The most dramatic example of Ledyard's regard for the importance
of appreciating the native perception of reality occurs in his account of
the change in relations with the Hawaiian islanders that led to the death
of Cook. On their return visit after having made their exploration of the
northwest coast, the voyagers were met by the largest number of islanders they had yet encountered, thousands who, as Ledyard said, could
easily have trampled him to atoms were they so disposed. "The intrinsic
difference between us and them in every respect was certainly great,"
he said, "but the greatest difference was imaginary respecting them and
imputed to us, the moment therefore that this supposed superiority of
ours should cease to exist or be diminished, our consequence and importance would be at an end" (p. 107), and a ruinous resort to arms
would have to take place. The feared erosion soon began: first, predictably, with officers and then men making visits to the island women,
followed by a steady increase in everyday social relations which resulted finally in the removal of the white poles around the voyagers'

shore camp which, it had previously been agreed, represented a boundary not to be crossed by either party. As a consequence, Ledyard said, "they had every opportunity to form an opinion of our manners and abilities and contrast them with their own, nay, were even instructed in the nature and use of our firearms, and permitted to prove our own personal prowess in wrestling, boxing and other athletic exercises, and in some instances with success on their side" (p. 109). What might appear to be an admirable, fraternal blending, the disappearance of the markers of physical boundary symbolizing the evaporation of cultural separation, was read by Ledyard as the beginning of the end because the only difference that really disappeared was the mystical one upon which security depended.

To be sure, Ledyard's *Journal* is not literally a journal; that is, it is not a printing of his day-to-day observations but a reconstruction of them several years after the fact. When he exposes what he claims were the mistakes in perception that led to Cook's death, then, he does so with the wisdom of hindsight even though he may conceivably have had the same sense of the matter at the time since as a marine he was especially concerned with maintaining the shore camp's disregarded perimeter. What is certain, however, is that in order to dramatize what he took to be Cook's fatal insensibility to "the daily decline of his greatness and importance in the estimation of the natives" (p. 136), Ledyard constructed a fictionalized version of an event he regarded as crucial to the catastrophe that occurred.

Writing in the official report of the expedition, James King said that on the 4th of February 1779 Cook sent him ashore to Kealakakua on Hawaii directing him to purchase the wood that fenced the sacred burial ground, the Morai, so that the damaged *Resolution* could be repaired with it. King, then a lieutenant, admitted he was in some doubt about the decency of the proposal but that no surprise was expressed by those with whom he negotiated and the wood was procured without incident.

In Ledyard's rendering, Cook was in charge of the shore party and offered two iron hatchets for the fence to the presiding priests who were

The death of Captain Cook as reconstructed by eye witnesses (Cook & King, *Voyage*, 1786; Amherst College Archives and Special Collections).

unnerved at both the proposal and the price: "The poor dismayed chiefs dreading his displeasure, which they saw approaching followed him upon the Morai to behold the fence that enclosed the mansions of their noble ancestors, and the images of their gods torn to pieces by a handful of rude strangers without the power, or at least without the resolution of opposing their sacrilegious degradations" (p. 137). Neither Cook who is the protagonist in this drama nor Ledyard who is the dramatist were present at the actual scene. At this stage of his narrative—Cook was killed ten days later—Ledyard begins to bend the facts in favor of a presentation that will epitomize the differences that led to the catastrophe. Event is sacrificed to an interpretation of underlying cause; accordingly, "insensible" Cook offers two iron hatchets to "dismayed" islanders whose reaction to the sacrilege completes the process of de-mystifying him and prepares the way for his death. Hatchets and idols symbolize the sides of the cultural abyss that, Ledyard asserts, has not been crossed for all the interchanges that have taken place. (It is also intriguing to observe that the chiefs lack the "resolution" to oppose the taking of wood to repair Cook's *Resolution*.)

Unreliable as chronicle though it is, Ledyard's book is nevertheless significant as an interpretive narrative, at a few brief moments even a protonovel, of an American's experience of two cultures, neither of which were his: the exotic island culture and that of England, its class structure quintessentially captured in the distinction between commissioned officers and "the people" aboard a naval vessel. Never superior to the one in intrinsic worth and never inferior to the other in intelligence and ability, the author of the *Journal* tacitly presents himself as from yet a third culture. His narrative, appearing as it did at a time when Americans were compelled to question whether despite their newly won political independence they were not, at bottom, without a distinct cultural identity, could have owed some of its popularity to the positive answer embodied in its author's self-reliant attitude.

At Nootka Sound, April 1778, ten months before Cook's death, the expedition reached the North American continent, an arrival that Ledyard romantically regarded as a return to his homeland after a four-year absence. Recognizing the Aleuts as being related to the North American Indians with whom he was familiar he wrote:

> This was the first fair opportunity after our arrival that I had of examining the appearance of those unknown aborigines of North-America. It was the first time too that I had been so near the shores of that continent which gave me birth from the time I first left it; and though more than two thousand miles distant from the nearest part of New-England I felt myself plainly affected: All the affectionate passions incident to natural attachments and early prejudices played around my heart, and indulged them because they were prejudices. I was harmonized

by it. It soothed a home-sick heart, and rendered me very tolerably happy. I had no sooner seen these Americans than I set them down for the same kind of people that inhabit the opposite side of the continent. (p. 71)

As further ground for this sameness, he observed, "In their manners they resemble the aborigines of North-America," and then gave as one example, "if they sacrifice it is to the God of liberty" (p. 72), thus implying not only the common identity of differing groups of Native Americans but also of all who were from America, even those of European stock. There was a detachment to Ledyard's observations of the South Sea islanders, a considered, philosophical attempt to reveal their viewpoint. But with regard to the Aleuts, whom he perceives to lack the charm of the Tahitians or Hawaiians and whose lands are harshly unyielding, Ledyard's tone becomes more intensely personal and, finally, more admiring. He takes pleasure in the fact that they regard everything on their land as their property; Cook said that nowhere else in all his travels had he met with an uncivilized people who believe they had an exclusive right to all that their country produced. And so when they want to charge for wood and water, Ledyard reports with evident delight, "Capt. Cook would not credit this fact when he first heard of it, and persisting in a more peremptory tone in his demands, one of the Indians took him by the arm and thrust him from him, pointing the way for him to go about his business. Cook was struck with astonishment, and turning to his people with a smile mixed with admiration exclaimed, 'This is an American indeed!' " (p. 72).

Cook had earlier served on the St. Lawrence River, conducting marine surveys of the river's estuary, and knew Native Americans from this experience—indeed, he was the only observer other than Ledyard to discern that the Aleuts differed ethnically from the Eskimos. His remark, then, most obviously referred to a spirit of independence he regarded as American—ambiguously both native and colonial—although additionally there is a hint that their hardheaded trading practice was also what was American about the Aleuts.

Ledyard's admiration for, and perhaps unconscious identification
with, the Aleuts reaches its fullest in a passage that seems to sound a
keynote for the Melville of *Moby-Dick*, who, indeed, referred to Ledyard
in that novel. Characteristically, Melville treated primitive cultures as
parallel to advanced cultures, measuring achievements within each in
terms relative to that particular culture rather than by an absolute standard. So, for example, Queequeg, the South Sea islander in *Moby-Dick*,
was a George Washington cannibalistically developed rather than a
man who under other circumstances could have become a Washington.
Occasioned by his observation of Alaskan whaling technology (thus further intensifying the Melville connection) Ledyard's proleptic passage
reads:

> They have a harpoon made from a mushel shell only, and yet
> they have so disposed of it as to subdue the great leviathan and
> tow the unweildy monster to their shores. Let not man think
> meanly of himself, but claim that glorious rank his amazing
> powers so justly entitle him to. If Descartes and Newton from the
> improvements of age could produce at last the magnificent sys-
> tem of Philosophy that hath immortalized them; why should not
> these glorious savages, who, without any of those great collat-
> eral assistances, without which THEY could have done nothing,
> have discovered such astonishing sagacity, be intitled to equal
> veneration, and the name of Ben Uncus be as great as that of
> Isaac Newton. (pp. 76–77)

One might at this point also remember that Uncus (i.e., *Uncas*) was chief
of the Pequot tribe that gave its name to the ship that pursued the white
whale. Of primary importance here, however, is not the Melville parallel, striking as it is, but rather the implication that grows out of the
earlier identification of native American and European American, the
implication that the new nation's achievements are to be measured in
accordance with a standard internal to it rather than comparatively.

It seems appropriate that the only point on the voyage at which Ledyard was singled out by other reporters (although not always by name) occurred on the North American coast. Moored off the island of Un-alaska, Cook determined to explore further after a native, astoundingly, presented him with a gift of a pie made of rye wheat with peppered salmon baked in it. Ledyard volunteered to search out the Europeans who must have prepared that pie and on the recommendation of his friend, the American-born Lieutenant Gore, was given the task. Entirely unarmed on the advice of Cook, he set out with the natives and traveled two days and a night with them, spending the final stage of the journey lying flat on his back in the hull of a kayak between the holes in which the paddlers sat. Finally lifted from the dark of the hull, he was led through the dark of night into the light of the Russians' hut: "When I reached the end of the room I was seated on a bench covered with furr-skins, and as I was fatigued, wet and cold, I had a change of garments brought me, consisting of a blue silk shirt and drawers, a furr-cap, boot and gown, all which I put on with the same chearfulness they were presented with. Hospitality is a virtue peculiar to man, and the obliga-tion is as great to receive as to confer" (p. 94). Thus spoke a born trav-eler. Ledyard observed life at the Russian trading station, remarked with satisfaction the natives' veneration for the icons of the Russian Orthodox Church, contrasting this method of conversion with attempts to inculcate the history and principles of Christianity (an implicit crit-icism of Wheelock's Dartmouth), and led the affable Russians back to Cook's ship where an exchange of gifts and goodwill took place although none in either party could find a language they had in common.

While Cook's third voyage is most notable for the discoveries made and the terrible death of its leader, it is the Alaskan interval that not only gave Ledyard the greatest personal satisfaction—his statement that he was "harmonized" can be taken literally—but also set him on the course he was to pursue for the remainder of his brief and adventurous life. In his Memorial to the Connecticut Assembly he said his book would be useful to America in general but "particularly to the northern States by opening a most valuable trade across the north Pacific Ocean to China &

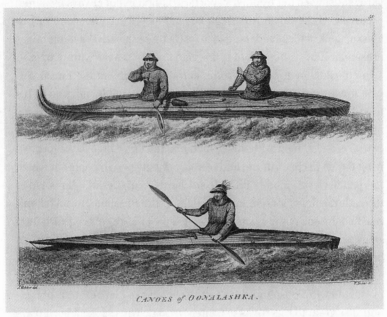

CANOES of OONALASHKA.

Lying in the hull between the rowers of a kayak such as the one depicted here by Webber, the expedition artist, Ledyard was transported to the Russian trading outpost (*Plates to Cook's Voyage,* 1784, first impression; The John Work Garrett Library of The Johns Hopkins University).

the east Indies." With the book published, he set forth to attempt to make good on these words.

The "valuable trade" was the fur trade in which the Russians alone were at that point engaged. The natives in the vicinity of what is now called Vancouver Island sold their skins—beaver, fox, sable, hare, ermine, wolverine, and others—to the Russian station at Kamchatka, and while in the region, Ledyard wrote, we purchased "about 1500 beaver, besides other skins, but took none but the best, haveing no thought at that time of using them to any other advantage than converting them to the purpose of cloathing, but it afterwards happened that skins which did not cost the purchaser sixpence sterling sold in China for 100 dollars" (p. 70). Had they known they would have met with such a profit, he said, they could easily have procured three times as many skins.

In May 1783 Ledyard left Hartford for New York and Philadelphia in search of backers for his plan to sail to the northwest coast and establish a fur trade. Robert Morris, the Philadelphia financier, for a time did agree to back him, but after a year during which Ledyard unsuccessfully attempted to find a ship for the venture, Morris withdrew. No other Americans showed interest, because, one of Ledyard's friends said, his description of the profits to be made was so glowing as to be implausible. If Ledyard's romantic fervor made those in the financial community uneasy, their distrust was not allayed when to the rosy picture of the profits to be made he added what could only be regarded as the insane proposal that once a station had been established and a vessel loaded with furs he would return to the Atlantic coast by walking across the continent!

As later traders were to demonstrate, however, Ledyard's projection of profits was accurate, and his hunch that the trade should be anchored by an overland as well as a maritime connection was shrewd. In Alaska Cook's party had seen natives wearing copper bracelets but could receive no account of where they came from. This led Ledyard to reason that "commerce is defusive and nothing will impede its progress among the uninformed part of mankind, but an intervention of too remote a communication by water, and as this cannot be the case with regard to the inhabitants of a continent, it seems intirely conclusive to suppose no part of America is without some sort of commercial intercourse, immediate or remote" (p. 77). As wild, then, as was the idea of a single-person transcontinental trek, it was, nevertheless, anchored in the reasonable conjecture that a chain of trades between contiguous peoples marked the way. Lewis and Clark, whose sponsor, Jefferson, was to be influenced by his conversations with Ledyard, found the links of just such a chain, encountering, for example, items from the Pacific coast on the eastern slope of the Rocky Mountains.

In June 1784 Ledyard took his plan to France where after months of negotiating he received backing from a group in the port of Lorient. Subsidized by them he entered upon months of preparation only once again to have the backing withdrawn before he could engage a vessel. The reasons for the reversal are unclear but since the Lorient failure did not expose any flaw in the intrinsic merit of the plan itself, Ledyard remained confident if now also all but penniless. He proceeded to Paris and the community that centered on Jefferson, then American minister to France, where he met John Paul Jones and arranged a partnership with him. They planned to fit out two ships, set up a station in Nootka Sound, and while Jones sailed to Asia in one ship to sell the furs initially gathered Ledyard would remain in North America with the other ship and trade coastally for more furs, after which both ships would trade in Asia for tea, silk, and porcelain and return to France. The profit was going to be huge, as much as 1,000 percent in Ledyard's estimate, and financing was to come from the prize money due Jones for his feats during the American Revolution as well as from Louis XVI, whose administration knew Jones's abilities and could be expected to venture into so profitable an area, especially to beat the British to the scene. So in the summer of 1785 Ledyard in Paris was sustained by money given him by Jones who went in search of suitable ships as well as to collect his prize money. But again the scheme collapsed. Jones did not get the money he expected and the French crown, allied with Spain against England's expanding naval interests, was made aware that Spain regarded the Pacific coast of America as her territory and disliked the encroachment represented by a French station.[10]

That third major frustration convinced Ledyard that he was not going to advance his ambition in combination with others, and, since a commercial venture was totally dependent upon large financial backing, he abandoned that goal. But he did not abandon his plan to travel to the northwest coast. Rather the frustration of the trading scheme returned Ledyard to himself, as it were, and allowed him to see that his primary interest had not been financial gain, as great as that would have been had he only found those who would venture with him, but the adventure itself; that is, the fame to be achieved by exploring unknown territory. As he later wrote in a letter to his cousin in America, a "new Ass," meaning hobby horse, had "sprung from the Ashes of my Ass Commerce" (Watrous, p. 107). Ledyard was now determined to walk from the area of Nootka Sound across the entire continent to the settlements of the United States. And since it appeared he could find no ship that would land him at Nootka he would simply proceed across Russia and then Siberia on foot or by whatever conveyance came his way until on the Siberian coast he could locate some trading vessel that crossed to the North American shore; in other words, he planned to walk around the world. "A blush of generous regret," he wrote in the same letter, "sits on my Cheek to hear of any discovery there [America] that I have not part in, & particularly at this auspicious period: The American Revolution invites us to a thorough discovery of the Continent and the honor of doing it would become a foreigner. But a Native only could feel the pleasure of the Atchievement. It was necessary that an European should discover the Existance of that Continent but in the name of Amor Patria. Let a Native of it Explore its Boundary. It is my wish to be the Man I will not yet resign that wish nor my pretension to that distinction" (pp. 106–7).

If there is vanity in this ambition it is steeled by courage and tempered by a genuine identification of personal achievement with the advancement of knowledge and the welfare of society. Cook's fame provided an example. It was an age in which discovery in geography and the sciences, the contrivance of a practical invention, or the success of a social experiment wedded the distinction of personal accomplishment to that of public benefaction. Ledyard's discussions with Jefferson frequently turned to the national advantages that would result from the information to be gained from a continental crossing and Jefferson had

suggested to him that if his plans to trek from west to east did not mate-
rialize he should return home and attempt the journey from east to west
(Lewis and Clark's expedition was to do this in 1804–5).

Internal passports were required of travelers within the Russian Empire and Lafayette endeavored to procure one for Ledyard from Baron
de Grimm, Empress Catherine's personal representative in Paris. Introducing Ledyard to Lafayette in February, 1786, Jefferson spoke of his
having been with Cook and said, "He has genius, an education better
than the common, and a talent for useful and interesting observation."
He believed him to be honest, "a man of truth," Jefferson said, and "to
all this he adds just as much singularity of character and of that particular kind too, as was necessary to make him undertake the journey
he proposes."[11] Since the imperial government had recently commissioned a survey of the Siberian coast to be conducted under the direction of Joseph Billings, an Englishman who had sailed with Cook as an
astronomer's assistant and was now a captain in the Russian navy, as
part of his claim for a passport Ledyard apparently mentioned his acquaintanceship with Billings and his willingness to assist in the survey
because while awaiting her majesty's response Baron de Grimm advanced Ledyard twenty-five guineas against the payment he would receive once he was appointed to Billings's group. Lafayette too gave financial assistance. Thus provisioned for the moment, Ledyard went
into training for his journey. He worked on his French, believing it the
language that would be of greatest single service in his travels, and he
followed a regime of running several miles a day and taking walks of as
long as twenty-four miles a day.

When the summer of 1786 arrived, however, Ledyard had not yet
received his passport and was living on the outskirts of Paris and making occasional sojourns into the country on whatever funds he could
procure from one or another well-wisher. If you want to know how I
live, he wrote, "ask vice consuls, consuls, plenipotentiaries, ministers
and whores of fortune all of whom have had the honor to be tributary to
me."[12] Beyond Jefferson's circle of acquaintances, Ledyard because
of his extraordinary travel plan was also known to the community of

gentlemen travelers and amateur scientists, principally British, who passed through Paris. One of them, Sir James Hall, roused him from sleep early one morning to tell him that he had called at that unusual hour because he was on the point of departure for London. The point of the visit the sleepy Ledyard did not know, but during an awkward silence Hall walked across the room and, Ledyard wrote: "laughingly put his hand on a Six Livre piece and a Louis d'or that lay on my toilet & with a half stifled blush asked me 'how I was in the money way' blushes commonly beget blushes and I blushed partly because he did, and partly on other accounts: If fifteen Guineas interrupting the answer he had demanded will be of any service to you, there they are and put them on the Table—. I am a traveller myself and tho' I have some fortune myself to support my travels. yet I have been so situated as to want money which you ought not to do" (p. 103). Then wishing Ledyard a good morning, Hall departed.

Ledyard's voyage with Cook also continued to gain him attention, and on another occasion, he reported, he was at an inn in Normandy where out of pocket as usual he was compelled to prepare his own meal. While he was doing so the kitchen servants asked about the markings on his hand, and when he told them they were tattoo marks he had received in Tahiti, word quickly spread throughout the village and he was soon summoned to dine with the Lord of the Manor.

The long wait for a passport ended abruptly that summer because before Baron de Grimm received a reply from St. Petersburg, Ledyard heard from Hall that an English ship preparing to trade in the Nootka region had agreed to carry him there. He quickly crossed the Channel and with a further twenty guineas presented to him by Hall, *pro bono publico* Hall said, he bought two large dogs, an Indian pipe, and a hatchet. Such would be his basic equipment on his long march. As he wrote to Jefferson from London on August 16th: "My want of time as well as more money will prevent my going otherwise than indifferently equipped for such an Enterprise; but it is certain I shall be more in want before I see Virginia" (Jefferson, 10:259).

In London Ledyard also had a long visit with William Stephens Smith, son-in-law of John Adams the American minister, who was acting as minister plenipotentiary in Adams's absence. Reporting on this interview to John Jay, secretary for foreign affairs of the Continental Congress, Smith wrote that since Ledyard seemed to be preparing to accept English sponsorship of his journey, "I endeavour'd to convince him, that it was his duty as an American Citizen, to exercise his talents and Industry for the immediate service of his own Country, and if the Project he was upon, could be beneficial to any, his Country upon every Principle was entitled to these services." Geographical knowledge translated into political power and Smith gained Ledyard's assurance that what he learned would be placed at the service of the United States:

> If he succeeds, and in the Course of 2 or 3 years, should visit our Country by this amazing Circuit, he may bring with him some interesting information, if he fails, and is never heard of, which I think most probable, there is no harm done. He dies in an unknown Country, and if he composes himself in his last moments with this reflection, that his project was great, and the undertaking what few men were capable of, it will, to his mind, smooth the passage. He is perfectly calculated for the attempt; he is robust and healthy, and has an immense passion to make some discoveries which will benefit society and insure him, agreeable to his own expression, 'a small degree of honest fame.' (Jefferson, 10:315–16n)

Smith's coolly remarking that if Ledyard disappeared off the face of the earth no harm would be done is not, in all probability, a reflection of his own attitude but seems very much in keeping with the stoic view of the superior power of fate that tempered Ledyard's large ambition. The strong and positive impression he made upon almost all who met him is one of a man who knew what he had to lose as well as gain and realized that although his success could bring great public distinction his failure was, in the same scale, of no consequence to any but himself. Jefferson who wrote that "The moment a person forms a theory, his imagination sees in every object only the tracta which favor that theory," was not himself immune from the implications of that pronouncement and so was more sympathetic than censorious when he said of Ledyard, "Unfortunately he has too much imagination," and then added, "if he escapes safely, he will give us new, various, and useful information" (Jefferson, 12:159). So far as he knew when the summer of 1786 drew to a close, Ledyard had finally embarked on his adventure.

And then in November Jefferson received a letter from Ledyard in London addressing him as "My friend, my brother, my Father" and telling him, "After all the fair prospects that attended me when last I wrote—I still am persecuted—still the slave of accident and the son of care. The Ship I embarked in was seized by the Custom House and is this day exchequered" (Jefferson, 10:548). Apparently the merchants who underwrote the voyage intended to trade in violation of the monopolies held by other companies; to be exchequered was to be proceeded against in the Court of Exchequer administered by the Treasury.

By this time in his life, however, Ledyard was undeterred by any setback not of his own making. Members of the Royal Society, headed by Sir Joseph Banks, the wealthy patron of science and distinguished botanist whose activities on Cook's first voyage had given Australia's Botany Bay its name, put together a modest subscription on his behalf, and with it, Ledyard informed Jefferson, he was going to proceed by way of Hamburg, Copenhagen, and Stockholm to St. Petersburg, which he intended to reach by crossing the frozen Gulf of Bothnia. It is unclear whether he knew that several months earlier Baron de Grimm in Paris had finally heard from the empress, who denied the passport and declared Ledyard's scheme to be chimerical. At any rate he hoped to obtain the document by applying in person at St. Petersburg.

After November Jefferson next heard from Ledyard in a letter written from St. Petersburg in March 1787: "I cannot tell you by what means I came to Petersbourg, and hardly know by what means I shall quit it in the further prosecution of my tour round the world by Land: if I have any merit in the affair it is perseverance, for most severely have I been buffeted and yet still am I even more obstinate than before—and fate as obstinate continues her assaults" (Jefferson, 11:217). Although he furnished no details of his months-long journey to St. Petersburg, to know the outline is to recognize that Ledyard's claim to perseverance in response to fate's buffetings is so far from bravado as to be understatement, because at Stockholm he found that that winter the Gulf of Bothnia had not frozen solidly enough to permit a crossing on foot. What he quite extraordinarily did as a result was to point his nose in the direction of the Arctic Circle and circumambulate the gulf, traveling some 1,200 miles to gain the point that lay 120 miles directly across the gulf's treacherously uncertain ice.

So accustomed had he become to the opposition of conditions both unpredictable and beyond his control that Ledyard characterized his feat rather as a passive adjustment to circumstances than as the active triumph of personal fortitude it might well seem to others. In yet another presaging of Melville's wanderer, Ishmael, who recognizes early in *Moby-Dick* that the first kick he receives will not be the last that destiny deals him but that a "universal thump" is passed round the world, Ledyard wrote in the March letter to Jefferson, "How the matter will terminate I know not: the most probable Conjecture is that I shall Succeed, and be kicked round the world as I have hitherto been from England thro Denmark, thro Sweden, thro Swedish lapland, Swedish finland and the most unfrequented parts of Russian finland to this Aurora Borealis of a city."

Now without a clean shirt he was off to dine with Peter Simon Pallas, professor of natural history at St. Petersburg, who was an expert on Siberia. He would speak French with Pallas, "a most extraordinary language: I believe the wolves, rocks, woods and snow understand it for I have addressed them in it and they have all been very complaisant to me." This acquaintanceship, which Ledyard owed to Sir Joseph Banks's activity in the international network of natural scientists, served Ledyard well. Pallas as had so many others obviously took an immediate liking to him and offered a good deal of assistance. He also served as Ledyard's post office during his Russian sojourn, receiving his letters from the hinterland and forwarding them on to the addressees. It was probably through Pallas that Ledyard connected with a Scotch physi-

cian, William Brown, who was bound on business to Barnaul, more than
2,500 miles into the interior, for which city the two departed by horse-
drawn carriage in June 1787. The empress was not in St. Petersburg at
the time, and Ledyard still lacked a passport although he may have had
a quasi-official appointment as messenger to Billings who was then
surveying for the government in Siberia. If so, this permitted him to
travel without expense in the empire. Tenuous though his status may
have been, finally he was eastward bound across Russia to Siberia and
the Pacific.

Were it not for the admirable scholarship of Stephen D. Watrous, little would be known of Ledyard's Russian journey except for what exists
in two fragmentary transcripts of his lost journal, neither in his hand.
Reconstructing the journal in *John Ledyard's Journey Through Russia
and Siberia, 1787–1788,* Watrous added information he unearthed in
letters to, from, and about Ledyard, and in references to his Russian
travel in the writings of Russian and English contemporaries. The itinerary he established took Ledyard to Barnaul by way of Moscow, Nizhni
Novgorod, Kazan, Tobolsk, and Ekatarinburg, a journey of nearly 3,000
miles—past the Urals, across the Volga, and down the Baraba Steppe—
that took nearly eight weeks. Parting company with Dr. Brown, in late
July he proceeded to Irkutsk by way of Tomsk and Krasnoyarsk, reaching there on August 15th, and after ten days at Irkutsk, during which
time he was entertained by the town's leading citizens, he set out for
Yakutsk and arrived there on September 8th having spent the final part
of the journey on a 1,500-mile ride down the Lena River. An excursion of
a little more than three months and of many thousand miles had taken
him to within 500 miles of his target, Okhotsk on the Siberian coast,
whence he could expect shipping to the Kamchatka Peninsula and
thence across to North America. His accomplishment was considerable—he was the first American to have traveled in Siberia—and he was
well situated to accomplish far more.

But eager though he was to continue eastward, he was detained by
the local commandant who insisted that winter travel in the region was

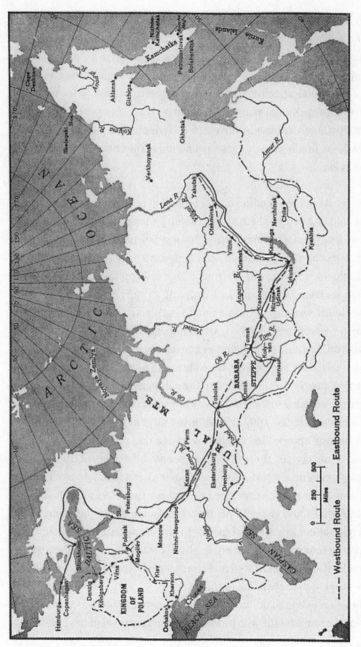

Map of the Russian Empire with Ledyard's routes to and from Yakutsk (Stephen D. Watrous, ed., *John Ledyard's Journey Through Russia and Siberia, 1787–1788.UF* 1966; reprinted by permission of the University of Wisconsin Press).

too treacherous. Ledyard who had circumambulated the Gulf of Both-nia in winter was certain he could manage the remaining distance to Okhotsk but could make no headway against the commandant's pro-hibition. Unhappy about it but unable to do otherwise, he accepted the prospect of a stay in Yakutsk until the spring. In November, however, Billings arrived on his way to pick up supplies in Irkutsk and faced with the continued monotony of his enforced halt Ledyard decided to accom-pany Billings, even though it meant backtracking. When he had passed through Irkutsk earlier he had been welcomed by the governor general and the bank director, wined and dined by them. Now in addition to the diversion of Billings's company he could anticipate a renewal of these local relations to alleviate the boredom of a winter of delay.

He had, however, unsuspectingly reached the end of his Siberian journey. Immediately upon his arrival in Irkutsk he was arrested and in the custody of two guards hurried back from stage to stage to Moscow. There he was interrogated, then taken to the Polish border, questioned again, and deported with his guards' cheerful assurance that if "he returned to Russia he would certainly be hanged, but that if he chose to go back to England, they wished him a pleasant journey."[13] Such, at least, is what he told friends in England after his return. In his journal, however, his farewell to Russia was less chipper. His last entry reads, "Let no European put entire Confidence in a Russian of whatever Condi-tion and none at all in the lower & middle Ranks of People" (p. 232).

After making his impoverished way across a Poland he detested, in April 1788 he reentered the western world at Königsberg. In that city he managed to have a note he drew on Sir Joseph Banks accepted and with the money was able to continue on to London.

Earlier, in October when he first learned he would have to remain in Yakutsk for a season, Ledyard had written to William Stephens Smith, "It is certainly bad in theory to suppose that the seasons can triumph over the efforts of an honest man" (p. 137). But it was not the seasons. When she learned of his presence in Siberia, the Empress Catherine, who had never granted him a passport, issued the orders that halted him and sent him westward under guard to the Polish border. To the imperial gaze, an American who proposed to wander across the fur-trading region had very much the look of a spy.

The greater part of Ledyard's journal of his Russian and Siberian travel was written in Yakutsk when he thought he was merely halting before moving onward to his goal. As a result it is composed with eyes fixed beyond the sights it records on the lands where what he regarded as his real journey would commence. From St. Petersburg he had written Jefferson, "I am hastning to those Countries where goodness if natural to the human heart will appear independent of example and furnish an Annecdote of the character of man not unworthy the attention of him who wrote the declaration of American Independence" (Jefferson, 11:217). He clearly meant the "Countries" of North America where he would travel among previously unreported primitive nations. The greater part of his ethnographic observations to the point of arrival at Yakutsk were, therefore, concerned with arguing that the Asiatic groups he encountered—such as Yakut, Calmuc, or Chuckchi—were all part of the larger group he designated as Tartars, and to which, he claimed, the native North Americans, whom he called "our Tartars," also belonged. The Asiatic peoples were for him introductory to what would center his attention. America, his experience told him, was a part of Asia, and when the history of Asia becomes as well known as the history of Europe, he wrote, it will be found that those who previously "have written the History of Man have begun at the wrong end" (p. 200).

Manifestly, the two poles of Ledyard's world were the region of the primitive, as represented by native Americans and Pacific islanders, and the region of the highly cultured, as represented by such as Jefferson, Banks, and Pallas. He had not previously in his travels been compelled to contemplate the vastness of the region in between. The peasant culture of Russia and Siberia with which he now came in daily contact presented a striking contrast to both primitivism and cultivation and he was appalled. "I looked for certain Virtues of the heart that are called natural," he wrote. "I found them not in the most remote & obscure Villages in the Empire but on the contrary I find the rankest vices to abound as much as in their Capital" (p. 182). If he felt this way during what seemed a vexing delay in Yakutsk the sentiment was intensified as he was hustled back to the western edge of the Russian Empire. And in Poland although he was no longer guarded the sentiment did not abate: "If I had believed from Information I never could have formed an adequate Idea without the little Tour I have made of the inferiority of the Eastern to the Western World & that so vast a difference could be found in the qualities of the Hearts & even of the Minds of men" (p. 223).

When Ledyard said "men" he meant men, not people, because he believed that the differences in men from culture to culture were enormous but the same was not true of women: "My general Remark is that Climate & Education makes a greater difference in the character of Men than Women." In a passage that in the nineteenth century achieved a wider circulation than anything else written by him, he said, "The Woman is never haughty, arrogant, or supercilious; full of courtesy & fond of Society; economical, ingenious; . . . & in general have more virtue & perform more good actions than [men]." The belief was not mere gallantry but the practical principle arrived at by an impecunious traveler who all too often had to rely on the courtesy of strangers in a hostile environment: "I never addressed myself in the Language of Decency & Friendship to a Woman whether civilized or savage without receiving a decent & friendly answer. . . . With Man it has often been otherwise" (p. 183).

But running through Ledyard's expressions of disgust for the peasants he met is a strain of altruism characteristic of his sense of himself not just as a citizen of America but of the world. Like other democratic optimists he thought of American independence as the first stage in a universal movement for the liberation of mankind and he thought of being an American as being a member of the international community that was aborning. While in custody he sustained himself with vaunting journal entries that under other circumstances might be considered bombastic but, given his need to retain his sense of worth in extreme adversity, are entirely understandable if not, indeed, commendable. Harassed by the "Snuff box Serjeant" set over him, for example, he wrote, "I consider Resignation as Cowardice, nor will I set the base Example, debase my honour, or sin against the Genius of my noble

Country. They may do wrong & treat me like a Subject of this Country, but by the Spirit of my great Ancestors, & the ignoble Insult I have already felt they shall not make me one in Reality" (p. 201). But he was no chauvinist. When he said that he could not stand the sight of a Polish peasant—it "becomes the occasion of so much uneasiness to me"—he added, it was because "I become interested to think & act for him, & have not time to do either" (p. 223). Very much like Tom Paine, Ledyard thought of his American identity as conferring upon him a responsibility to contest the reign of oligarchs and oppose the systems by which they rendered the lives of others unworthy. "Daring villainy" on the part of rulers and "base temerity" on the part of the ruled, he said, had led to the deplorable eastern European conditions in which he found those he called "my Brethren & my Sisters in this world" (p. 206).

Perhaps the most remarkable passage in the Russian journal is the one in which Ledyard sought to recover from the devastating banishment that had blocked yet another road to his goal, rallying himself with a declaration characteristic both of his unsinkable self and the revolutionary fervor of his age's radical thinkers:

> My anxious hopes are once more blasted, the almost half accomplished wish! what secret machinations has there been? what motive could direct to this? but it suits her Majesty of all the Russians and she has nothing but her pleasure to consult she has no nation's Resentment to apprehend, for no State's, no Monarch's Minister am I, but travel under the common flag of humanity. Commissioned by myself to serve the world at large, and so the poor, the unprotected wanderer must go where sovereign will ordains. If to death why then my Journey is over sooner and rather differently from what I had contemplated. If otherwise why then the Royal Dame has taken me rather much out of my way but 'I may take another route—' The rest of the world lies uninterdicted. (pp. 196n–97n).

Unmistakable in the passage is the model of the Shakespearean soliloquy that sounded in Ledyard's head as he wrote and in this case at least served him to good effect. As previous quotations from his writing have indicated, he was a careless writer. Frequent lapses in syntax, careless grammar that joins plural subjects with verbs in the singular, confused grammatical antecedents, and totally arbitrary punctuation often force the reader back up the page to reread in order to clarify. Yet what he writes about holds the interest not just because of its exoticism but because of the passionate intelligence of the authorial voice that, as in the passage just cited, can rise to a unique eloquence. Milton, too, informed his style at his most ardent moments; the Bible he tended to use as a source of information about other cultures, less often as a prose model.

With explorers' accounts of alien races multiplying in scientific centers such as London and Paris, some philosophers in the late-eighteenth-century became attracted to the theory that the different races were to be accounted for by different origins rather than by the idea that all humankind descended from common ancestors. Even though he never explicitly subscribed to this polygenetic theory, Jefferson in his *Notes on the State of Virginia,* which he had privately printed in Paris in 1784, came close to an implicit endorsement of it in the extreme manner in which he differentiated Negroes from all other races. Given their common ethnographic interests it is probable that Ledyard and he touched on this subject a number of times in their Paris conversations.

But whatever he and Jefferson may have said on the matter in Paris, during his Asian travels Ledyard's observations indicated that polygenetic theory was wrong. Taking note of persons who were genetically half-European and half-Asian he inferred: "the difference of Colour in Man is not the effect of any design in the Creator; but of causes simple in themselves. . . . It is an extraordinary circumstance but I think I ought not on that account to conclude that it is not a Work of Nature" (p. 158).

More generally, in his Russian journey Ledyard became increasingly sensible of the way a lack of field experience misled the scientific theorists of his day even as he became increasingly conscious of the way his own lack of scientific training qualified the usefulness of his reports from the field: "It is a pity Men of Science will or cannot travel themselves & that Fate should so whimsically ordain to sally forth such as I am for example for the purpose of adding Knowledge & it appears very demonstrable to me that they ought to be hung for staying at home as much as I do for going abroad" (p. 217). To travel was to learn but a traveler would learn better if he was knowledgeable before he traveled even as a scientist would know better if he traveled.

The two areas in which Ledyard felt his lack of training most strongly were physiology and linguistics. In his journal he lamented these wants which prevented him from accurately characterizing the physical features peculiar to each ethnic group he encountered and accurately rendering in writing words from their basic vocabularies. Aware of the gaps in his knowledge, he said he could only write what he thought without knowing whether it was of importance and would leave others to judge of it. "It is better," he felt, "to write many pages in vain than that one of Service to Mankind shall not be written" (p. 212). The specific power of Ledyard's travel writing stems from this awareness of his inability to report his experience in the scientific language of his day and his consequent reliance upon his literary instincts. He offers his reader cultural history in place of ethnographic data and the validity of his observations is all the more telling for the undisguised idealism through which the reader is enabled to read them.

Ledyard best summed up the relation of travel to learning (and by implication to writing) in a letter he sent to William Stephens Smith from Yakutsk. Pondering the difficulty of accommodating himself to the people there, he wrote, "The only consolation I have of the argumentative kind is to reflect that him who travels for information must be supposed to want it, & tho a little enigmatical it is I think equaly true that to be traveling is to be in error" (pp. 137–38). Although he did not consider the matter in such terms, this paradox at the heart of his wanderlust brought him back full circle to the ancient idea of the traveler (theor) journeying to view the sights in order, finally, to acquire a broadened mental view (theory).

A number of the members of the London social group, the Saturday's Club, were keen followers of the rapid additions to geographical knowledge that were accumulating in the final decades of the eighteenth century. Especially interested in the fact that so little was known about the interior of Africa they agreed to expend some portion of their money and influence in sponsoring projects for the gathering of such knowledge and, accordingly, formed the Association for Promoting the Discovery of the Interior Parts of Africa. The group's most prominent member was Sir Joseph Banks, president of the Royal Society, and like him the others in the association were Whigs, men who had been opponents of the war with the American colonies.

When Ledyard returned to London from his Siberian venture in May 1788 he went immediately to Banks to tell him, among other things, that he had without authorization used the letter of introduction Banks had given him as a letter of credit and on its strength had received twenty guineas in St. Petersburg on outward travel and five guineas in Königsberg on the return leg. This gave Banks no concern. His affection for Ledyard was strong; besides he had larger plans for him.

On Thursday June 26, Sir Joseph Banks and Henry H. Beaufoy, as an executive committee acting for the African association, commissioned John Ledyard to proceed to Cairo, stating that from there he "shall traverse the Continent of Africa, as nearly as possible in the direction of the Niger, and with the Towns and Countries on its borders, he shall endeavour to make himself acquainted—and that he shall return to Britain by way of any of the European settlements on the Western Coast."[14] He was to be paid seventy guineas initially and was authorized to draw up to eighty pounds more in Cairo but advised that "in such an Undertaking Poverty is a better protection than Wealth, and that Mr. Ledyard's address will be much more effectual than money" (p. 243). The association was not just trying to save money in advising Ledyard to rely upon his "address." His physical bearing was what instantly impressed all who met him. When Banks first sent Ledyard with a note to Beaufoy, the latter remembered, "Before I had learnt from the note the name and business of my visitor, I was struck with the manliness of his person, the breadth of his chest, the openness of his countenance, and the inquietude of his eye."[15]

It is not likely that Ledyard either required or disagreed with the advice to proceed without much money. He had always traveled in poverty, and although this was of necessity rather than choice he also recognized after his experience of widespread thievery in the Pacific and petty thefts in Russia that it was quite impossible for a single traveler in an unknown country to expect to retain anything of value. The scheme he and Jefferson discussed in Paris was born of such a realization. Particularly concerned that Ledyard in his travels be able to record significant geographical data such as the height of mountains, aware that he could hardly be expected to carry surveying instruments with him—or keep them from being stolen even if he did start out with them—and probably inspired by the tattoo marks on Ledyard's hands, Jefferson suggested that he tattoo two marks on his arm exactly a foot apart. Carrying such a measure with him he could always break off a stick at that length and estimate heights by measuring shadows. (This scheme also gave rise to the idea that other relevant data might be recorded in a kind of tattooed shorthand should writing implements fail.) Whether Ledyard ever got that foot put on his arm is not known.

On June 30, less than two months after he returned to London from the buffetings of his Siberian journey, Ledyard departed for Cairo. Having not quite managed to cross Asia and with plans still eventually to cross America—he had promised Jefferson that if his west-to-east trek fell through he would return to the States and attempt one from east to west—he was on his way to cross Africa. While the speed with which he entered upon the undertaking is stunning when one considers the physical ordeal through which he had recently passed and the extreme difference of climate he would have to endure in Africa, it is quite likely he had been mentally prepared for the venture for some time. That he had talked with Banks about such a possibility at the end of 1786, just before he set out for St. Petersburg and a half-year before the African association was formed, is suggested by an isolated entry in his Russian journal. In Yakutsk awaiting the spring and permission to proceed to the Pacific, Ledyard felt his empty pockets but reflected that once he got to Okhostsk, " I shall be beyond the want or aid of money, until emerging from her deep deserts I gain the American Atlantic States and then thy glow[i]ng Climates Africa explored, I lay me down and claim a little portion of the Globe I've viewed—may it not be before" (p. 167). The Pacific he had seen, Asia he had all but crossed, and America he thought he would soon be crossing. There in Siberia he probably had some reason other than his romantic fervor for thinking he might someday explore Africa.

Ledyard arrived in Cairo in July and established his credentials with Rosetti, the Venetian who acted as the English chargé d'affaires in Egypt. From him he procured an interpreter and set about planning his trek. Obviously he needed whatever political protection could be extended to him once he entered the Sudan, and with the interpreter supplied by Rosetti visited the confidential minister of the most powerful of the ruling beys and gained the promise of letters of protection and support through what he called "Turkish Nubia." A less-obvious part of his preparation and one very characteristic of him was his visits to the slave market, to, that is, one terminus of the trade with the interior. Since the authorities did not approve of Europeans attending that market he dressed as a Turk and with his interpreter talked with the slaves from the interior, noting they were adorned with Venetian beads and attempting to trace the chain that led from the stores in Cairo to their homeland. He also began to take a measure of their outlook since he believed he would soon be traveling among their people.

As a result of such conversations as well as discussions with the merchants in the market Ledyard decided that the surest way into the interior was for him to join the annual caravan to Sennar. Until it departed he continued to gather what information he could, especially from the traders who annually traveled into the interior. He wrote back to the association: "I wonder why travellers to Cairo have not visited these slave markets, and conversed with the Jelabs, or travelling merchants," because they, he said, are the best sources of information and without having expended a crown "I have a better idea of the people of Africa, of its trade, of the position of places, the nature of the country, manner of travelling, &c. than ever I had by any other means; and, I believe, better than any other means would afford me" (*Association*, p. 39).

He wrote this in October and for another month he continued to report enthusiastically on one or another piece of information that would aid him in his journey. But as the days passed to his exasperation he learned that the "annual" Sennar caravan sometimes did not depart for two or three years. In November, however, he was sure he was on the eve of departure and the association could expect next to hear from him from Sennar. Instead there arrived a dispatch with the scarcely believable news that still waiting in Cairo for the delayed caravan Ledyard had been struck with a "bilious complaint" (that is, dysentery), and when the acid of vitriol he took to remedy it caused a burning pain had countered it with a strong dose of tartar emetic. In violent reaction an unstemmable bleeding commenced. On January 10, 1789, less than two months into his thirty-ninth year, John Ledyard died in Cairo and was buried there. The news had reached London almost three months after the event.

In Paris Jefferson had been receiving letters from Ledyard that were livelier in tone than those sent the association, brimming with the verve Jefferson had come to admire. They were in good part iconoclastic, embryonic contributions to the debunking travel literature that Mark Twain was to bring to a peak in the following century. "Sweet are the songs of Egypt on paper," he wrote in one such letter. "Who is not ravished with gums, balms, dates, figgs, pomegrannates with the circassia and sycamores without knowing that amidst these ones eyes eare mouth nose is filled with dust eternal hot fainting winds, lice bugs mosquitoes spiders flies—pox, itch leprosy fevers and almost universal blindness"; and then he cheerfully added, "I am in perfect health" (Jefferson, 13:596–97). That letter was written in September. Two months later he continued in an iconoclastic vein, blaming the self-love of historians and the mischief done by religion for the false views in the books about Egypt. He concluded that letter, "I shall not forget you. Indeed it would be a consolation to think of you in my last moments" (14:182).

Rumors of Ledyard's death reached Jefferson in May, the day he received Ledyard's November letter saying that he was just about to depart for Sennar. This being so, said Jefferson, the rumor that he died in Cairo in January must be false and he wrote to Tom Paine in London asking him to tell Banks why he thought the rumor was false. But in a June reply Paine told Jefferson that Banks had written him confirming the rumor. "We have," said Banks, "lost poor Ledyard." In that same letter to Paine, primarily concerned with the iron-arch bridge that Paine had invented and was seeking to promote with Banks's aid, Banks wrote that he expected "many improvements from your Countrymen who think with vigor, and are in a great measure free from the shackles of Theory which are imposed on the Minds of our people before they are capable of exerting their Mental faculties to advantage." After confirming that "poor Ledyard" had died, he completed the circuit of his thought: "We sincerely lament his loss, as the press we have received from him are full of those emanations of the Spirit which taught you to construct a Bridge without any reference to the means used by your predecessors in the art" (15:193–94).

The next day Paine again wrote Jefferson, whom he knew would be saddened and distressed at the certainty of Ledyard's death, with words of intended comfort: "Ledyard was a great favourite with the Society. They consider him as falling a sacrifice to integrity and lament him with an affectionate sorrow. His manner of writing had surprised them as they at first conceived him a bold but illiterate adventurer. That man said Sir Joseph one day to me 'was all Mind,' " (15:199).

The last word of consolation, however, belongs to Ledyard himself: "I have known what it is to have food given me as charity to a madman; and I have at times been obliged to shelter myself under the miseries of that character to avoid a heavier calamity. My distresses have been greater than I have ever owned, or ever *will* own to any man. Such evils are terrible to bear; but they never yet had power to turn me from my purpose. If I live, I will faithfully perform, in its utmost extent, my engagement to the Society; and if I perish in the attempt, my *honour* will still be safe, for death cancels all bonds" (*Association*, p. 46). The words as recalled by Beaufoy carry the mark of the man: a

Shakespearean self-dramatization in the implicit likening of himself to
King Lear's Edgar, undercut by the resemblance consisting unheroically
in a shared madness.

The peoples among whom Ledyard traveled and about whom he
wrote in his attempt to win a small degree of fame were strangers,
exotically different from him and from those to whom his writings were
addressed. And yet he also saw from within the lives of those whom
he encountered and so realized he was the different one, all the more
strange in that they were many and he was not, they were home and he
was homeless. He saw that if anyone appeared insane it was not the
island cannibals or the grease-encrusted Aleuts or the stony-hearted
Tartars but the one who visited them. He saw that the true alien is the
traveler.

"All the recent work on what is called colonial discourse," John Barrell said in 1991, "and on the relation of the West and East has started
from the binary distinction, however much it may come to be compli-
cated, between the western self and its exotic or oriental other, in which
the other is conceived in terms of whatever in the western psyche is
an object of disgust and terror: the East as embodiment of western
fears."[16] In a good example of such discourse, Mary Louise Pratt has
noted that in eighteenth- and nineteenth-century travel accounts portraits of the manners and customs of indigenous peoples are usually
presented in units separate from those concerned with descriptions
of the terrain, the natural resources, and the outstanding aesthetic
features of the landscape being traversed. The native inhabitants are
placed, as she nicely phrases it, "in textual homelands or reservations"
so that the landscape that has been emptied of them becomes available
for whatever economic, political or aesthetic ends the European observer has in mind.[17] While the European locates her-or-himself in a
history that is moving inexorably to western leadership in the East,
peopling or repeopling the visited land through colonization and subor-
dinating it to the imperial center, the natives of the observed region are
described as so fixed in their different ways as to have no temporal

existence; as they are at the moment of encounter they have always been, and, save for western intervention, will always be.

John Ledyard's travels were an inescapable part of the West's extension of its imperial frontier. He was a member of Cook's third voyage which sought a shortcut that would accelerate the spread of English influence in the Pacific; his scheme of opening a triangular fur trade from Northwest America to Asia to the Atlantic nations would have expanded western dominance of native people through introducing them to a dependency upon the world capitalist system; and behind the scientific interests that sponsored his attempt to cross Africa loomed the commercial interests of the London financial world.

Yet curiously, and attractively, his fragmentary writings and the brief records of him made by his contemporaries (in the main, illustrious men) combine to present a man whose outlook countered the racist, polygenetic views that worked to accomplish the imperial task. Although his plans to become a fur trader collapsed in Philadelphia, and then again in Lorient, Paris, and London, through circumstances that seem to have been beyond his control, as one traces these defeats the suspicion grows that the inherent flaw that doomed each reinvention of the enterprise is to be traced to Ledyard himself and the fact that his ultimate interest in the plan was an interest in the pursuit of knowledge under the most adventurous circumstances possible. One suspects that one after another of his tentative financial backers came to spot the underlying appetite for exploration itself that drove him and accordingly withdrew from association with so imprudently venturesome a partner. And one senses in addition Ledyard's relief when, freed of the commercial responsibilities that were never at the core of his ambition, he set forth to walk around the world.

Ledyard was the Cook chronicler who strove most notably to understand and represent the natives' viewpoint and in his subsequent travels he continued against the imperial current to view the indigenous peoples he encountered as subjects like himself, not objects. In pointed contrast to the travelers who, in Pratt's phrase, presented the "face of the country" as an essentially unoccupied landscape, Ledyard regarded the occupants as the very essence of the lands he visited. Directly opposite to what came to be the common practice of travel writers he offered few physical descriptions; no descriptions, for example, of the Russian steppes he crossed, Lake Baikal that he went out of his way to view, or the Lena River down which he coasted for hundreds of miles. For Ledyard the Pacific islands are the islanders, North America is the Indians, Siberia the Tartars.

A half-century after Ledyard's death in Cairo, Egypt became a fashionable destination for tourists, and the literature of that tourism, as Barrell shows, is consumed with distancing the people through whom and with the aid of whom travelers journeyed from both the sights that were the object of their journey and the travelers themselves. The ruins visited were left by "civilizations" akin to that of the European visitors but alien to the subhuman specimens who now lived in squalor among those ruins. In contrast, Ledyard's distress at what he encountered there—filth, pestilence, poverty—is not assigned to the character of the people themselves and does not dehumanize them. His criticism is, rather, directed at the historians who glamorized Egypt by gazing past the people at the celebrated ruins. In none of his dispatches from Egypt did he concern himself with the artifacts and monuments celebrated in travel literature. He wrote instead about Turkish administrators, Egyptian villagers, slaves from the interior, and traveling merchants. These for him were Africa.

As a young man Ledyard had gone to college to learn how to convert the Indians. As it turned out, the principal thing he seems to have learned in his year there was how to make a dugout canoe; rather than learning to instruct the Indians, that is, he received instruction from them. This realignment of interest was predictive of his subsequent encounters with other cultures. He moved through them as an undergoer not a shaper and it is perhaps because of this that he failed. He did not cross North America; he did not cross Africa; he published but one book and one-fifth of that was not his own composition.

But the attractive power that drew the interest of such men as Banks and Jefferson, retained it through his apparent failures, and made it so

difficult for them to think of him as dead continues to engage the reader
of the records that he left. America for all its provincialism presented
Ledyard with two gifts: the opportunity to live simultaneously in a European and a primitive—a cultivated and a natural—world; and the will to
test the consequences of the belief that inherited distinctions of privilege are unnatural. A great deal of his appeal stems from his unstudied
application of both these gifts. Like Whitman afoot on the open road he
is an observer who sees nothing so clearly as he sees the equality of the
seer and the seen. His imagination preceded him on whatever road
he took and he traveled to keep up with it.

CHAPTER 2

John Lloyd Stephens

—————◆————

Incidents of Travel in Egypt, Arabia Petraea, and the Holy Land (1837)
Incidents of Travel in Greece, Turkey, Russia, and Poland (1838)
Incidents of Travel in Central America, Chiapas, & Yucatan (1841)
Incidents of Travel in Yucatan (1843)

"I very well remembered staring at a man . . . who was pointed out to me by my aunt one Sunday in Church, as the person who had been in Stony Arabia, and passed through strange adventures there all of which with my own eyes I had read in the book which he wrote. When the church was out, I wanted my aunt to take me along and follow the traveler home. But she said the constables would take us up if we did; and so I never saw this wonderful Arabian traveler again. But he long haunted me; and several times I dreamt of him." Although the words were spoken by the fictional Redburn the memory was that of Herman Melville, his author.

The traveler who so magnetized the young Melville was John Lloyd Stephens; his book, "arid-looking" but the opposite of dry in its contents, was *Incidents of Travel in Egypt, Arabia Petraea, and the Holy Land*. Its two volumes had been published by Harper & Brothers in 1837 and in defiance of the great financial panic of that year went through six reprintings in its first twelve months quickly earning Stephens $15,000, an extraordinary amount for an American author. Just about every review, and it was widely reviewed, was enthusiastic. In the *New York Review,* the best critic of his time, Edgar Allan Poe, discussed it at length, taking the opportunity to deploy his own knowledge of biblical lore as he declared Stephens to be a man of good sense and sound feeling. In the following year Harpers, eager to solidify their author's instant fame, rushed into print his *Incidents of Travel in Greece, Turkey, Russia, and Poland,* again in two volumes. This work sold well also and Stephens's reputation was established. In the popular press his name and the epithet, "The American Traveler," became interchangeable.

The best was yet to come. *Incidents of Travel in Central America, Chiapas, & Yucatan* (1841) and *Incidents of Travel in Yucatan* (1843), each also in two volumes, excelled their predecessors in the popularity they enjoyed in their day and the esteem in which the world of curious readers has since held them. After many reprintings in the years immediately following their publication, both appeared in annotated editions in the twentieth century, and as recently as 1993 an abbreviated, "scholarly" edition of *Central America* was published.[1]

Stephens made his remarkable impress in a crowded field. During the first half of the nineteenth century only religious writings exceeded in quantity the number of travel books reviewed and the number of travel narratives published in American journals. For example, in its ten-year career (1827–37) the *American Quarterly Review* reviewed sixty travel books. It seemed as if no literate person left for a journey abroad without promising one or another editor to send back publishable letters, even though few expected to be paid. Moreover, if they received even a mildly favorable reception no series of such letters could fail eventually to find publication as a book. Over a period of several years the most popular items in the *New York Mirror* were the letters sent it by its traveling editor N. P. (Nat) Willis, which then gained even greater popularity when gathered into a multivolumed book, *Pencillings by the Way* (1836). Willis's appeal derived, among other things, from his coy peepings at women in scant native dress—exotic settings frequently licensed a male naughtiness unacceptable in scenes at home—and his insouciant mix of attention to hallowed tourist sites, gossip about high society gatherings, and visits to lazarettos, funeral vaults, and burial pits, the prurient and the ghoulish never far apart in his teasing prose. At the opposite end of the scale of moral purpose stood the eminent pioneer of women's education, Emma Willard, whose *Journal and Letters from France and Great Britain* (1833) mixed parochial American prudery—she believed the plot of *The Barber of Seville* would undermine the morals of the young—with shrewd social observation—for all that she found shocking in the conduct of French women she commended French society for being free of the prejudice against women earning their own money which, she asserted, degraded American women.

A multitude of writers thronged the field between the poles of Willis and Willard, but in a six-year burst John Lloyd Stephens rose above them all. He was remarkably adept at moving back and forth between the particularity of his own lively adventures and issues of general interest to his readers—the historicity of the Bible, for example, in *Egypt,* or modern European politics in *Greece*. Indeed, a distinguishing mark of all Stephens's books is the attention paid to the history of the peoples he visits. He does not pause before a pyramid or an alp in order to produce a framed prose picture as is common with authors who feel obliged to lecture their readers on the aesthetics of landscape appreciation—James Fenimore Cooper in his five travel books published from 1836 to 1838 provides stultifying examples of such insistent pedantry. For Stephens, rather, sites are not unchanging but have a history and therefore a narrative of their own that connects them with the enfolding narrative of his visit to them.

Most famously, in his second two books Stephens in effect founded the field of Maya archaeology at a time when archaeology itself lacked system. A modern archaeologist writes: "What is significant and modern-sounding about Stephens's books, especially in contrast to most other discussions of Maya sites, are his careful descriptions of the archaeological materials, his eye for detail, and the relative lack of speculation amid his observations. He saw the cultural similarities among lowland Maya sites and inferred that the lowlands had been occupied by a single cultural group who had built their cities before the Spanish conquest (but not too much earlier) and whose descendants still lived in the same area. Moreover, he viewed the Maya as an indigenous people and did not attribute their achievements to long-distance diffusion from Asia, Africa, or some mythical land."[2] Another modern archaeologist sees Stephens as "practical intellectual, sober and precise,"[3] but although such terms may characterize his approach to the ruins he discovered, his narratives while precise are also crammed with events and colored with a consistent good humor.

While famous today for his contribution to the study of Maya civilization, in his day Stephens owed his wide readership to the attractiveness of the personality that shone through all of his books: easygoing yet purposeful, knowledgeable but never pedantic, and quicker to laugh at himself than at others. The risks, sometimes mortal, that he takes as a traveler—and so the suspense he generates as a writer—are not taken for the thrill that is attached to danger itself but because they must be encountered if the desired goal is to be reached. When at times he becomes conscious that his account of an incident—say of defying the chief of an armed Bedouin band upon whom he is completely dependent for guidance in the Arabian desert—may be read as a display of courage, he is quick to remind his reader that in his desperation he acted from bravado rather than bravery. Not only did John Lloyd Stephens have the capacity to construct a literary persona remarkably like himself—goodnatured, curious, and enterprising—but in so doing he also constructed an American readership that could imagine itself as very much the same as he in character and so apt to react in a similar manner to the incidents he depicted.

Born in Shrewsbury (Monmouth County), New Jersey, on November 28, 1805, John Lloyd Stephens moved with his family to New York before he was two years old, his father correctly discerning that the prosperity of his merchandising firm was tied to the growth of that city.

Young Stephens grew up in step with a burgeoning New York, his development shaped by the way of life of Manhattan's more prosperous citizens. Although the descendants of the old Dutch families were still at the top of the social ladder, their landed, conservative outlook no longer gave the tone to society. The style that replaced it was vividly exemplified in the ebullient literary output of Washington Irving and his friends who in *Salmagundi* (1807–08), modeled on the eighteenth-century London *Spectator,* prattled on entertainingly about social life in New York, refusing any awareness that they were treating as a metropolis a city that was as yet but a provincial commercial center. When Irving's *Knickerbocker's History of New York* (1809) gave the city the label it has cheerfully worn ever since, it also, in effect, sounded the end of the old Knickerbocker style by making it an object of burlesque.

The young New Yorkers with whom Stephens grew up were not from landed families but rose on the cresting wave of commerce. They did not presume upon their wealth to provide their station in life but actively pursued politics and the professions. Although they had received conventional classical educations, they more often displayed their literary knack in song and light verse than in sober stanzas. Young Knickerbockers gave the world "Home Sweet Home," "Woodman, Spare That Tree," "The Old Oaken Bucket," and "A Visit from St. Nicholas," (" 'Twas the night before Christmas"), not "Thanatopsis" or epics on the rising glory of America.

At the age of ten Stephens was sent to the Classical School, then at thirteen entered Columbia University, well prepared in Greek and Latin. Graduating in 1822 he went on to spend fourteen months studying law at Tappan Reeve's famous Law School in Litchfield, Connecticut, and then before seeking admission to the bar accompanied his cousin on a tour of the American West: Pittsburgh, Cincinnati, the Illinois Territory, New Orleans, and back to New York by steam packet, February 1825. Not just the routes of travel but the means of transportation (ships and rail) fascinated him and were to continue to engage him throughout his professional career as well as his personal life.

Admitted to the bar in 1827 Stephens also entered his father's prosperous merchandising firm and took a vigorous part in pro-Jackson, Democratic party politics until a severe throat infection prostrated him. His heavy schedule of political speeches was diagnosed as the cause and a journey abroad was prescribed as the cure. He left for Europe in 1834.[4]

Landing in France, Stephens crossed the continent to Greece and Turkey, then sailed from Constantinople to Odessa and proceeded by way of Kiev—he was the first American ever to have visited that city—to Moscow, St. Petersburg, Minsk, Warsaw, and Vienna, arriving back in Paris in November 1835, the month in which he turned thirty. His plan was to return to New York on that month's packet from Le Havre, but he could not procure a booking and while lingering in Paris awaiting another arrangement he reread two old favorites, Constantin-François Volney's *Ruins* and his *Travels*. These led him to other works on the Middle East, and the subject so seized him that he abruptly changed direction. By way of Malta he voyaged to Alexandria, thence to Cairo, the Nile Valley, Arabia Petraea, Jerusalem, and the Levant before reappearing in New York in 1836.

During his travels Stephens wrote letters to Charles Fenno Hoffman* who published four of them in numbers of his *American Monthly Magazine* during 1835 and 1836, as might well have been expected of a magazine editor. Yet V. W. Von Hagen, Stephens's biographer, reports that Stephens before his departure had said to Hoffman, "You who have a tender regard for my character, will not publish me" (p. 34). Why, then, send Hoffman publishable letters?

The paradox arises from the attitude toward professional authorship that prevailed in the America of the first decades of the nineteenth century. While a gentleman was expected to be well acquainted with the "higher forms" of literature, that is, history and poetry, and prestige attached to those who contributed to them, to write for financial reward

*Hoffman was the son of the attorney in whose firm Washington Irving studied law and the brother of Matilda, Irving's fiancée, whose premature death is said to have consigned the mourning Irving to life as a bachelor. He was the author of a notable travel work, *A Winter in the West* (1835).

was to move to the margins of social acceptability. In bustling, commercial America, literary leisure was easily identified with idleness. Consequently, "The writer was caught in a double bind," as literary historian Michael Davit Bell explains the situation. "On the one hand, to devote oneself exclusively to literature rather than 'business' was perceived as mere 'idleness'. . . . On the other hand, to the extent that one pursued literature *as* a 'business,' one was betraying its true 'gentlemanly' nature."[5]

Washington Irving exemplified the predicament. Although he contributed greatly to breaking the bind described by Bell, he did so while maintaining the mask of a gentleman of leisure writing for amusement rather than gain. The full title of his most famous work is *The Sketch-Book of Geoffrey Crayon, Gent.* (1819–20). In it the gentlemanly Geoffrey represents his tales as mere sketches, verbal equivalents of the sort of drawings that every educated person learned to make in order to preserve memories of his travels. They were to be placed in a portfolio and shared with friends, not displayed for money.

Stephens's injunction to Hoffman, then, may not have been as disingenuous as it seems. He would have known that his letters were going to be printed, but this did not compromise him so long as his observations as opposed to his private person became the object of the public gaze. And, indeed, Hoffman did omit personal details before he printed.

"Apparently there was an understanding between Stephens and Harper as early as the fall of 1836," Von Hagen surmises, "for by May 1837, Harper was already setting up for publication the work [*Egypt*] in two duodecimo volumes" (p. 67). It was Stephens to whom Mayor Harper is reported to have said that "travels sell about the best of anything we get hold of. . . . They don't always go with a rush, like a novel by a celebrated author, but they sell longer, and in the end, pay better."[6] By that time Harper had read the pieces that appeared in the *American Monthly* and knew he was talking to a promising author about a very promising book.

In his review of *Egypt,* Poe praised Stephens for being free "from the degrading spirit of utilitarianism, which sees in mountains and waterfalls only quarries and manufacturing sites,"[7] but Poe is only relatively accurate. To be sure Stephens did not gauge the value of what he saw in terms of its financial potential, but his persona—the genial, open-minded, decently educated, democrat—is also frankly that of a man of business from a land of business. He recognizes that the increased facilities of traveling from which he benefits have come about as the result of extended commercial relations and he addresses his book—a "picture of the widely-different scenes that are now passing in the faded and worn-out kingdoms of the Old World"—to fellow countrymen who are "in the midst of the hurry, and bustle, and life, and energy, and daily-developing strength and resources" of the New World,[8] an ambience from which he does not exempt himself. While lighthearted rather than crassly commercial, remarks such as the following about Alexandria are earnest: "The genius of my native land broke out, and with an eye that had some experience in such matters at home, I contemplated the 'improvements': a whole street of shops kept by Europeans and filled with European goods, ranges of fine buildings, fine country houses, and gardens growing upon barren sands, showed that strangers from a once barbarous land were repaying the debt which the world owes to the mother of arts, and raising her from the ruin into which she had been plunged by years of misrule and anarchy" (*Egypt*, 1:14–15).

Stephens's visit to Egypt was part of an Anglo-American invasion that had commenced in the early 1830s when the Nile came into fashion as a winter resort for the wealthy.* If his visit was prompted by intellectual curiosity rather than the search for sensual pleasures he nevertheless did not ignore those pleasures. Engaging Paul, a Maltese, as his servant, cook, and interpreter, he hired a boat, captain, and crew of eight, for about thirty-five dollars a month and stocked it with coffee, tea, sugar, macaroni, and "a few dozen of claret." As they proceeded up the Nile, Paul bargained for lambs (from fifty to seventy-five cents each),

*Appended to later editions of *Egypt* is a notice of the Egyptian Society that is forming to establish a library in Cairo. Since there is an increase of travelers to Egypt, the notice says, men of letters and science will welcome a rendezvous where information can be exchanged and garnered from a collection of works on Egypt and its environs.

Ascension de Pyramide N°8

Tourists climbing a pyramid with ample assistance from the local tourist industry, photographed by an unidentified Turkish photographer around 1890 (Reprinted by kind permission of the Wilson Centre for Photography, London).

fowl (about a shilling a pair), and eggs (so cheap they were practically free). When the wind failed the crew leapt ashore and towed. At one point Stephens was a guest aboard the boat of English tourists and with them was hauled above a powerfully resisting cataract by more than one-hundred, straining, slipping, faceless men: "I have no hesitation in saying that, with a friend, a good boat well fitted up, books, guns, plenty of time, and a cook like Michel [from the English boat], a voyage on the Nile would exceed any traveling within my experience" (*Egypt,* 1:160).

In common with other visitors, Stephens found that the Egyptians through whose land he traveled kept getting in the way of the object of his travels, but also in common with other visitors he managed to train himself to disregard them. Once at the pyramids when he could not walk free of the throng of would-be guides ceaselessly offering their services he struck out with a club to punctuate his rejection; the importuning, however, continued unabated.

Those who occupied the land lived in huts "so low that a man can seldom stand up in them, with a hole in the front like the door of an oven, into which the miserable Arab crawls, more like a beast than a being made to walk in God's image" (*Egypt,* 1:26). Ignorant of the relation of shape of dwellings to sun and blowing sands, such an observation displaces the ignorance from the observer onto the observed. The modern Egyptians are barbaric; they cannot possibly be related to the men who built the great ancient monuments since those are the products of a civilized people. The civilized tourists who visit the monuments are more closely akin to the ancient Egyptians who built them than are the degraded people now living among them. Although Pompey's Pillar had to be reached through "long rows of Arab huts, where poverty and misery, and famine, and nakedness stared me in the face," he gazed past the sight at the site to conclude "this was indeed the work of other men and other times" (*Egypt,* 1:16). "In a land of comparative savages," Stephens further writes, the traveler "hails the citizen of any civilized country as his brother" (*Egypt,* 1:87).

The savage/civilized distinction that Stephens accepted operated in his homeland as a persuasive rationale for the westward movement of its citizenry onto Indian land. It was routine to gaze past the native inhabitants to the landscape that they occupied and discern that the Creator had destined it for "civilized" peoples. Abroad the distinction served to justify the tourist's contempt for the native who came between him and the culture he came to see. Stephens's participation in this rationale was positioned between two alternatives, both of which, to judge from the reports of other travelers, were more common: either a belief that modern Egyptians, like other "backwards" people, were inferior by nature (polygeneist theory supporting such a view); or an ardent embrace of Eastern manners—an adoption of the fancied languor, sensuousness, and spirituality of the Orient—that accepted a debased, indeed enslaved, class as necessary to the provision of such a condition. In contrast, Stephens's faith in the spread of commerce and technology served to reconcile his contempt for the Egyptian peasantry with his republican ideals. He believed that these progressive forces would serve eventually to lift the peasantry from its degraded position into a realization of its humanity. To the pragmatic American eye, the admired civilization of ancient Egypt manifested itself in monuments that were a technological triumph and modern technology would return civilization to a modern Egypt. The parallel between the enslaved masses who built the pyramids and those who would serve the masters of the new technology was not then present to his mind although he was later in his life not just to theorize but to enact it. His sense of cultural differences was to become more responsive to the daily reality of others as his travels continued and his writings digested their lesson.

In *Egypt,* John Lloyd Stephens produced the first of the four books that, taken together, exceed the commonplaces of American travel literature to achieve the status of what Daniel Boorstin has characterized as "travel epic."[9] Most obviously, they earn that ranking because of Stephens's adventurous departures from the beaten track. After touring the Nile Valley he chose to go to Jerusalem by way of the Arabian desert and Petraea rather than to follow the route along the Mediterranean coast and to follow him along this path is to witness his transformation from tourist to traveler. The sites he visits now acquire their significance from his experience rather than from the kind of previously assigned significance that governs tourism. The ardors of the journey are now tests that he welcomes rather than inconveniences that should have been avoided. The knowledge that the traveler seeks about people and places is, finally, inseparable from self-knowledge.

The change from tourist to traveler registered in the sequence of incidents in *Egypt* had important literary consequences. For example, although *Greece,* the book that was written after *Egypt,* deals with travel that took place prior to Stephens's visit to the Nile and is concerned, in the main, with less-hazardous undertakings, it nevertheless applies the literary lesson arrived at in *Egypt* and subordinates the sites visited to the narrative of the visiting traveler.

Stephens chose to begin every one of his titles with an emphasis on *Incidents* rather than places, but the appeal of his works does not derive from adventures alone. Even when he is on the beaten track his narrative manages to convey the singleness of his experience. Prepared as he is by his reading, he nevertheless sees what he sees directly. His readings provide him (and hence his reader) with the history of the sites he visits but they do not tutor his response: "I have observed that travellers generally, when they arrive at any place of extraordinary interest, find the right glow of feeling coming over them precisely at the right moment" (*Egypt,* 2:199). Realizing this, however, he does not swerve from the conventional simply for the sake of novelty. When he is moved at a site that others have also found moving he manages to make the experience his own. He climbs Mount Sinai and on it reads the Law, believably conveying to the reader an experience that, he says, is more uplifting than any he has had on the classic grounds of Egypt, Greece, and Italy. Thinking of the many enthusiastical hermits who once infested the area he writes: "I too felt myself lifted above the world, and its petty cares and troubles, and almost hurried into the wild enthusiasm which had sent the tenants of these ruined convents to live and die among the mountains." But, characteristically, he then descends from such transcendence to his fallible self: "Blame me not, reader, nor think me impious, that, on the top of the holy mountain of Sinai, half-unconscious what I did, I fired at a partridge" (*Egypt*, 1:220).

On at least one other occasion also Stephens's gun impiously spoke for him, this time committing sacrilege against the gods of high culture. At the Temple of Dendera he sat down and

> even while admiring and almost reverencing the noble ruin, be-
> gan breaking off the beautifully chiselled figure of a hawk, and
> perhaps in ten minutes, had demolished the work of a year. I felt
> that I was doing wrong, but excused myself by the plea that I was
> destroying to preserve, and saving the precious fragment from
> the ruin to which it was doomed, to show at home as a specimen
> of the skill of the Old World. So far I did well enough; but I went
> farther. I was looking intently, though almost unconsciously, at a
> pigeon on the head of Isis, the capital of one of the front columns
> of the temple. It was a beautiful shot; it could not have been a
> finer if the temple had been built expressly to shoot pigeons
> from. I fired; the shot went smack into the beautifully sculptured
> face of the goddess, and put out one of her eyes; the pigeon fell at
> the foot of the column, and while the goddess seemed to weep
> over her fallen state, and to reproach me for this renewed insult
> to herself and to the arts, I picked up the bird and returned to my
> boat." (*Egypt*, 1:84–85)

There is little regret here—the goddess is left to do the weeping—and while the act may not have been deliberated neither was it unconscious. His behavior at Dendera is something other than an act of Philistinism; ancient monuments, as indeed, most other arts, had not as yet achieved the sacred status they were to enjoy later in the century.[10] Graffiti at a site, for example, were not the crass leavings of the vulgar but marks made by cosmopolitan visitors as notices to those that followed that they were to be enlisted among those who had been there, just as one might sign a guest book. Their names were sought out by subsequent visitors who regarded the traces of previous visitors, especially prominent ones, as an integral part of the site's history. While Stephens's defacement at

Dendera is more damaging than graffiti (which he also sought out and contributed to, most notably at Petraea) it is, nevertheless, the result of the same attitude.

More than this, however, is manifestly at issue in the Dendera incident. The face is "beautifully sculptured," but the shot also is "beautiful" and its "smack" resonates. There was for Stephens something satisfyingly defiant in what he did, and that satisfaction reaches the reader, who comes to share his impatience with the indolent pleasures of tourism even as he apparently delights in them. At times this impatience surfaces in explicit comments: "Something was yet wanting in my voyage on the Nile. It was calm, tame, and wanting in that high excitement which I had expected from travelling in a barbarous country" (*Egypt*, 1:134). At other times it is displaced, as when he says, "The fact is, I know nothing of architecture, and never measured anything in my life" (*Egypt*, 1:103) before offering a clear, concise description of Philoe, followed by a longer, more personal appreciation of the history conveyed by the graffiti accumulated there. And at yet other times this impatience bursts forth in apparently gratuitous, bad behavior, as at Dendera. Such restlessness enlivens the narrative even when it remains, as it does for long periods, beneath the surface, and it appeals—even the sacrilege at Dendera—because at some level the reader too has had enough of veneration and wearied by the abasement of the present in the presence of the past welcomes a dash of iconoclasm. Instead of remorse, why not just pick up the bird—whether stone hawk or dead pigeon—and get back to the boat? Consciously or not, Stephens was declaring his independence from the protocols of tourism. He was ready for the desert.

Stephens took the hawk he had broken off back to New York with him. In reasoning that it would inevitably come to ruin if left where it was, he was on a tiny scale not far from the logic that in his day removed antiquities from their original locations to public and private collections in London and Paris. This trifling example of his "collecting" was predictive of his later career. The sites he had visited were sites of the Old World, not just the ancient as opposed to the modern, but the old Eastern Hemisphere as opposed to the new Western Hemisphere. The fame that was in store for him would arrive in greatest part because he uncovered the remains of Maya civilization, monuments that, whatever their age, he regarded as part of the New World, his world. He was driven to those discoveries by the competitive feelings invoked on his tour of Egypt.

As he had been one in the army of tourists who combined winter relaxation in the warmth of the Nile Valley with intellectual uplift in the presence of the pyramids, so Stephens also in common (but not in company) with many tourists visited biblical sites in Egypt and the Holy Land. The practice, prevalent in his day, of assigning events recorded in the Bible to specific sites in the modern world served to create a Holy Land that was an idea as much as, if not more than, a place. Once designated as a biblical locale, often on the basis of wishful thinking, a site was then pointed to as evidence of the truth of the biblical text.[11] Stephens, too, used the Bible as his guidebook, locating, as he believed, the most probable point on the Red Sea where the waters parted. But he was skeptical about the claims to historicity of many of the venerated sites and repelled by the Holy Sepulchre, seeing it as a business conducted by the monks who clearly gave preferential treatment to the wealthier pilgrims.

The departure from well-traveled routes in order to visit Petraea, not on the itinerary of Western travelers, was inspired by Stephens's reading of Leon Laborde's *Voyage de Larabie Petree*. To reach his goal he required not only guidance but protection and accordingly engaged a Bedouin sheik and his band, donned native dress (both as suitable for the physical conditions and a disguise should hostile nomads be encountered), and sallied forth into the trackless waste. Although potentially hostile bands were sighted and evaded the greatest peril, at least the most persistent trouble, came from the sheik who constantly haggled for larger payments than had been agreed upon, sometimes threatened to abandon Stephens in the midst of the wasteland, and other times seemed on the point of outright robbery if not murder also.

Extraordinary as the journey is, however, the appeal of its account comes from the consistently human scale on which it is presented. The narrative is not a saga of triumph but a small chronicle of endurance with Stephens battling illnesses that frequently left him all but unable to keep his mount as he over and over again wheedled, or faced down, or pretended not to comprehend his armed escort in order to reach Petraea and then return safely from the barrens. He satisfied both an intellectual curiosity invoked by his reading and the yearning for high excitement that had made him restive on the Nile and in narrating his travel makes no pretense of higher or more consequential ends. He is never possessed of powers beyond those a reader could imagine himself having although he is perhaps a shade more forceful in his insistence upon going on when, after all, unlike the journey of an epic hero, it would make little difference to anyone else if he turned in another direction or even simply went back. But if he is not an epic hero he is a representative one; not the hero who displays at large attributes that lie as yet unrealized in his fellows,* but the modern American hero whose schooling in classical texts, faith in the democratic experiment, experience in the world of business, and humorous awareness of his own vulnerabilities add up to a character who believes himself adequate to whatever the world will present to him. This character is implicit in Stephens's narratives. As the century advanced Melville's Captain Delano and James's Christopher Newman were to share his attributes with less-happy results.

About the route from Akaba to Petraea Stephens writes, "I have found it throughout difficult to give any description which can impart to the reader a distinct idea of the wild and desolate scenes presented among the mountainous deserts. . . . In the few rough and hurried notes I made on the spot, I marked rather the effect than the causes which produced it" (*Egypt,* 2:48). What he mentions here as a possible weakness is actually a strength characteristic of a great deal of his narrative. Although in this instance the sparseness of his notes compelled him to reconstruct his experience after the fact rather than copy the impressions

*It is this sense that Ralph Waldo Emerson, Stephens's contemporary, intends when he writes *Representative Men.*

made on the spot, even when his notes are fuller Stephens rarely in his narratives conveys the sense that he is reproducing them. Rather his narratives are so composed that the notes seem to have served as temporary scaffolding for a structure that by the time it reaches print stands free of them. His narrative proceeds chronologically but it does not proceed in a day-by-day fashion as do transcribed diaries. The units of composition are units of travel, incidents, not units of time.

Stephens emerged from the desert at Hebron, to be welcomed back to civilization by "friendly and hospitable Israelites," to whom he had been sent by the local pasha because he was not a Muslim and so could not be entertained by Muslims. "I had seen," he reflected, "enough of the desert, and of the wild spirit of freedom which men talk of without knowing, to make me cling more fondly than ever even to the lowest grade of civilization" (*Egypt*, 2:118). His pride in being an American—"I hope I may be pardoned a burst of national feeling, and be allowed to say, without meaning any disrespect to any other country, that I would rather travel under the name of an American than under any other known in Europe" (*Egypt*, 1:92)—did not extend to a fervid, romantic identification with the wild such as was soon to be on display in the writings of Thoreau, a voracious reader of travel literature. Republicanism and the commercial and technological enterprise that it generated marked the America with which Stephens identified himself.

At Jerusalem Stephens learned of the death several days before of an Irish traveler who, found by Arabs on the shore of the Dead Sea, would have been left by them to die there if an old woman had not compelled her sons to carry him to her hut. "With his dying breath," Stephens noted, "he bore the same testimony to the kindness of woman under the burning sun of Syria, that our countryman Ledyard did in the wilds of Siberia" (*Egypt*, 2:202). As for the society that but for that woman would have left the Irishman to die untended, it made him prize civilization all the more.

Yet even as he made these observations and even before he returned to New York, Stephens was beginning to speculate about the possibility of a journey away from civilization into an unvisited region for which no guidebooks existed. In Jerusalem he had toured the holy sites with the aid of a map executed, as the small print indicated, by "F. Catherwood." It was a name he recognized as having seen incised on Egyptian monuments he had visited as well as entered into the registers of convents in which he had spent the night. Then in London in 1836 en route home he noticed that a panoramic display of Jerusalem together with a lecture by Frederick Catherwood, the artist who had mounted it, was showing at Robert Burford's rotunda in Leicester Square. He visited, chatted with Catherwood about sites he had visited and Catherwood knew intimately, and then about rumors they had both heard of stone cities in Central America that had receded behind the green curtain of the jungle. Neither then realized they were entering upon a friendship and an enterprise of major consequence in the annals of travel literature as well as the history of archaeology.

The second Stephens travel book, rushed into print by the Harpers within a year of the enormous success of the first, was based on the travels he had made across Europe prior to his Egyptian journey.[12] Although he had begun that European tour in France and then passed through Italy, he began his narrative with his arrival in Greece, uncertain that he was able to add to, or unwilling to test himself against, the acres of prose already expended on those countries in travel literature. The English upper classes, after all, had been sending their sons abroad for their education since as early as 1500 and by the middle of the seventeenth century the itinerary for what was called the "Grand Tour" had become fairly well established together with a prolific literature on travel in France and Italy.[13] Moreover, there was a large body of contemporary American travel writing about those countries, of which Willis's was the most prominent and also possibly the best.

Although classical Greece was hardly unvisited in travel literature, the modern Greece that Stephens visited was newly of interest to the West, and especially to Americans. The Greek struggle for liberation from Turkey had taken place in the previous decade and while it remained most vividly in the Western imagination because of the death of Byron at Missolonghi in 1824, that site was just as well, if not better, known in America because of "Marco Bozzaris," the poem by Fitz-Greene Halleck, New York's poet laureate, in celebration of the Greek patriot who had lost his life there leading a Souliot force against the Turks in 1821.

> At midnight, in his guarded tent,
>> The Turk was dreaming of the hour
> When Greece, her knee in suppliance bent,
>> Should tremble at his power

So began a poem that quickly became a favorite recitation piece for American schoolchildren. In praising Bozzaris whose "Fame" would endure because he fought for "Freedom," Halleck was implicitly placing him in the company, as every American recognized, of Washington.

Stephens entered Greece at Missolonghi and his narrative begins with his visit to Bozzaris's widow and daughter there. In reporting it he realized he might appear in breach of a protocol that regarded social calls as private matters; to publish the details of a private visit, and especially to name names, was generally regarded as a betrayal of confidence that put the betrayer beyond the pale of good society.* "True, I was received by them in private, without any expectation either on their part or mine, that all the particulars of the interview would be noted and laid before the eyes of all who choose to read," Stephens explains, "but I make no apology; the widow and children of Marco Bozzaris are the property of the world" (*Greece,* 1:27).

The Greek travels that follow this opening continue to appeal to the American interest in a revitalized Greece. The progenitor of classical democracy had in its recent revolution become, as it were, the heir of

*Nat Willis was notorious for dealing in personalities, and when attacked for naming names in his newspaper letters on English society brazenly replied that it couldn't harm those named because they didn't read American journals. Fifty years later Henry James's Henrietta Stackpole (in *Portrait of A Lady,* 1881) offered another version of the Willis defense, saying she was not violating the rules of privacy when she wrote to her newspaper about her English hosts because she was not writing about herself.

modern democracy. Americans popularly believed their nation to be both the child of ancient, and the parent of modern Greece, and American engagement with that country took the form of financial support and missionary efforts, educational as well as religious. Stephens reports, for example, that "when the strong feeling that ran through our country in favour of this struggling people had subsided, and Greece was freed from the yoke of the Mussulman, an association of ladies in the little town of Troy . . . formed the project of establishing at Athens a school exclusively for the education of females" (*Greece,* 1:65). The chief mover in that project, although Stephens does not state it, was Emma Willard who had published her travel book—made up of what were initially letters back home to her students—in order to raise money for the Athens school.

The vivid sense of history existing in the present moment rather than in the past that informed Stephens's *Egypt* also vitalizes his *Greece.* But he does wish to visit the great classical sites, and to do so, he realizes, is to accept, however reluctantly, the responsibility of reporting on them. On one hand, "the reader need not fear my plunging him deeply into antiquities. Greece has been explored, and examined, and written upon, till the subject is almost threadbare; and I do not flatter myself that I discovered in it anything new." Yet, on the other, "no man from such a distant country as mine can find himself crossing the plain of Corinth, and ascending to the ancient city, without a strange and indescribable feeling. We have no old monument, no classical associations; and our history hardly goes beyond the memory of that venerable personage, 'the oldest inhabitant'" (*Greece,* 1:47). His characteristic solution is to give, for example at Corinth, a brief and lively history of the city-state rather than an extended description of the existing site.

The lack of places on the American landscape that had what were called "classical" or "historic" or "poetic" associations is what sent most American travelers of the day to foreign lands. "Had I been merely a lover of fine scenery," explained Geoffrey Crayon, Gent., "I should have felt little desire to seek elsewhere its gratification: for on no country have the charms of nature been more prodigally lavished" than on

America. "But Europe held forth the charms of storied and poetical associations." In so saying he spoke for all nineteenth-century American travelers who crossed the Atlantic to visit the fabled sites about which they had read. While, however, these sites were, for the most part, the places at which one or another memorialized event had actually taken place, the "associations" that stirred the emotions of the visitor did not inhere in the site—it was, after all, a building, a field, a stone—but were brought to it by the visitor who arrived prepared to have the appropriate experience. A voluminous travel literature existed to supply "associations," but it is the mark of a superior account such as Stephens's that it neither, on one hand, continues to say what has always been said, nor, on the other, seeks to escape the obvious through debunking it, an approach that also, in effect, depends upon "associations."

In sentences such as the following Stephens smiles at the kind of American travel accounts that Poe praised him for not writing: "There is a good chance for an enterprising Connecticut man to set up a hotel in Constantinople. The reader will see that I have travelled with my eyes open, and I trust this shrewd observation on entering the city of the Caesars will be considered characteristic and American" (*Greece,* 1:218). But he was not entirely in jest. The remark was as much a sly smile of self-awareness as it was a glance at others and it is a strength rather than a weakness of his work that he saw things with the educated eye of an American man of business. Although he did not crassly talk of the money value of what he saw, in his accounts there is an unstated perception that cultural or aesthetic value and monetary value are not entirely different. In the uncultivated, "beautiful region" of Anatolia, he sees greater inducements for European emigrants than exist in any portion of the United States now that steamboats are becoming common and this leads to the further consideration that "wonderful as the effects of steamboats have been under our own eyes, we are yet to see them far more wonderful in bringing into close alliance, commercial and social, people from distant countries, of different languages and habits; in removing national prejudices, and in breaking down the great characteristic distinctions of nations" (*Greece,* 1:209). Within ten years of his European travel Stephens was to become director of the Ocean Steam and Navigating Company of New York. It would be wrong, however, to conclude that he traveled in search of business opportunities. The vitality of his books derives from the same source as the vitality of his business enterprises, an ability not just to see the past in the present but the present in the future and to believe in the ultimate compatibility of technological progress and human betterment.

Athens, then, posed a particular problem for Stephens because there modern progress and cultural preservation were clearly at odds: "Even I, deeply imbued with the utilitarian spirit of my country, and myself a quondam speculator in 'up-town lots,' would fain save Athens from the ruthless hand of renovation; from the building mania of modern speculators. I would have her go on till there was not a habitation among her ruins; till she stood like Pompeii, alone in the wilderness, a sacred desert where the traveller might sit down and meditate alone and undisturbed among the relics of the past" (*Greece,* 1:83). The paradox inherent in his contention is that tourists' interests both increase the cultural value of a site—the more it is visited the more it is celebrated—and, prior to the age of mass tourism, decrease its financial potential—its environs are thus rendered exempt from profitable commercial development. Unresolved here the dilemma was to recur in inverted form in the Central American jungle where it became a practical rather than a theoretical issue as he pondered the purchase of Maya sites whose cost increased dramatically only because he had identified them as culturally precious.

Travel beyond geographical boundaries encouraged the trespassing also of the moral boundaries of the homeland, and Stephens was not unlike other male visitors to the East, who found such transgression especially tempting when they crossed from Europe into the lands of exotic harems, Turkish baths, hashish, and bodies openly for sale.[14] Whatever explicit sexual encounters may have occurred did not, to be sure, find their direct way into their travel books but were there, nevertheless, in barely suppressed form when they paused to undress with their gaze the native women whom they encountered. Willis provides a number of examples of this rather common practice, one that to modern eyes is far more objectionable than would have been a blunter admission of desire. At a village outside Smyrna, in one instance, the curtain of a tent is lifted as he passes to reveal "a beautiful girl, of perhaps thirteen" whom he proceeds to describe in some detail, heightening the suggestiveness of what is exposed with a description of the jewelry or costume that guides the eye to it: dark, rounded arms with silver bracelets, fine eyes between which a gold coin on a yellow thread is suspended, a naked bust beneath which a girdle loosely sustains a long pair of full Turkish trousers.[15] Stephens too participated in this convention although less frequently and in less detail than Willis. What Americans such as they were experiencing was a society in which the extremity of class—even caste—differences created a population that seemed explicitly at the disposal of men with money. Nothing like it existed back home, and whether or not they physically surrendered to temptation they were unable to resist a literary refraction of the desire this aroused. "She was not more than sixteen, with a sweet mild face, and a figure that the finest lady might be proud to exhibit in its native beauty;" Stephens writes of a Nubian girl, "every limb charmingly rounded, and every muscle finely developed. It would have been a burning shame to put such a figure in a frock, petticoat, and the other et ceteras of a lady's dress" (*Egypt,* 1:115). It seems apparent that the "burning shame" is actually located in an observer conscience-stricken by what excites him.

The ultimate subjection of women to male desire was to be found in the institution of slavery. No defender of that institution as it existed in the United States would admit this was an inherent feature of it—it was slavery's opponents who raised and melodramatized that point—but abroad the traveler's visit to the slave market conventionally dwelt upon the sexual possibilities on display there. Willis, for example, visited the slave market in Constantinople for the avowed purpose of looking at the women there and did so with such avidity that he felt compelled to undercut his fervor with an anticlimactic description of a fat slave eating a pie, as if this would mitigate the prurience which had brought him to the site.

Stephens, however, is emphatically aware that slavery in America "will not admit of any palliation," and writhes, as he perhaps too energetically puts it, with mortification whenever in his travels he is taunted by the fact that slavery in his homeland puts the lie to America's claims to be a free republic. For him, then, the observation of slavery in the Turkish Empire was not a matter of self-indulgence but of self-realization. "Bad, horrible as this traffic is under any circumstances, to my habits and feelings it loses the shade of its horrors when confined to blacks; but here whites and blacks were exposed together in the same bazar" (*Greece,* 1:237). In nature black deepens shading, but in moral shock at the sight of white slaves Stephens's language reverses nature: the slavery of blacks is lighter than the slavery of whites.

As he became more knowledgeable about the nature of Turkish slaves both black and white, however, Stephens's racial outlook modulated. Then in Russia, where like Ledyard before him he was appalled by the condition of the serfs, he rejected his previous notions of a natural link between racial difference and human bondage. The marks of physical and personal degradation on the Russian serf "were so strong, that I was insensibly compelled to abandon certain theories not uncommon among my countrymen at home in regard to the intrinsic superiority of the white race above all others. Perhaps, too, this impression was aided by my having previously met with Africans of intelligence and capacity, standing upon a footing of perfect equality as soldiers and officers in the Greek army and the sultan's" (*Greece,* 2:40–41).

His knowledge of French, Italian, and a crude form of conversational Latin served Stephens in Greece and Turkey but in Russia he sometimes found himself unable to communicate. Since he traveled alone he made it a practice never to eat alone in his apartments in the hotel but to use the public dining room in order to make acquaintances and acquire the information he wanted in a strange city. But perhaps because of his occasional linguistic isolation he sometimes fell back upon the kind of guidebook description he was usually so skillful at avoiding. A sentence from his description of the Cathedral of Our Lady of Cazan illustrates, by contrast, why his travel writing is so rewarding. This is the kind of thing one does *not* often encounter in Stephens: "Within, fifty noble columns, each of one piece of solid granite from Finland, forty-eight feet high and four feet in diameter, surmounted by a rich capital of bronze, and resting on a massive bronze base, support an arched roof richly ornamented with flowers in bas-relief" (*Greece,* 2:131).

Characteristically, Stephens carries a lore with him as a backdrop against which to animate the places he visits. As that lore is the Bible in his Egyptian journey and both the ancient classics and modern Greek history in his Greek and Turkish journey so in Eastern Europe it is the history of the Napoleonic wars and of the unsuccessful uprisings in Poland. Always in the foreground of a place visited are distinct portraits of the people who live there; in Minsk, for example, the Jews, whose outcast and persecuted state he sympathizes with, although when he encounters Jews on the road, as he frequently does since they are the principal keepers of posthouses, he finds them dirty, grasping, and disagreeable. Many a potentially dull stretch of road is made lively on the page by his haggling with posthouse keepers in mutually incomprehensible languages. Since there was nothing resembling public transportation—the closest thing would have been to engage room, not even a seat, just some space on one or another totally uncomfortable and wildly unpunctual vehicle bound in one's direction on business— Stephens was forced to engage his own carriage, driven by hired coachmen who since they spoke only Russian and were, he maintained, always drunk were oblivious to any directions he offered. His journey out of Russia was happier, enlivened by his sharing a coach with a minor nobleman whose company both pleased and amused him, not the least because this amiable companion paid court to the women of every city in which they halted: "He was a capital fellow, a great beau in his little town on the frontiers of Poland, and one of a class by no means uncommon, that of the very ugly men who imagine themselves very hand-some" (*Greece*, 2:119).*

Incidents of Travel in Greece, Turkey, Russia, and Poland followed its predecessor in galloping through edition after edition. It became abundantly clear to Stephens that unlike any American traveler before him he could finance future travel on the proceeds from the books about his previous travels. He was not a professional writer, nor did he intend to become one; the chief end of his travels was not the income to be earned through writing about them. But the income he did derive served to enable him to undertake travel for other ends, and within a year of the publication of *Greece* he was once again traveling, this time not in the footsteps of any but on a journey of exploration.

When he returned to New York in 1837 Stephens found that Frederick Catherwood, the English artist whom he had met in London, had preceded him and was with good success displaying his "Splendid Panorama of Jerusalem" at a rotunda expressly built for the purpose near Broadway at the corner of Mercer and Prince Streets. Impressed by Catherwood's artistry and his profound knowledge of the Middle East, he had lived there for seven years and spoke Arabic, French, and Italian, Stephens renewed their acquaintanceship and in the preface to later editions of *Egypt,* promoted Catherwood's exhibit: "In justice to one who deserves it. The author would endeavor to direct the attention of the public to MR. CATHERWOOD'S PANORAMA OF JERUSALEM."[16] He went on to declare that in London the panorama had created a sensation and was visited by more than 140,000 persons in one season.

Catherwood was an artist-architect, a master depicter of architectural detail. He was among the last members of a profession which was soon to be made obsolete by the development of photography, a technology that could accomplish in minutes what it took months for the artist

---

*A degree of self-irony may be at play here. The red-bearded Stephens had protuberant eyes. Melville called him "lobster-eyed" and a woman acquaintance fondly referred to him as her "gargoyle."

Portrait of John Lloyd Stephens from a woodcut reproduced in *Harper's Monthly* for
January 1859.

to render, albeit without the ambience of the drawing. Catherwood had
grown up in the same London neighborhood as Joseph Severn, John
Keats's close friend, like Severn had studied at the Royal Academy,
where his principal mentor was Sir John Soane (both Fuselli and Turner
also lectured there in the days of his attendance), and after Keats's
death he joined Severn and roomed with him in Rome. In 1828 he joined
the team organized by Robert Hay, Marquis of Tweeddale, that undertook a systematic description of Egyptian ruins, going from site to site to
make plans of the grounds and drawings of the monuments and murals.
The team was in the field for ten years but in 1832 Catherwood was
back in Cairo working for Pasha Mehmet Ali on mosque restoration

after which he went to Jerusalem where among other accomplishments he made amazingly detailed drawings of the Mosque of Omar.

In New York Catherwood and Stephens once again took up the subject of the rumored ruins of Central America. The literature they had consulted, three books "shadowy in evidence and exaggerated in illustration," as Catherwood's biographer characterizes them, were principally concerned with Palenque in the Mexican province of Chiapas. But in New York the bookseller, John Russell Bartlett, brought them the newly published *Voyage pittoresque et archéologique* of Jean-Frédéric Waldeck which mentioned other sites, and even though Catherwood suspected that the illustrated monuments looked suspiciously like some in Egypt* the book, nevertheless, provided the final push that sent them on their way.

They realized that there was a good chance that the reports that lured them were so inaccurate as to be downright false, but with confidence in his ability to produce a marketable travel book even should this prove to be so, and with certainty about the importance and profitability of a well-illustrated book should discoveries actually be made, attorney Stephens drew up a contract with Catherwood. It stipulated that the artist would accompany him on his journey through Central America, Chiapas, and Yucatan, make drawings of any ruins deemed desirable by Stephens, not publish his own account of the journey, and not interfere with Stephens's right to the exclusive use of the information and materials gathered, including the drawings. Catherwood received a down payment of $200 and was guaranteed all travel expenses and a fee of $1,500, against which $25 a week was to be paid the family he left in New York while he was traveling. This agreed, they set off on the journey that was to establish the field of Maya archaeology and introduce

---

*That the Waldeck illustrations were inaccurate in this direction undoubtedly derives from the fact that most antiquarians who considered the matter attributed Central American ruins to migrating or just plain lost Egyptians, Israelites, Vikings, or Celts, and assigned them to a remote period in antiquity. It seemed impossible for them to have any relation to the Indians who now lived among them.

that civilization to the world. It was also to result in Stephens's best book, one of the greatest works of American travel literature.

Just before their departure for the Gulf of Honduras, Stephens learned of the death of William Leggett, the American minister to the Republic of Central America, and, Democratic Party loyalist that he was, applied to President Van Buren and received the post. He did not seek it for financial remuneration. Indeed, his charge was to close the legation in Guatemala City and send the papers back home because no one was certain that the Republic which once consisted of Guatemala, Nicaragua, Salvador, Costa Rica, and Honduras still held together or if it did where its present capital might be. Stephens, that is, was sent in search of a government. While genuinely committed to fulfilling his charge, Stephens sought the post because he believed that a diplomatic passport and diplomatic uniform would be useful in gaining the respect of officials, from village alcaldes to provincial gobernadores to national authorities (if they existed), who could expedite his explorations. In the event, the passport proved nearly valueless because so harried was the Republic by civil war that the only useful document was a pass signed by whatever military commander at that moment controlled the region through which he was passing, and even such was not helpful when he was confronted, as he was from time to time, by armed men who could not read. When that occurred he was detained or imprisoned until either a literate officer arrived or he procured his release by sheer blustering. It was unlikely that an armed group of Guatemalan Indians would be shaken by the threat that their bad behavior would be reported back to some place called Washington, but the oral display that conveyed the threat sometimes did the trick. As for the uniform, he never had occasion to wear it officially although he had frequent occasion to laugh at himself for thinking it would be useful.

In October 1839 Stephens and Catherwood arrived in Belize by boat, and after a brief stay there where they began gathering news of the distracted state of the Central American Republic continued by sea to the coastal town of Livingston, whence they proceeded into the Guatemalan interior by sailing up the Rio Dulce to Izabal. There they prepared for entry into the Sierra Madre range gathering an equipage of five mules, one each for Stephens, Catherwood, and Augustin, the young French Spaniard from Santo Domingo they had engaged as a servant, and two for their luggage, which included equipment Catherwood needed for his work and a stock of medical supplies as well as items of clothing. They also carried some equipment for camping but in the event almost always managed to find lodging in the dirt-floored building that served in every village as a town hall when they could not, as they more often did, purchase a room from a native farmer, receive hospitality in a larger hacienda, or obtain lodgings with the local priest, generally the proprietor of the best accommodations in town.

Additionally a helpful Guatemalan acquaintance knowledgeable in the ways of travel in his country had engaged four Indian carriers for them. "If we had been consulted," Stephens said, "perhaps at that time we should have scrupled to use men as beasts of burden, but Señor Ampudia had made all the arrangements for us." His conscience, however, seemed to have been assuaged when he observed a fat, amiable priest who not only had Indian carriers for his luggage but also for himself. He "set off on the back of an Indian, in a *silla,* a chair with a high back and top to protect him from the sun. Three other Indians followed as relay carriers, and a noble mule for his relief should he become tired of the chair. The Indian was bent almost double, but the canónigo was in high spirits, smoking his cigar and waving his hand till he was out of sight" (*Central America,* 1:37). At least, Stephens reasoned, his carriers were used only for the baggage.

The instant portrait of the traveling canónigo is one of a myriad of brief and vivid verbal illustrations that enliven Stephens's narrative. Whatever the larger purpose of his travel, however impressive the major sites he visits or exciting the incidents in which he participates, his pen is also quick to capture the passing details of people going about their lives: loin-clothed Indians bearing to burial an unwrapped corpse bouncing on its bier as they make their way over the uneven trail; a man and wife on horseback, he with a gamecock under his arm, she with a guitar, a little boy hidden away among the bedding of a luggage mule, and four lads trailing along, each with a gamecock wrapped in matting, only head and tail visible; elegantly dressed society women stepping around drunken soldiers sprawled in their path as they return from a ball. Such pictures actualize his travels as depictions of landscape cannot.

Although he says, "I regret that I cannot communicate to the reader the highest pleasure of my journey in Central America, that derived from the extraordinary beauty of scenery constantly changing" (*Central America,* 1:237), his narrative benefits from not being slowed by attempts to render aesthetic effect through verbal landscape painting. One or another sentence may remark on how stunningly beautiful the sight before his eyes is, but he records its physical details without emotive embellishment. While in good American fashion he had sought out sites in the Old World that had historical associations, the New World sites presented a different challenge. Of Guatemala City seen from a distant height, Stephens says, "It had no storied associations, but by its own beauty it created an impression on the mind of a traveler which could never be effaced" (*Central America,* 1:149–50). The absence of associations cleared the mind to receive a direct impression even as the clarity of the mountain air permitted the eyes to see a sharper image. When his imagination begins to grapple with the scope and grandeur of Maya sites, a good deal of the excitement he conveys derives from his awesome realization that with each stroke of the machete another detail of a major civilization is emerging before his eyes massively, mysteriously, silently, unclothed by historical or poetic associations.

After leaving Izabal and crossing Mount Mico to Zacapa, Stephens and Catherwood turned with some trepidation toward Copán where only a month or so into their expedition they were about to ascertain whether they were, in effect, on a fool's errand. "Of the great cities beyond the Vale of Mexico—cities buried in forests, ruined, desolate, and without a name—Humboldt never heard; or, if he did, he never visited them. It was only lately that accounts of their existence reached Europe and our own country, accounts which, however, vague and unsatisfactory, had roused both our curiosity and our skepticism—Mr.

Catherwood and I arrived at Copán with the hope rather than the expectation of finding wonders" (*Central America*, 1:75–76).

Their arrival, however, was delayed, and suspense prolonged when at Camotán, the nearest village to Copán, they were arrested by an armed band whose members demanded the surrender of their passports. This they refused even though they were seated within three feet of muskets pointed at their breasts. Instead Stephens proffered a pass he had procured from the general to whose army the band belonged, only to have that disregarded, which led him for the first but far from the last time in Central America to a foolhardy defiance that, he admitted, resulted more from his being treated with what he called ignorance and rudeness than from the detention itself. Haranguing the officer in charge, he insisted his captors send to their commanding general a letter that he proceeded to compose on the spot, sealing it, for want of anything else that looked imposing, with the imprint of a new American half-dollar. They were set free soon after although Stephens admits that he was not at all certain just why; but, then, neither did he quite know why they were arrested. The whole scene is marvelously captured: the menace mortal and convincing, the outrage rather comic, and the shabby contrivance an implicit comment on the worth of a diplomatic passport. As he reconstructs this and other scenes Stephens is engagingly aware of how decentered his important American self is in a land where educated persons learn American history from a four-volume work portentously titled *La Historia de la Revolución de los Estados Unidos del Norte,* that is in actuality a translation of Cooper's novel, *The Spy,* and the uneducated know only that he is white and foreign, neither, their experience teaches them, a particular warrant of his good intentions. The result of such decentering is that in a land where he mingles with a small upper class that has a powerful old Spanish sense of decorum and moves among a large underclass for whom death is an everyday companion he becomes more concerned with his dignity than with his life. To stand on one's character, especially on one's national character, when such a posture bears little coherence to its setting and can scarcely be comprehended by those present is to risk pomposity.

But with his flair for self-awareness Stephens also sees its comic potential and carries his reader in that sympathetic direction even while, at the same time, quite unapologetically defining himself as an American gentleman.

Nearing Copan Stephens finds that those who live in the vicinity know little and care less about whatever ruins might lie behind the masking foliage. But as Catherwood and he follow the Indians they have hired to open a way for them they come upon walls, columns, and carved figures distributed so as to indicate that a multitude more of such remains are dormant behind the obscuring foliage. Clearing the tropical growth from around one impressive stele, Stephens affirms, "The sight of this unexpected monument put at rest once and forever all uncertainty in our minds as to the character of American antiquities and gave us the assurance that the objects we were in search of were not only interesting as the remains of an unknown people, but were works of art as well, proving, like newly discovered historical records, that the people who once occupied the American continent were not savages" (*Central America,* 1:79). Addressing readers whom, he knew, had been schooled in the notion that the European colonization of America constituted the arrival of civilization in a savage world— a notion he, too, had once shared—he became expansive: "Savages never reared these structures, savages never carved these stone. . . . There were no associations connected with this place, none of those stirring recollections which hallow Rome, Athens, and 'The world's great mistress on the Egyptian plain.' But architecture, sculpture, and painting, all the arts which embellish life, had flourished in this overgrown forest; orators, warriors, and statesmen, beauty, ambition, and glory had lived and passed away, and none knew that such things had been, or could tell of their past existence" (*Central America,* 1: 80–81).

Clearly, that none knew the history of the civilization of the site as they knew the history of the classic civilizations of the Old World was a matter of patriotic pride for Stephens. Old as the ruins might have been they were new not just in the sense that they were in the New World but also in the profounder sense that they presented a new field of investigation and it rightly belonged to Americans since it offered them a cultural genealogy independent of Europe. If there was a difference between such cultural possession and actual material possession it was quickly erased by the entrepreneurial attorney from bustling New York. He wanted to buy Copán in order to "to remove the monuments of a bygone people from the desolate region in which they were buried, set them up in the 'great commercial emporium,' and found an institution to be the nucleus of a great national museum." If transporting them proved an insuperable problem he could at least take casts: "The casts of the Parthenon are regarded as precious memorials in the British Museum; would not the casts of Copán be similarly regarded in New York? Other ruins might be discovered that would be even more interesting and more accessible. Very soon their existence would become known and their value appreciated, and it would be the friends of science and the arts in Europe who would get possession of them. They belonged by right to us and, I resolved, ours they should remain" (*Central America*, 1:89).

However grossly the "us" that refers to those in the United States rather than to the descendants of the Maya builders may now sound in the reader's ear, it must be remembered that in Stephens's world the only other possible proprietors were either the French or the English. There was no Central American government and the local population was uninterested in exposing the ruins and incapable of preserving them. Stephens was, moreover, keenly conscious of the sense in which the discoverer is the worst enemy of the purchaser because discovery renders valuable land previously regarded as worthless. Indeed, in later negotiations at Palenque he was to be thwarted by this circumstance, frustrated as purchaser by the rising price caused by his activity as discoverer. At Copán, however, he succeeded. Although his Panama hat was soaked with rain and his white pantaloons were yellow up to the knees with mud, he opened his trunk, took out his diplomatic coat with its profusion of large eagle buttons, put it on, and thus arrayed entered into negotiations with Don José María the site's owner, who, he reported, thought him a fool for offering so much. Copán cost Stephens fifty dollars.

With the site thus secured there was work aplenty for Catherwood and he prepared to remain to draw in the extraordinary detail that may be seen in the book's illustrations not only the remains of the buildings and the figures on the stela but the precise shape of each of the many hieroglyphs on their facades. Aldous Huxley dramatically but not inaccurately describes Catherwood's ordeal and his achievement:

> From dawn till dusk, day after day and for weeks at a stretch, this martyr to archaeology had exposed himself to all the winged and crawling malice of tropical nature. Ticks, ants, wasps, flies, mosquitoes; they had bitten him, drunk his blood, infected him with malaria. But the man had grimly gone on drawing. Itching, swollen, burning or shuddering with fever, he had filled whole portfolios with the measured plans and elevations of temples, with studies of Mayan sculpture so scientifically accurate that modern experts in pre-Columbian history can spell out the date of a stele from Catherwood's representations of its, to him, incomprehensible hieroglyphs.[17]

Stephens, meanwhile, assembled his tiny caravan and pushed on to Guatemala City in search of the government to which he was accredited but which he was already fairly certain no longer existed. In his journeying he was no less exposed to illness, injury, and death than was Catherwood at Copán, frequently seized by the alternating extremes of malaria and sometimes leveled by food poisoning. But his physical woes while mentioned are not dwelled upon. Rather, on the road again he is his best narrative self fascinated by everything he sees but always critically and often amusedly so. He enters into friendly relations with priests, politicians, businessmen, and foreigners who speak Spanish, English, or French but his exchanges with Indians are rudimentary. In Guatemala City on the Feast of the Conception he attends the ceremony of a nun taking the veil (curiously anticipatory of a similar scene in Henry James's *The American* a half-century later), goes to the

Catherwood's drawing of a stele that, Stephens wrote, "is eleven feet eight inches high, three feet four inches on each side, and stands with its front to the east on a pedestal six feet square" (*Incidents of Travel in Central America, Chiapas, & Yucatán,* 1841).

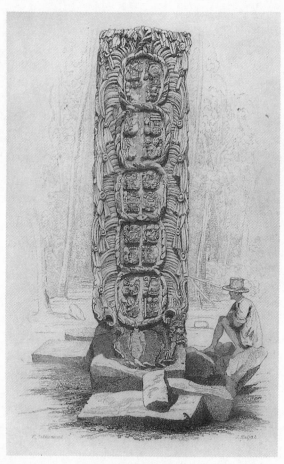

The reverse of the same stele, of which Stephens wrote, "It has nothing grotesque or pertaining to the rude conceits of Indians, but is noticeable for its extreme grace and beauty" (*Central America*).

bullfights, looks in on the street parties, visits dances, feasts, and a cock-fight (which disgusts him), and is awakened one night by the clamor that accompanies the son of his host when he arrives home after a street brawl in which his hand has been severed from his arm. Dress, or the lack of it, a woman's figure, and Indians beyond the spill of light gazing at a society dance flow into and animate his narrative which never indulges the exotic for its strangeness but receives such sights as tributaries to its larger course.

The lore that informs *Central America* is the modern history of the land. Prior to his first meeting with Carrera, the twenty-three-year-old Indian leader of the disquietingly undisciplined army that was then in the process of overthrowing the central government of the Republic of Central America, Stephens gives an account of that incipient dictator's skirmishes against the force of the president, General Morazán, describes the policies of the warring Centrist and Liberal parties, discusses the church's role in the revolution, and estimates what is at stake for foreigners. His account of the manner in which a threatened oligarchy allies with a populist demagogue in order to defeat democratic reform is an exceptionally shrewd description of the bases of the kind of political dictatorships that were to dominate Central American countries for over a century. His movement across the landscape is also a movement through the land's history as he encounters native inhabitants, village priests, Creole descendants of the Spanish invaders, and the armies then fighting to define the area's future. Private narrative and public history intersect and enliven one another.

In the war between Morazán's Liberal Party and the Central Party of the Indian revolutionaries led by Carrera, the church backs Carrera because he will return to it the power and privileges that the Liberals have been redistributing. The merchant princes, heirs to the import monopolies bestowed upon their families in the days of Spanish dominion, also back Carrera because the Liberals have been democratizing their inherited entitlements. In doing so "they were hurrying back the country into darkness," writes Stephens of these privileged classes, "and, in the general heaving of the elements, there was not a man of nerve enough among them, with the influence of name and station, to rally round him the strong and honest men of the country, reorganize the shattered republic, and save it from the disgrace and danger of truckling to an ignorant Indian boy" (*Central America,* 1:245). He wrote this on his return. On the spot Stephens was silent in political discussions for three very good reasons: he was a diplomat and could not take sides in an internal war; he benefitted from the hospitality of priests and landowners, genuinely liked them as individuals, and did not wish to offend them; and he could never be certain of who would control a town on the next day and so to express a preference was to place himself in mortal danger. On one remarkable day, for example, he arrived in Ahuachapán on the Salvador-Guatemala border to find its streets empty, the townspeople having gone into hiding in anticipation of the arrival of Carrera's undisciplined soldiers. When those soldiers arrived the residents emerged to cheer them, only to hide again when Morazán's army approached and caused the rebels to flee and then re-emerge to cheer the new occupiers. Jeopardized by the suspicious character both sides assigned foreigners, Stephens, although he refrained from cheering, took care to visit and mollify each commander in turn in order to secure the safety of his passage back to Guatemala City. Aware of the evasiveness he himself practices he is amused by, but not critical of, the way the townspeople hide, cheer, hide, and cheer again. The engrossing account of his day in Ahuachapán offers on the level of a specific series of events a model of the technique that informs the narrative at large. His personal history and the public history unfold in tandem and he brings as wry a detachment to observations of his own behavior as he does to observations of the political scene.

Stephens was in Ahuachapán because he was en route to El Salvador, Morazán's stronghold, in search, he said, of the government he had failed to find in Guatemala. Since, however, he already knew that the federation had disintegrated he surely could have excused himself the perils of such a journey. Even though it could be said to be strictly in accordance with his diplomatic charge, his decision to undertake the journey appears to have been more strongly determined by his desire to see the Pacific Ocean and visit the narrowest parts of the Central American isthmus. Explorer and diplomat he my have been, but he was also an attorney and heir to a prosperous mercantile firm in a city that was profiting from the recently completed Erie Canal. He was, accordingly, curious about the prospect of a canal between the oceans and especially keen to view the route that had been surveyed by the English engineer who had been commissioned but then left unpaid by the crumbling federal government.

"On Sunday, the fifth of January [1840], I rose to set out in search of a government" (*Central America*, 1:249). This meant going from Guatemala City to Iztapa on the Pacific coast while burning under an attack of malarial fever, sailing from there down the coast to Acajutla on a boat that was flea-infested but nevertheless provided him for the first time since he left Belize with the opportunity to rest while traveling, and then proceeding inland by mule to Sonsonate where the government should have been. There he did locate Don Diego Vigil, vice-president of the federal government, but he declined to present his credentials because he felt that Don Vigil's Republic of Central America no longer existed. That, of course, he knew well before he arrived at Sonsonate. What he did learn during that journey had to do with a possible canal route. He managed to acquire a set of the engineer's plans, the details of which he published in his book, and was able to visit the Pacific end of the proposed route. Although the times obviously were not ripe for so massive an undertaking Stephens was profoundly moved by its implications:

> Many in established businesses will oppose it as deranging the course of their trade. Capitalists will not risk their money in an unsettled and revolutionary country. The pioneers will be denounced and ridiculed, as Clinton was when he staked his political fortune on the 'big ditch' that was to connect the Hudson with Lake Erie; but, if the peace of Europe be not disturbed, I am persuaded that the time is not far distant when the attention of the whole civilized and mercantile world will be directed toward it, and steamboats will give the first impulse. (*Central America*, 1:336)

The isthmus might be inhabited by a fairly primitive population and torn by war, but a canal would inspire Central Americans with a taste for money, "which, opprobrious as it is sometimes considered, does more to civilize and keep the world at peace than any other influence whatever" (*Central America,* 1:338).

Stephens could joke about his commercial eye. In Nicaragua he undertook an arduous climb—even his native guide could not keep up— simply because he was curious to see the crater of a volcano. Curiosity satisfied, he became facetious: "At home this volcano would be a fortune; there would be a good hotel on top, with a railing round to keep children from falling in, a zigzag staircase down the sides, and a glass of ice lemonade at the bottom" (*Central America,* 2:7). But while he thus caricatured the American travelers who saw, as Poe scornfully said, quarries when they saw mountains and manufacturing sites when they saw waterfalls, Stephens had an instinct for the more global, commercial implications of his travels. His governing business interest was not, however, to capitalize on natural resources but to develop the networks of transportation on which new manufactories and new markets would depend. Fascinated by the future of travel itself, he saw that accelerating improvements in steamboat navigation were making possible the opening of sea routes independent of prevailing winds, and he also foresaw the need for a modern transportation link across the isthmus. And indeed, before the 1840s had ended he became head of the company that established the first scheduled steamship service between New York and Bremen and then, a canal still beyond financial reach, invested in and took charge of the construction of a rail line across the isthmus, choosing the route that was eventually to be followed by the Panama Canal.

After his excursion to the isthmus Stephens was joined in Guatemala City by Catherwood, who arrived worn and haggard from his labors at Copán but, nevertheless, in possession of a wealth of illustrations. Together they turned toward Mexico to explore the ruins at Palenque in Chiapas, the reports of which, as Stephens said, first "awakened attention to the existence of ancient and unknown cities in America" (*Central*

America 2:245). Indeed, it was Waldeck's work on Palenque that had put them in motion. But although better known than other sites, Palenque was hardly well known. It lay in a remote area and those who had visited it had provided descriptions that did not seem reliable. Certainly Palenque had never received the kind of precisely detailed verbal and pictorial attention given Copán by Stephens and Catherwood who were, without quite realizing it, founding the field of Maya archaeology.

On the mountainous climb away from Guatemala City, Stephens, badly shaken by fever, let go of his resolve and decided to ride in a silla as he had seen the fat, cigar-smoking canónigo do when he first entered the Sierra Madre. His lapse, however, was only momentary: "It was bad enough to see an Indian toiling with a dead weight on his back; but to feel him trembling under one's own body, hear his hard breathing, see the sweat rolling down him, and feel the insecurity of the position made this a mode of traveling which nothing but constitutional laziness and insensibility could endure" (*Central America,* 2:330–31). He slid off and resumed the climb, step by aching step, pause by gasping pause.

Finally arrived at the ruins they found there was no habitation in the vicinity that could receive them and so prepared to live at the site. Stephens was excited by the prospect of actually occupying a building that had housed the aboriginal inhabitants of the region but his enthusiasm was quickly qualified when during the first night rain poured through and mosquitoes arose to commence an attack that knew no remission until dawn. Screening was improvised around bedding and canvas hung above it; neither expedient proved highly successful. But the work commenced and the work went on. Each day Stephens with the aid of native laborers cleared dense overgrowth to reveal wall, column, and stele, and to decide which of them should be drawn by Catherwood who stood at an easel under a parasol and with the aid of a camera obscura focused on his subjects. When the sun faded Catherwood folded his equipment and Stephens sat down to record details of the dimensions of the remains Catherwood pictured. Food was procured by Juan, a young man who had once been a muleteer but whose pride and ambition it was *servir a mano,* to be, that is, a menial servant instead of a toiler on the land. He scoured the villages each day for the chocolate and eggs that formed their staple diet together with tortillas. The latter because they went rancid rapidly had to be baked afresh on the spot and for that a woman was necessary. None would remain at the ruins, to do so would have compromised her reputation, but Juan finally persuaded a matron to come out each day to do the baking. She was accompanied by her child who served as warrant that her errand was chaste. Some nights there was no food at all and they were thankful for the solace of tobacco. Thus battling uneven diet, heat, sunstroke, stings, bites, swelling limbs, fevered heads, bone-deep chills, and drenching downpours—Stephens said that at home he once was pleased to get an Englishman to admit that American thunderstorms were more awesome than English but that honesty now compelled him to abandon patriotism and grant that nothing compared with a tropical tempest—they filled the portfolios and notebooks to be carried by luggage mule on the first leg of the road to publication.

Industrious as they were, it was clear that they could but accomplish a preliminary survey of the extensive and mostly hidden remains at Palenque. Accordingly, Stephens, as he did at Copán, made preparations to purchase Palenque. Ownership would secure the site so that future investigations could proceed systematically rather than hastily for fear of competition, and ownership would guarantee his right to transport to New York selected objects together with casts of the more monumental, less-portable ones. Negotiations for the purchase went slowly but confident of a successful outcome Stephens left an agent, a young American who had had Central American experience as manager of a cochineal plantation, charging him to make casts and complete the details of the purchase. He and Catherwood then set off for a briefer survey of ruins in the Yucatan before returning home.

For part of their journey they moved up the Gulf of Campeche on a bungo, a barely maneuverable, desperately unsafe native boat that clumsily hugged the shore: "Oh you who cross the Atlantic in packet ships, complaining of discomforts and threatening to publish the captain because the porter does not hold out, may you one day be caught on

"Casa No. 1," depicted by Catherwood. Stephens wrote that it represents "the actual condition of the building surrounded and overgrown by trees, but no description and no drawing can give effect to the moral sublimity of the spectacle" (*Central America*).

board a bungo loaded with logwood" (*Central America,* 2:334).* At Merida they luxuriated in the food, finery, and social life of that charming provincial capital. Entertained by members of the prosperous class Stephens learned not just what was known about the ruins in that part of the Yucatan, but of equal importance, just what hacienda owners in their vicinities could be visited and asked for further information. They visited Uxmal, Catherwood making drawings of the ruins, and, now experienced at discerning the presence of hidden ruins from the lay of a landscape which to the untutored eye presented but tropical growth,

*Five years later in *Typee,* his first novel, Herman Melville was to echo the traveler whose presence in church one Sunday had awed him: "Oh! ye state-room sailors who make so much ado about a fourteen-days passage across the Atlantic; who so pathetically relate the privations and hardships of the sea."

they realized that a great many more cities awaited exposure than any-one, even the natives who lived in their vicinity, were aware of. But Catherwood and he were exhausted, not just physically worn down but intellectually drained, overwhelmed by the extraordinary overabun-dance of what they had been prepared to find on a much smaller scale, if at all. They had acquired more than enough material for the book that Stephens had planned when he first signed Catherwood on to the proj-ect. It was time to return.

At the port of Sisal on June 24th they boarded the Spanish brig *Alex-andre* bound for Havana where they planned to procure passage on one of the frequent ships that traded between that port and New York. From Sisal to Havana was normally an easy journey, but they were caught in so deadly a calm that three weeks later having made only about 200 miles headway the ship was drifting off Cape Catoche with its sup-plies exhausted. On July 15th another ship was finally encountered and when Catherwood and Stephens boarded it to request water and food for the desperate *Alexandre,* they learned that this ship, the *Helen Maria,* was en route to New York. Accordingly, once the *Alexandre* was supplied they transferred to the *Helen Maria.*

"On the thirty-first of July we arrived at New York ten months less three days since we sailed. . . . Deducting the time spent at sea, we had spent but seven months and twenty-four days in the prosecution of our work," Stephens wrote in the final paragraph of his book. After which, with a sly nod at his countrymen's distrust of wasted time, he added, "This, I am sure, must recommend us to every true American" (*Central America,* 2:395).

Throughout his Central American journey Stephens had employed local Indians as laborers of one sort or another: carriers, muleteers, machete-wielding clearers, lifters, and haulers. Each of these scantily clad men carried his own supplies: tortillas, mashed corn, and a cup into which to blend the corn with water and make the cold porridge that was his chief sustenance. Iguana when encountered supplemented the diet; Stephens in a second trip to the Yucatan noted with fascination that the animal was not killed at once but that parts of it were removed for a meal while the rest was kept alive for further amputations at further meals with death postponed as long as possible. The procedure was repellent yet, he knew, entirely reasonable; with no refrigeration the iguana would begin to spoil as soon as killed. But while making observations about costume and diet, Stephens frankly recognized that he had acquired no particular sense of any one of the Indians with whom he spent his days and on whose hired labor he depended; that he recognized none as an individual, a separate person: "So little impression did any of our attendants make upon me, that I have entirely forgotten every one of them. Indeed, this was the case throughout the journey. In other countries a Greek muleteer, an Arab boatman, or a Bedouin guide was a companion; but here the people had no character and nothing in which we took any interest except their backs" (*Central America,* 2: 220–21).

The harshness of the observation is to some degree deflected by the fact that Stephens candidly offers it rather than pretending otherwise. He was bent on his mission and the native peoples were at this stage—he was to change his outlook on his second visit—of no interest save as laborers whose services he needed in order to attain his end. The Greek, Arab, and Bedouin referred to were each encountered and dealt with singly rather than as members of a group and so were readily distinguishable whereas no Indian was encountered except in a group. Even with such considerations, however, the last sentence stings. Stephens's gathering sense of the discrepancy between the immense potential of the land and the primitive uses to which the natives put it nudged him toward depersonalizing them. Consciously or not, he came to think of them as alien to the promise of the land they occupied rather than in natural coherence with it and in so thinking was perilously close to recapitulating the kind of reasoning that at home justified the dispossession of North American Indian tribes with the claim that since they were not fulfilling the land's economic potential it was only right that they give way to those who would.

At one point in his travels Stephens had set out to climb volcanic Mount Mayasa. In the village closest to the crater he hired a native guide who had been upon the mountain all his life. But before long Stephens's desire to view the crater took him above the paths with which his guide was familiar and in exasperation he had to blunder along on his own. "Throughout my journey," this led him to comment, "my labors were much increased by the ignorance of the people concerning the objects of interest in their immediate neighborhood. A few intelligent and edu-cated men knew of their existence as part of the history of the country, but I never met one who had visited the volcano of Mayasa, and in the village at its foot the traveler will not obtain even the scanty information afforded in these pages" (*Central America*, 2:9). What Stephens's guide did know was every foot of the mountain on which straying cattle were to be sought, but such paths were not "objects of interest."

When drunken Indians were encountered in a Guatemalan village situated in the midst of mountain splendor "it gave us pangs to think that such a magnificent country was in the possession of such men" (*Central America*, 2:197). At the time that he wrote this Stephens's im-perial motives were confined to securing the rights to explore and col-lect ruins, but the image of the Central American character his popular book presented to his fellow North Americans shaped their view and contributed to the self-justifications of military adventurers and profi-teering adventurers.

As in his earlier books so in *Incidents of Travel in Central America, Chiapas, and Yucatan* Stephens constructs a compelling narrative that stands free of the day-by-day journal structure from which it emerged. "Public interest in the Maya discoveries," writes Stephens's biographer, "was as intense as the curiosity which prevailed during the twentieth-century raid on the grave of Tutankhamen. Stephens had promised the public a book on his adventures, and the public sat back impatiently waiting for it" (Von Hagen, p. 188). Harper urged him to complete the work speedily, fearing that the Maya rage would soon be met by other publications, and Stephens did work with remarkable speed, gaining Harper's agreement that Catherwood would supervise the reproduc-tion of all illustrations and that the book would have a sensible not a luxury price despite its two-volume format and the many reproductions. It was published on June 25, 1841 at a price of five dollars, within three months sold 20,000 copies, and rolled on into edition after edition. While readers thus satisfied their curiosity about the newly discovered civilization at their back door, what sustained the book's continued popularity was the personality of the narrator: knowledgeable but unpretentious, daring yet fallible, international in outlook yet American in character—good company and a good writer. He continued to be the man they had come to like so well in the earlier books. Poe said *Central America* was the best travel book ever written.

Home in New York Stephens quickly raised $20,000 from business friends to lay the foundation of a Museum of American Antiquities in that city, hoping to attract the support of the government. He planned to draw into it the gallery of North American Indian paintings by George Catlin, which was then on display in the city in its own quarters, and eventually to add "every other memorial of the aboriginal races, whose history within our own borders has already become almost a romance and a fable" (*Central America,* 2:401). But even as he published these words in the appendix he foresaw obstacles. The very appearance of his work had so increased—Stephens said "exaggerated"—the value those in Palenque set on their ruins that the price was rising beyond his reach, while the Mexican government was blocking the export of anything from Palenque, even the casts. At the time of writing, however, Stephens believed the difficulties could be overcome and with Catherwood was eager to make a rapid return to the Yucatan to explore in depth what they had all too briefly glimpsed. Hopeful that he could persuade the Mexican government to lift its opposition, he argued that in so doing they would amplify the world's, especially the United States', knowledge of their country without any loss to themselves. But with his sense that objects of cultural interest were rightly the possession of nations capable of valuing them as such, he was more fearful of interference from England and France "whose formidable competition has already been set up, as it were, *in terrorem,* by one proprietor;" that is, the Mexican owner of Palenque who under French influence was driving up the price beyond his reach. London and Paris, Stephens argued, were already enriched by the remains of art they had collected in the Old World, could they not respect the "rights of nations and discovery" and "leave the field of American antiquities to us?" (*Central America,* 2:401). It is ambiguous as to where this left Mexico, save as a supposedly willing, even grateful, contributor to the cause of a science practiced by others.

Within four months of the publication of *Central America* Stephens and Catherwood were back in the Yucatan, financed by the proceeds from that book and also hurried by its popularity and the consequent fear that others would soon be in the field. They were accompanied by Dr. Samuel Cabot, a personable, young Boston physician who enthralled by Stephens's recent book joined them at his own expense in order to do some exotic sightseeing as well as to pursue his scientific interests. Not the least of these was paleontology, a science that had only recently begun to concern itself in a systematic fashion with American vertebrae. Pioneering work had been done by Dr. Samuel Morton of Philadelphia who in 1831 had published a scientific description of the prehistoric bones brought back by the Lewis and Clark expedition in 1806. Now Morton was at work gathering for analysis a collection of human skulls from all parts of the world and Cabot was to send him specimens from Mexico. Archaeological sites were obvious grounds for such collecting. Well aware that they could not hope to escape the illnesses that had plagued them on their last journey, Stephens and Catherwood welcomed the company of so pleasant and competent a physician. The two had always maintained a warm relationship even under the severest trials of their earlier journey and now with Cabot they were again to undergo the difficulties that awaited them with uninterrupted cordiality. Despite his highly ambitious project, Stephens, the leader of the expedition, was obviously as amiable in the field as the persona he presented on the page.

Before their arrival in Merida portions of *Central America* had been translated and published in newspapers there and pronounced to be *lleno de verdad,* full of truth. Stephens was welcomed back as a celebrity. The social attraction of his party was further heightened by the two modern innovations they brought to the Yucatan. Catherwood had with him a daguerreotype camera with which he planned to capture images of the ruins in order to assist his drawings, much as the camera obscura had served him earlier. In the event the experiment was not successful, but the novelty of the daguerreotype charmed Merida society and especially attracted young women who visited them in numbers, properly chaperoned to be sure, in order to have their portraits taken.

Of greater moment was Cabot's mastery of a recently developed surgical technique for the easing of strabismus (*biscos*) through the severing of an optical muscle. The affliction was, apparently, far more common in the Yucatan than in the United States* and wherever they went Cabot was implored to perform the operation, which he did *pro bono publico,* Stephens often assisting as a nurse. His descriptions of those who visited either for the operation or to have their portraits taken animate the opening chapters of *Incidents of Travel in Yucatán.*[18] As is usual with him, description folds into narrative so that Merida society is delineated not in set pieces but as part of the action.

The Yucatan visit also commenced with Stephens's attendance at fetes, bullfights, and the *lotería,* the gaming hall which, in the absence of theaters and other public entertainments, served as the great meeting place for all classes in Merida. The gambling itself, Stephens noted, was for trifling sums; what the *lotería* really was, he discerned, was a grand municipal *conversacíon*. All things he saw seem to have interested him, both for their own picturesque characteristics and for the inferences about the life of the natives that he could draw from them.

When they set off for their field of study, Stephens, Catherwood, and Cabot were mounted on horses as was Bernaldo their cook, while Albino, who translated between their Spanish and the Indian of the laborers, walked along with his supplies held on his back by a strap across his forehead. Arrived at a site they hired laborers to clear it with their machetes. One squad of seventeen worked so well that in addition to

*Ironically, among the ancient Maya strabismus was accounted a sign of beauty and infants had trinkets suspended between their eyes in order to encourage it.

their wages Stephens gave a half-dollar to be divided among them: Ave Maria, what thanks they're showering on you, Stephens's interpreter exclaimed as they departed. Stephens discusses the peculiar social organization of one closed cooperative community they visit, notes the social gradations at a village fiesta, attends a wake (*velorio*) and after describing it discourses on the difference between those for adults and those for children: "In the latter, as they believe that a child is without sin and that God takes it immediately to himself, the death is a subject of rejoicing, and the night is passed in card playing, jesting, and storytelling. But in the case of grown persons, as they are not so sure what becomes of the spirit, they have no jesting or storytelling, and only play cards. All this may seem unfeeling, but we must not judge others by rules known only to ourselves" (*Yucatán*, 1:233).

In the Yucatan unlike Central America, Stephens was sensitive to the daily realities of Indian life and his book, which made so major a contribution to the history of Maya archaeology, also in more modest particulars contributed to anthropological knowledge. One can only speculate on the causes of his changed responsiveness to the Indian presence: his warm welcome at Merida and therefore a more pleasant transition from there to the Indian villages? Better interpreters? The presence of Cabot? Perhaps all of these were factors but the strongest would seem to be that in the Yucatan Stephens became convinced that the people among whom he was living and whose work he was supervising were the descendants of the builders of the cities he was uncovering. Throughout his book he cites evidence in support of this, refuting prevalent claims that they must have been constructed by those from another civilization—Phoenician, Welsh, Viking, Israelite, Roman—because Indians were not capable of such architecture. He interests himself in contemporary native practices as signs of continuity between the villagers and the builders of the monumental cities among whose ruins they dwell and affirms that although those cities were built before the Spaniards arrived unlike the classic ruins of the Old World they flourished well into the Christian Era. His and Cabot's interests intersect as he compares the structure of disinterred skeletons with the build of modern Mayans, and it is ironic that the collection to which Cabot sent the specimens he gathered was eventually used by Samuel Morton in advancement of his thesis that the differences between races was so distinct as to argue that humans were descended from separate sets of ancestors. This carried as a corollary the doctrine of the inherent superiority of the Caucasian race. Stephens in his linking of modern Indians to ancient Mayans was moving in the opposite direction, recognizing that if the Indians he saw were the children of the Maya builders their degraded condition had nothing to do with natural inferiority but was the result of historical factors.

"Society in Yucatán," Stephens wrote, "stands upon an aristocratic footing. It is divided into two great classes: those who wear pantaloons, and those who do not; the latter, and by far the most numerous body, going in *calzoncillos,* or drawers" (*Yucatán,* 2:69). His new awareness of Indian life stirred his republican sentiments and moved him to take a critical view of such a society. Characteristically, his critique although at moments explicit is made more manifest in the pictures he draws. At Jalacho: "For the last night of the fiesta the neighboring villages had sent forth their all; the ball was larger and gayer of whites and those in whose veins white blood ran, while outside, leaning upon the railing, looking in, but not presuming to enter, were close files of Indians, and beyond, in the plaza, was a dense mass of them—natives of the land and lords of the soil, that strange people in whose ruined cities I had just been wandering, submitting quietly to the dominion of strangers, bound down and trained to the most abject submission, and looking up to the white man as a superior being" (*Yucatán,* 1:135–36).

Stephens's journey had been facilitated by the assistance of Don Simón Peón, whom he had met in Merida. A wealthy landowner whose holdings included the area of the monumental ruins of Uxmal, Don Simón did not usually visit his hacienda in that region during the fever season but made an exception in order to see Stephens and lend him the aid of his authority. Together they visited a cornfield where since it was harvest time the workers slept in the field in hammocks despite its being the season of fevers. When he arrived at the field: "Don Simón threw himself into one of the hammocks and held out one of his legs which was covered with burrs and briers. These men were free and the independent electors of the state of Yucatán; but one of them took in his hand Don Simón's foot, picked off the burrs, pulled off the shoe, cleaned the stocking, and restoring the shoe, laid the foot back carefully in the hammock, and then took up the other. It was all done as a matter of course, and no one bestowed a thought upon it except ourselves" (*Yucatán,* 1:153).

Later on his travels Stephens for the first time encountered an Indian proprietor of a rancho: "The Indians on the rancho were his servants, and we had not seen in any village or on any hacienda men of better appearance, or under more excellent discipline. This produced on my mind a strong impression that, indolent, ignorant, and debased as the race is under the dominion of strangers, the Indian even now is not incapable of fulfilling the obligation of a higher station than that in which his destiny has placed him. It is not true that he is fit only to labor with his hand; he has within him that which is capable of directing the labor of others." The enthusiasm Stephens felt at the encounter was governed as much by his feeling that the proprietor confirmed his theory about the Maya builders as it was by his feeling that the proprietor confirmed his democratic principles. He saw that Indian as the descendant of a long line of caciques. And with characteristically wry self-awareness, he admitted that his admiration might not have been as idealistic as he would have liked it to be:

> Involuntarily we treated him with a respect we had never shown
> to an Indian before; but perhaps we were not free from the influ-
> ence of feelings which govern in civilized life, and our respect
> may have proceeded from the discovery that our new acquain-
> tance was a man of property, possessed not merely of acres and
> Indians and unproductive real estate, but also of that great de-
> sideratum in these trying times, ready money; for we had given
> Albino a dollar to purchase eggs with, who objected to it as too

large a coin to be available on the rancho, but on his return informed us, with an expression of surprise, that the master had changed it the moment it was offered him. (*Yucatán,* 2:42–43)

When Stephens made his second visit to the Yucatan the world knew of only three Maya cities: Copán in Honduras, Palenque in Chiapas (Mexico), and Uxmal in the Yucatan, which at that time considered itself independent of Mexico. The extent of the discoveries he made is astounding: "In our long, irregular, and devious route, we have discovered the crumbling remains of forty four ancient cities, most of them but a short distance apart, though, from the great change that has taken place in the country and the breaking up of the old roads, having no direct communication with each other; with but few exceptions, all were lost, buried, and unknown" (*Yucatán,* 2:290). Among these discoveries were Chichen Itza and Tulum. Stephens announced that the findings gave an entirely new aspect to "the great continent on which we live." What was now clear was that Uxmal, Palenque, Copán were not separate cultures but that the many cities that extended over the Yucatan and down to Honduras were part of a single, comprehensive civilization—that of the Maya.

In May 1841 Stephens and friends departed the Yucatan. Throughout their seven-month expedition the three had intermittently undergone severe malarial seizures, so badly so that at times one or another of them had to travel lying in a *coche,* a covered litter stretched between poles that rested on the shoulders of carriers. The ship that bore them from the port of Sisal to Havana was the *Alexandre,* the bad-luck brig of their first visit, but the passage went smoothly; in Havana they boarded the *Anna Louisa;* and on June 17th reached New York.

At Merida, on the eve of departure, Stephens received yet one more sign of the influence of his work. While he was dining at his inn the diligence from Campeche arrived and one of its passengers accosted him, saying that Stephens had been the cause of his coming to the Yucatan, and adding facetiously that if he did not succeed in his venture he would sue Stephens for damages:

Mr. Clayton had already created, perhaps, a greater sensation than any stranger who ever visited that country; he had obtained a hold upon the feelings of the people that no explorers could ever win, and will be remembered long after we are forgotten. He had brought from the United States an entire circus company, with spotted horses, a portable theater, containing seats for a thousand persons, riders, clowns, and monkeys, all complete. No such thing had ever been seen before; it threw far into the shade Daguerreotype and curing *biscos*. He had turned Campeche upside down, and leaving his company there to soothe the excitement and pick up the *pesos,* he had come up to make arrangements for opening in Mérida. (*Yucatán,* 2:299)

It was perhaps fitting that the portal to Central America opened for North Americans by Stephens's work was entered first not by the agricultural or mining interests but by the entertainment industry. It was also predictive of a cultural imperialism that did not depend upon military conquest or the control of natural resources. Indeed Stephens himself was not apart from the industry: his projected Museum of the Americas would have entered a New York market served by the amusements offered at Niblo's Gardens and the exhibitions on display at P. T. Barnum's museum.

Incidents of Travel in Yucatán was published by Harper and Brothers in March 1843, nine months after Stephens returned to New York. Its two volumes ran to eight hundred pages and contained eighty-five engravings. Like its predecessor, the book was eagerly awaited—in a letter home Cabot had begged his family not to repeat anything because Stephens did not want to be anticipated—and it sold rapidly, quickly running through twenty-two editions, albeit of small runs compared to modern printings. Because of the enormous extent of the archaeological findings reported on, the narrative of *Yucatán* unlike its predecessors pauses time and again for a detailing of the remains found at each site. The book asks its reader to bring more background and greater intellectual curiosity to it than did previous Stephens works. But those who sought it out in order again to be in the company of the famous traveler's graceful personality and to enjoy his narrative gift had an abundance with which to satisfy themselves. The fourth and final book by John Lloyd Stephens, *Yucatán* both established him as the founder of Maya archaeology and confirmed him as the greatest of American travel writers, a position that 150 years later, it may well be claimed, he still occupies.

Stephens reentered the commercial and political life of New York with vigor. A fervent Democrat he was further attracted to James K. Polk's candidacy by Polk's commitment to the acquisition of California which promised to advance his own interest in promoting an isthmian canal, a venture that relied on the United States reaching the Pacific. He was a founder member of the Century Club, and Whigs as well as Democrats elected him to the Constitutional Convention of 1846 that rewrote the New York State constitution.

A strong interest in a Central American linkage of the Atlantic and Pacific did not preclude other marine interests and in 1847 Stephens became vice-president and director of the Ocean Steam Navigating Company that established a line between New York and Bremen. In that capacity he was on the maiden voyage to Bremen of the *S. S. Washington* and went from there to Berlin in the hope of gaining an interview with Alexander Von Humboldt, the world's greatest living scientist, an entire institution in himself as his fellow scientists called him. Humboldt's thirty-volume masterpiece was based on botanical, zoological, geological, and geomagnetic data he had collected during five years of travel in South and Central America during which he had also examined pre-Columbian remains in Peru and Mexico, and in his book Stephens had respectfully disagreed with certain of Humboldt's conclusions. In Berlin Stephens learned that the great man, then seventy-eight years old, was at the Royal Court in Potsdam where he served as a privy councilor, was in frail health, and did not usually receive visitors. Stephens ventured, nevertheless, and found when his name was sent in that Humboldt had read his work and would grant him an hour. To Stephens's disappointment, however, the great man did not want to discuss Mayan ruins. Rather Humboldt, who had visited the United States and met with Jefferson at the conclusion of his momentous South American travels, and who professed himself an admirer of its institutions, wanted to discuss the current American war with Mexico. "I was well aware that in the conduct of the war, General Taylor was drawing upon himself the eyes of all Europe," Stephens reported, "and whatever might be the differences of opinion as to its necessity or justice, it was producing everywhere, in monarchical and anti-republican countries, a strong impression of our ability for war—which in *enlightened* Europe, even at this day, more than all the fruits of peace, industry, and extended commerce, more than the exhibition of twenty million people abounding in all the comforts of life, raises us to the rank of a 'first-rate power,' and makes us 'respected.' "[19]

Democrat though he was, Stephens regarded the Mexican War as retrogressive. His hopes for the extension of American influence both in the underdeveloped regions of Latin America and the advanced nations of Europe centered on the power of "extended commerce" rather than military force. That was the principal political lesson he had taken from his travels and he staked his commercial future on developing lines of transportation and communication. Nothing challenged his imagination so strongly as the prospect of circumnavigating the globe by steam power and when a canal proved beyond his financial reach he proceeded to raise money in New York for the construction of a railroad across the isthmus, the steam locomotive linking the steamships at either end of the line.

As one of the directors of the newly founded Panama Railway Company, Stephens returned to Central America where he conducted two surveys—the route finally decided upon was almost identical with that which was to be followed by the Panama Canal more than a half century later—and then proceeded to Bogotá to finalize terms with the New Granadian (present Colombian) government. Back in New York in 1850 he was made president of the company and in August of that year returned to the isthmus to direct the work of clearing the right-of-way and laying track.

When during his Egyptian visit he had studied the Mahmoudya Canal that connected Alexandria with the Nile, Stephens observed "it could only have been done in that time, in such a country as Egypt, where the government is an absolute despotism, and the will of one man is supreme law" (*Egypt,* 1:22). Now directing a similar project under hellish circumstances, he may not have recalled his observation but he acted out its implications. So harried were travelers along the proposed route by land pirates who pillaged supplies and murdered resisters that he coerced a timorous provincial governor into granting his company supreme policing rights over a forty-mile long and ten-mile wide route, the "Yankee Strip," and then brought Randolph Runnels, a reformed criminal, out of retirement on his Texas ranch to organize a secret service to operate against the pirates. On one memorable night Runnels and his crew hanged thirty-seven men without trial.

Piracies ceased but death had a wider dominion. By 1853 there were 1,590 workers on the payroll, 1,200 of them black. While no exact figures can be arrived at, it seems conservative to estimate that one in five workers died every month of cholera, dysentery, yellow fever, or small pox, diseases that came so unceasingly on top of one another that they were indiscriminately lumped together as "Chagres fever." With the land too swampy to permit burials the company hit on the idea of pickling the bodies and selling them to medical schools around the world. Specimen skeletons of men of "different races" were also supplied for the advancement of science. As a result the company hospital became financially self-supporting on the profits from its failures.[20] It took five years to finish building the forty-mile road that began in great financial difficulty but was boosted into healthy profitability by the discovery of gold in California and the enormous demand for a quick way across the continent that followed. Even before the line was completed California-bound travelers insisted upon being transported on whatever construction vehicles were available for whatever distance was then in rails and paid whatever sum was demanded.

But Stephens was not to see the finish. A body already weakened by infectious fevers contracted on his earlier visits to Central America deteriorated further under the atrocious conditions in which he lived and worked. Increasingly his supervision took place between spells of wracking fever until, in February 1852, he collapsed entirely and had to be taken back to New York. In October of that year, a month short of his forty-seventh birthday, he died of hepatitis, his liver having become infected by malarial plasmodia.

At his workstation in Panama, Stephens had often talked with travelers en route across the isthmus. One of them was a twenty-eight-year-old German merchant who was on his way to claim his deceased brother's estate in California. What they talked about is not known. But twenty years after their encounter, that visitor, Heinrich Schliemann, tracked the Homeric epic to Turkey and unearthed Troy. It does not violate truth to conjecture that Stephens, who had visited Mycenae and Argos, and who, a rank amateur, had with monumental success taught himself archaeology through the trial and error of practice, stimulated his fellow man of business's amateur interest in that scientific art.

"The traveler," Daniel Boortsin writes, "was active. He went strenuously in search of people, of adventure, of experience. The tourist is passive; he expects interesting things to happen to him. He goes 'sightseeing' (a word . . . with its first use recorded in 1847)" (p. 85).

With a more specific interest in the topic but in a somewhat complementary vein, Eric J. Leed contends (p. 10) that for the "real and genuine traveler" travel is a test rather than a pleasure. Only the journey that involves fatigue and suffering leads to wisdom; pleasurable travel is mere tourism. The distinctions fit John Lloyd Stephens well. In Boorstin's terms it can be seen that he began in Europe and then in Egypt as a tourist—there to see the sights—but dissatisfied with tourism's complacencies veered off the path into Arabia Petraea and in the process became a traveler. Thereafter in Central America as well as the Arabian peninsula travel was, in Leed's terms, a test rather than a pleasure albeit not without its pleasures. To follow Stephens on his journeys is to follow a man who is trying himself: matching his will in the desert against that of the head of an armed band; climbing a volcanic mountain beyond the range of his native guide; forcing his fevered body out of hammock and onto horseback in the jungle. The amiable, self-amused voice of his narrator deflects the narrative away from the severity of these trials toward what they permitted him to observe; away, that is, from the subject to the object. But the energy of his narratives derives in great part from the tension between the experiences narrated and the understated self-testing that accompanied them.

Although the writer may be a traveler, the reader is a tourist who expects to be provided for in his journey: shown what is worth seeing, supplied with the information that makes a stop at one or another place worthwhile, briefed on the customs of the people visited, and cautioned about the dangers that are to be avoided. In that regard, the travel book is also inevitably a tourist book (to be distinguished from a guidebook) and Stephens was a master at the art of sustaining the two dimensions, the writer as traveler and the reader as tourist. The people and places he visits become significant because of what his account makes of them and although his discoveries give a scientific importance to his books his literary achievement resides in the narrations not the discoveries. He was not unaware that just as his discoveries would forever change the sites he had unearthed, so his books would alter the places and even the peoples he described. The paramount mark of his literary achievement is that while exposing his subjects to the changes that will inescapably follow from his work, he also holds them unchanged in his luminous pages.

CHAPTER 3

Bayard Taylor

————→»·•·«←————

Views A-foot (1846)
Eldorado (1850)
A Journey to Central Africa (1854)
The Lands of the Saracen (1855)
A Visit to India, China, and Japan in the Year 1853 (1855)
Northern Travel (1857)
Travels in Greece and Russia with an Excursion to Crete (1859)

By the 1870s, a number of American authors had acquired the kind of reputations that encouraged their publishers to present their works in collected editions. The fiction and histories of Washington Irving, the novels of James Fenimore Cooper, the poetry and prose of Henry Wadsworth Longfellow and John Greenleaf Whittier, and the essays of Ralph Waldo Emerson were each available in an edition that in the uniformity of its format invited the reader, already familiar with the individual works, to look at the collection not as a sum of parts but as a whole, not as the stages of a literary career but as its consummation. And in 1874 alongside these editions, the patriotic American collector could also shelve the eleven volumes of *Bayard Taylor's Travels,* issued by G. P. Putnam's Sons in a "Household Edition," bound in deep blue.

Views A-foot, Taylor's first travel book, had appeared in 1846—it was eventually to run through twenty editions—and from then until the year of the collected edition ten more appeared individually, most clustering in the 1850s. They had been compiled from travel letters, almost all written for Horace Greeley's New York *Tribune,* a newspaper that, as Taylor observed, exerted an influence outside of America's metropolitan centers second only to that of the Bible. A ready audience was thus provided for the books that followed. Far from the first to have book sales benefit from previous periodical appearances, Taylor, nevertheless, was foremost among American authors in the profits derived from such an arrangement.

Earlier American travel writers had written about journeys undertaken for ends other than the writing. It was the pursuit of these ends—Ledyard's explorations, for example, or Stephens's search for the Maya—that provided both the pulse that beat through their narratives and the imagination that fused them into singular experiences. But it is Bayard Taylor's distinction to have been the first who traveled for no leading purpose other than to write about that travel. Although his lifelong ambition was to be recognized as a major poet, the success of his first book—based on travel reports he wrote as a means of financing his youthful two years of self-education abroad—led him to an increasing dependency on further travel writing as the principal source of his income. This in turn kept him on the road in order to collect new material for presentation in the familiar format he had established. He traveled to feed the writing that fed him and the more he reported the farther he had to travel to find new places to report on—the Sudan, the Arctic Circle, India, Japan—and the more ingenious he had to be about the means of travel—dhows, reindeer sleighs, banghy-carts, warships—in order to add variety to his accounts. The ever more exotic locale and the ever more unusual means of reaching it were to become the stock-in-trade of the professional travel writers who came after Taylor. He had, in effect, founded the profession. He also hated it.

From Cairo in 1852, launched upon a two-year journey that was to yield him three books, Taylor wrote to a friend about the youthful book that had set him on the literary path from which he now seemed powerless to diverge: "I am not insensible that nine tenths of my literary success (in a publishing view) springs from those very 'Views Afoot' which I now blush to read. I am known to the public not as a poet, the only title I covet, but as one who succeeded in seeing Europe with little money, and the chief merits accorded to me are not passion or imagination, but strong legs and economical habits. Now this is truly humiliating."[1] He longed to be recognized as the successor of the whiskered New England poets of the previous generation who with the English Romantic poets had formed his taste in the 1830s, but, unhappily, also drained all distinctiveness from his voice. His poetic peers were Edmund Clarence Stedman and Richard Henry Stoddard, not Henry Wadsworth Longfellow and John Greenleaf Whittier. Impatient with the fame attached to his travel narratives, a form of writing he regarded as crass because he pursued it for money, he withheld from them what he called his "passion" and his "imagination" and in so doing unconsciously ensured that his name, once ranked with those other worthies of the uniform editions, would become at century's end unrecognized by any but the frequenters of second-hand bookstores.

Since Taylor achieved large contemporary fame only to plummet out of public notice as soon as his day had passed, those who have since studied him at length have, understandably, treated him as a model illustration of how a literary career is both made and blasted by the cultural superficialities to which it attaches itself: "The career of Bayard Taylor furnishes a conspicuous example of the rise and decline of a literary reputation. Taylor was one of the most popular writers of his time. His books were widely read, his lectures attended by throngs, and he was held in high esteem by his fellow authors, who felt him to be one of themselves. . . . Yet his name is well-nigh forgotten now except in the more extensive literary histories, and his books stand unread on the library shelves."[2]

From the perspective of the postcolonial end of the twentieth century, however, Taylor's writings have other value. They provide a fascinating (albeit disturbing) account of the rise in America of the twinned ideologies of the culture of travel—"the notion that certain classes of people are cosmopolitan (travelers) while the rest are local (natives)"[3]— and that of imperialism: "Where a traveller has once penetrated," Taylor wrote, "he smoothes the way for those who follow, and that superior intelligence which renders the brute creation unable to bear the gaze of a human eye, is the defense of civilized man against the barbarian."[4] To read Taylor from this perspective is not to demonize him. He was a valiant and adaptable traveler—quick to learn languages, uncomplaining in pain, willing to go it alone, able to cover long distances on foot, keen to don the local garb, adept at passing as a native—and he traveled to extraordinary places. Were he not so remarkably capable of submerging himself in local ways his reports would not have carried to his readers the conviction they did convey. But his ability to penetrate an alien society in order to represent it amounted, finally, to a tacit assertion of his, and by extension his readers', ability to dominate it.[5] The connection between travel writing and cultural dominance that was always implicit in Taylor's work became explicit when he accompanied Commodore Matthew C. Perry on the expedition that "opened" Japan.

Bayard Taylor was born on January 11th, 1825 in Kennett Square, Pennsylvania into a rural family that had fallen away from its Quaker affiliations but not from a good many of the Quaker fashions. In later life he liked to point out that his birth year was the same as that of the first successful trial of a locomotive, "I am therefore just as old as the railroad" (*Life and Letters,* 1:5), a coincidence he stressed because it was presumably predictive of the fame as a traveler that he was to acquire although the coincidence is also curiously hollow because not one of his travel books is concerned with a journey by rail.

A good-looking boy who was to grow into a tall and handsome man with a strikingly photogenic profile, he very early evinced an intense dislike for the forms of manual labor connected with his family's rural way of life. He was certainly strong enough for the work—as an adult his feats of physical endurance were outstanding—but he had what he called a "constitutional horror of dirty hands" (*Life and Letters* 1:8) and went at chores such as the weeding of corn with disgust. Always a voracious reader he early developed into an ambitious writer of short pieces, principally poems, that began to find acceptance in local newspapers and then in Philadelphia magazines and he was an eager student through his years at a Unionville academy where his mathematical instruction extended to differential calculus and his literary learning included French literature and Latin poetry. Twenty years later, in a fictional account of such an academy, Taylor wrote that the headmaster "was fond of reading anecdotes of Franklin, Ledyard, Fulton, and other noted men who had risen from obscurity, and inciting his pupils to imitate them."[6]

Taylor left the academy to become an apprentice in a print shop in his native Chester County, a fitting decision for an impecunious young man with literary ambitions. The print shops of that day, publishers of local newspapers and other forms of popular reading, were practice fields for many aspiring writers. In the previous century Benjamin Franklin had famously shown the way that was to be followed by, among others, Mark Twain and William Dean Howells (ten and twelve years younger, respectively, than Taylor). Hands smudged by printer's ink were different from hands dirtied by the soil of the cornfield.

Yet in 1844, within a year of his entry into the apprenticeship, Taylor bought his way out of it in order to travel to Europe. In later years he accounted for this by remembering the strong influence exerted on his ten-year-old self by Nat Willis's *Pencillings By the Way*, the installments of which he avidly followed as they were copied into his local newspaper from the *New York Mirror* as soon as they appeared there. The longing they aroused was intensified in the following years by his reading Longfellow's *Outre-Mer*—a misty, idealized account of youthful wanderings in Europe—and Irving's sketches of foreign sites, which, curiously, managed to stimulate a widespread nostalgia for the Old World in Americans who had never left home. It was as if those foreign scenes were already in their memories, awaiting the prose that lifted them into consciousness.

The literary models who inspired Taylor, however, had entered upon their travels with funds sufficient to ensure their ability to make the visits they planned comfortably although they occasionally indulged in the persona of the wayfaring student. But Taylor was poor, markedly so after paying to be released from his apprenticeship, so that when, for example, he and the cousin who was to accompany him realized that they would need passports, they walked from Pennsylvania to Washington to procure them in order both to hoard what little money they had and to put into practice the chief means of locomotion they planned to employ in Europe. In plain and simple America, the impecunious youths called directly on the secretary of state John C. Calhoun, received the passports from his hand, and then walked back home.

Taylor left for Europe with $140: $40 from poems he had published and, after visiting them in Philadelphia, $50 each from the editors of the *Saturday Evening Post* and the *United States Gazette,* in exchange for twelve travel letters promised (and later dutifully supplied) to each. In New York prior to embarkation he called upon Nat Willis who gave him a letter of introduction to his brother Richard then studying in Germany. He also called upon Horace Greeley who, as Richard Croom Beatty wrote, "advised him to settle down in Germany, learn something real about the people with whom he stayed, and then write. Perhaps by that time, the publisher added, your letters will be worth buying. But no descriptive nonsense. Of that I am damned sick!" (Beatty, pp. 30–31). In the event Taylor did settle down in Germany, spending nearly half of his two years abroad there mastering the language and beginning a study of German literature that was to lead in his mature years to the translation of Goethe's *Faust* that stood for decades as the standard American version, as well as to books on German history and German literature. And once entered into German life, as Greeley had advised, he did succeed in placing letters with Greeley.

Taylor sailed from New York on July 1st, 1844. He landed at Liverpool, went to Scotland, came down to Dover, crossed the English Channel to Ostend, went to the Rhine, and sailed to Frankfurt where (assisted by Nat's brother Richard) he spent nearly a year living in a furnished room for thirty-three cents a day, meals, light, and fuel included, then walked and caught rides to Prague, Bohemia, Moravia, Vienna, and Italy by way of the St. Gothard Pass. He paused in Florence, went down to Rome, then Naples, took deck passage to Marseilles, and worked his way up through Lyons—where his scant funds ran out and he waited in distress for a journalistic fee that took too long to arrive—then Paris, Dieppe, and London. He returned to New York June 1st, 1846 where encouraged by friends, and especially by Willis, he sought out a publisher for the book he formed from the letters published in the *Post,* the *Gazette,* and the *Tribune.* Wiley and Putnam took the book with an agreement that he would be paid $100 for every thousand copies sold, and published it in the year of his return. It sold well and kept selling.

Today the flaws of *Views A-Foot* are all too apparent. Since it is made up of many letters written separately over a period of two years and insufficiently revised into a whole it presents one scene after another without modulation of tone or emphasis. In a periodical piece that is read apart in time from the reading of any other piece, superlatives— the most remarkable or memorable or beautiful scene ever encountered—may carry some conviction, but when the pieces are placed together in a book and "best" succeeds "best" repetitions are apparent and the superlatives become a literary tic.

The youthful Taylor also had a tendency to offer his excitement about a scene in place of the scene itself although he seemed to believe that he was describing the scene. For example, in the culmination of a rather engaging piece on Christmas rituals in Frankfurt (inspired by but not imitative of Irving's English Christmas in his *Sketch-Book*) Taylor is finally permitted to enter the room from which his German hosts have barred him in the days leading up to Christmas so that its effect upon him would be more striking. And, indeed, striking it is as the doors are flung open and Taylor at last enters the room. He showers phrases such as "how beautiful was the heart felt joy . . . a scene of unmingled joy . . . a glorious feast . . . chorus from happy hearts . . . full of poetry and feeling and glad associations"[7] but never provides a clear picture of just what was in that room to justify such excitement. Moreover, at times the letters are filled out with snatches of national history (lifted from a guidebook) that are quite apart from the personal experience of the young traveler, in contrast, for example, to the effective intertwining of public and private history achieved by Stephens.

What sustains *Views A-Foot* even today, however, is its direct expression of the enthusiasms of a young American traveler too captivated by what he experiences to feign sophistication. The information he supplies about art and architecture, the foreign words he intrudes, the costumes and the manners that catch his eye, do not so much accumulate into a picture of European culture as they do into the portrait of a young man from rural America validating the culture he had acquired from books read by lamplight and dreamed about by day. This is not without appeal.

Here, for example, is young Taylor on the Rhine:

> I sat upon the deck the whole afternoon, as mountains, towns, and castles passed by on either side, watching them with a feeling of the most enthusiastic enjoyment. Every place was familiar to me in memory, and they seemed like friends I had long communed with in spirit and now met face to face. The English tourists, with whom the deck was covered, seemed interested too, but in a different manner. With Murray's Handbook open in their hands, they sat and read about the very towns they were passing, scarcely lifting their eyes to the real scenes, except now and then to observe that it was "*very nice*"! (*Views,* pp. 98–99)

His fancied difference from the English tourists is naive because he, too, is seeing what he sees not directly but in terms of his reading—in this case, most likely *Outre-Mer.* But the book is not on his lap, it is in his memory; in effect, a part of him. Scotland validates Burns and Scott, London from the Thames confirms Byron, Vallambrosa corroborates Dante, Milton, and Ariosto.

The young Taylor's Europe is a book of pictures illustrating a text written by the sanctified poets. It possesses charm because if all seeing is inescapably mediated by the biases of the seer, his are, in the main, engagingly if ingenuously formed by aesthetic rather than social predilections. To be sure, his American upbringing occasionally informs a political comment. In Newcastle for example, he hears a body of miners singing a ballad in the streets and is told that they struck for higher wages because they could not support their families and as a consequence were replaced by miners imported from Wales. Their ballad was about their wrongs. "It made my blood boil," he wrote, "to hear those tones, wrung from the heart of poverty by the hand of tyranny," and he went on to a grandiloquent warning about the "gathering murmur" that would "ere long" reach the "dull ears of Power" (*Views*, p. 76). Even here, however, it is notable that the path into political commentary is opened by a ballad.

Nat Willis wrote an introduction for the first edition of *Views A-Foot*, published within six months of Taylor's return, and in August 1848 Taylor added to the eighth edition "a chapter containing some practical information for pedestrians, in answer to numerous letters from young men who desired to follow my example" (pp. v-vi). The first edition had told of his starting with $140, procuring a passage over for $10 to which he added $14 for the food and bedding he had to supply for himself, and from time to time mentioned one or another cost, most notably the thirty-three cents per day lodgings in Frankfurt. Understandably, young men who thought they never could afford Europe were attracted and wanted to learn more. In supplying that Taylor said "I must disclaim any particular talent for economy, which has sometimes been accorded to me, on account of having seen so much on such short allowance. Had I possessed more I should have spent more, and the only value of my experience is, to prove to young men of scanty means that they need not necessarily be debarred from enjoying the pleasures and the advantages of travel" (p. ix).

The new chapter advised carrying a knife and fork in the knapsack as well as solid tin boxes for articles that could not fit in one's pocket, having a pouch with pen and ink and a small bottle that could be filled with fresh stream water or sometimes with the country wine—price three to six sous the quart. On the road avoid post-inns, they are more expensive, and in the cities stay where the traveling merchants stay. Pay the night in advance once the price of a bed has been settled upon: four cents should get you in Germany a short box with coarse, clean linen sheets and a mattress of straw; in Italy, a very large bed stuffed with corn husks. Wake early, buy bread and cheese for breakfast, and then dine on it again after half the day's walk has been accomplished. Carry no more than fifteen pounds of clothing—single suit of good dark cloth, strong linen blouse, leather belt, slouched hat of good quality felt—and take along one or two pocket editions of classic authors as well as a guidebook. A cane may be useful but an umbrella is inconvenient, much better to have a foldable oilskin cape, and in the early weeks a small bottle of cognac will be needed to bathe the feet morning and evenings. Small amounts of money in the form of drafts on a Paris banking house can be cashed in any large city in Europe and the best coin to carry is English gold. With surprisingly few changes—ballpoints for pen and ink, for example, or traveler's checks for bank drafts—Taylor's advice still holds, to the dismay of American consular officials who ever since have had to cope with young countrymen stranded on their doorsteps. *Views A-Foot* originated the genre of "Europe on a shoestring."

Plagued with the many young people who, influenced by Taylor's book, offered him their letters from abroad as a means of financing their travels, Greeley growled: "He practiced a systematic and careful economy; yet he went away with money, and returned with the clothes on his back, and (I judge) very little more. My young friend, if you think yourself better qualified than he was, go ahead, and 'do' Europe! but don't ask me to further your scheme; for I hold that you may far better stay at home, apply yourself to some useful branch of productive industry, help pay our national debt, and accumulate a little independence whereon, by and by, to travel (if you choose) as a gentleman, and not with but a sheet of paper between you and starvation" (Smyth, pp. 52–53).

Before deciding upon the occupation that would have to support him as he continued to pursue his poetic vocation, Bayard Taylor on his return from Europe made a pilgrimage to Boston, the hallowed ground of the literati he had admired from afar since childhood. The popularity of *Views A-Foot* guaranteed him what passed for a warm reception in that stratosphere of the American intellect, and shepherded by James T. Fields, publisher of Hawthorne and the "fireside" poets and future publisher of his poetry, he met Longfellow and Whittier and commenced a correspondence with them that was to continue for the remainder of their lives: he sent them his poems, which they always received cordially, and he promoted their poems in the reviews and essays he wrote as part of his journalistic duties.

With the modest earnings from *Views A-Foot* Taylor purchased the *Phoenix Gazette* in Phoenixville, Pennsylvania, renaming it *The Pioneer,* and began his full-time journalistic career as a publisher as well as a writer, but remained at it for less than a year. Ambitious for literary fame he saw no way of achieving it in the provinces and sold his paper, determined to go to New York and somehow find journalistic work there. Learning of this, Nat Willis offered a bit of advice that was both characteristic of his flippantly shrewd personality and indicative of the volatility and virulence of the day's periodicals: "Write to every paper and everybody. Be willing to go in at a small hole, like a lean rat, trusting to increase so much that you cannot get out without destroying what took you in. This is fair play, where the property of an establishment is made by your underpaid industry" (*Life and Letters,* 1:101). On the other hand, Greeley with his conviction that the country's future was tied to the ability of young Americans to develop opportunities outside of the established cities urged him to stay put. But once Taylor was in New York working for Charles Fenno Hoffman's magazine, Greeley in 1847 brought him over to the *Tribune,* and for the rest of his life Taylor was associated with that newspaper, serving at various times as a reporter, a contributor, or an editorial staff writer. He also quite early in his relationship purchased stock in the newspaper and for most of his life derived from it an income that supplemented his chief source of support, earnings as a writer.

In his first year on the *Tribune,* Taylor chased stories of fires, crimes, and city life (he covered the Astor Place riots) in competition with reporters from the other dailies while always working at, and publishing, his poems: "One day, I hope, I shall be able to take your hand and tell you what happiness it is to be understood by one, whom the world calls by the sacred name of poet" (*Unpublished Letters,* p. 14), he wrote Whittier in September 1847. He was also thrilled at the entry he gained into New York literary salons excitedly writing home about his attendance at soirees peopled by such celebrities as T. B. Read, Grace Greenwood, and Anne Lynch. Today the roll call of these "notables" speaks not so much of his arrival as a poet as it does about his limitations.

Taylor was temporarily removed from such associates when the fever of the California gold discovery burned across the continent to heat the east and Greeley saw the need for reports not just on the gold fields but on the transcontinental routes to them, the government being formed in California, the nature of its inhabitants, its cities, and its climate, and the color of life there. In August 1849 Taylor set off on that assignment and, as he said with some pride in the speed with which he had accomplished the task, "finally reached my old working-desk in the Tribune office on the night of March 10th—just eight months and eight days from the time of my departure."[8]

Eldorado, the book based on Taylor's letters to the *Tribune,* appeared several months after his return. He knew a great deal more about compiling such a work than he had when he cobbled together *Views A-Foot.* In his preface he insisted, "Though the author's purpose in visiting California was not to write a book, the circumstances of his journey seemed to impose it upon him as a duty, and all his observations were made with this end in view" (p. vii). The difference between "purpose" and "duty" as he expressed it is unclear—he seems to claim that he did not intend to write a book even as he says he gathered materials in excess of what was needed for his newspaper letters because he was obligated (to whom?) by what he encountered to write a book. At any rate, *Eldorado* established the format for all the travel books that were to follow: a heavy reliance on the letters he had already published to which were added previously unpublished observations from his journal. Further to this formula, then established, the book was published very soon after the last newspaper letter had appeared in order to capitalize on a notoriety that was bound to fade quickly without such reinforcement, and it was long—more than 400 pages—offering value for the money. Right up to the collected edition of 1874, which was published soon after the first edition of the most recent book in the collection had been issued, Taylor and Putnam stayed with that formula.

Paul C. Wermuth, Taylor's most recent biographer, calls *Eldorado* "lively, full of detail, cheerful and vigorous, saying that "he shows more command of his prose, and also more confidence in his judgments," than he had in the earlier book. Moreover, since California was so raw, Taylor had "fewer opportunities to genuflect to art" and as a result the narrative was not as obstructed as it was in *Views A-Foot*.

Yet for all that, it is difficult to agree that "*Eldorado* is also one of his best travel books" (Wermuth, p. 41). The exuberance that lightened the clumsiness of *Views A-Foot* is gone and in its place is an essentially superficial series of reportorial observations. Taylor's journalistic responsibility to report details results in a series of accounts that hold little interest for anyone reading the material after 1850. Whatever profit resides in learning that San Francisco had grown from 500 to 5,000 people within a year and that the rates of labor there are exorbitant has long since been better provided by more penetrating accounts. The young narrator of *Views A-Foot* has been replaced by a narrator who however more confident his prose is also damagingly uncertain about his relation to his book. On one hand, the journalist in *Eldorado* strives to report what he sees. On the other, the narrator who turns the journalist's letters into a book appears in the moments when the journalist has nothing to report and describes one or another ramble simply because he took it. This, in turn, leads to the perfunctory insertion of descriptions of natural scenery: "no more lovely hermitage for thought" (p. 171) exists than the hills around Monterey, "no peak among mountains more sublime" (p. 434) than Orizaba. It is difficult to believe that someone who entered the New York literary scene so soon after the publication of John Lloyd Stephens's books was unaware of Stephens's presence both in New York and Panama, yet Taylor reveals neither an explicit nor a tacit knowledge of this work as he crosses the Central American isthmus on his eastward journey or traverses Mexico on his westward return.

It is true that nothing stales so quickly as yesterday's newspaper and the Taylor of *Eldorado* was yet to trust himself, to believe that what would hold the reader was not what he saw but that *he* saw it, not that something happened but that it happened to *him*. Put in journalistic terms, he was still a reporter rather than a correspondent. But the situation was soon to change.

Mary Agnew and Bayard Taylor had known one another from child-hood and as they grew older they effortlessly drifted into the assump-tion that they would some day marry. While not absolutely opposing their plan, her family disapproved: Taylor had no money, the profession he elected was not a promising one, and Mary was consumptive, con-stantly cared for by physicians. But Taylor was steadfast in his devotion, writing her long letters from Europe and then from Phoenixville and New York as he pursued an income that would enable them to marry. He visited her in Kennett Square as frequently as he could and wrote her encouraging accounts of the future he planned with her. When he re-turned from California in March 1850, however, he found her more ill than ever and at his own expense took her to Philadelphia for medi-cal consultations. But the only remedy the doctor suggested was hope. Impelled by Mary's desperate condition the two resolved to delay no longer. They were married on October 24th, 1850 in Kennett Square, where she remained while he commuted from New York to spend week-ends with her. Two months later, on December 22nd, 1850, Mary Agnew Taylor died.

The twenty-six-year-old widower determined to lose the pain of loss in travel to new scenes. He had acquired some savings and since this was insufficient—he no longer wished to be a virtuoso of shoestring travel—he threw himself into a flurry of activity to augment the amount. In addition to his assignments for the *Tribune* he wrote magazine pieces, published poems, and accepted a commission from a book publisher to compile an anthology. The summer of 1851 found him exhausted but also with $3,000 in savings. He sailed for Liverpool in August with the intention of visiting Egypt and the Holy Land along a path well worn by affluent Western tourists. Despite the conventionality of his planned route he was now so well regarded by Greeley that he could count upon the *Tribune* taking the letters he sent home as he made his way into Africa.

In the event, Bayard Taylor's recuperative tour turned into a series of journeys that kept him on the road for more than two years taking him across Asia to the Pacific and returning him home by way of South Africa. His cruise up the Nile began with the usual luxuries of the European tourist in Egypt but continued quite unconventionally when he did not return down the river from Aswan but continued up it beyond Khartoum. He then toured the Holy Land and Asia Minor and intended to go again to the Continent before returning home. But in Constantinople he received a dispatch from Greeley instructing him to discontinue this plan and instead make his way as best he could to the China coast in order to intercept and gain entry into the fleet of Commodore Matthew C. Perry which was heading across the Pacific to provide a show of force on behalf of American merchant houses trading in China before proceeding on its mission to knock on Japan's door—and then, if necessary, push it open. He accepted the assignment and succeeded in it.

When he reappeared in New York Taylor found he was famous. The letters he had sent back along his trail had excited a large reading public, but since he kept moving forward into more and more remote regions he had had no idea of the enthusiasm that had sprung up in his wake until it burst upon him at his return. He was in demand nationwide as a lecturer and he also quickly turned to the task of revising and supplementing his letters in order to make books of them while an eager audience existed. *A Journey to Central Africa, or Life and Landscapes from Egypt to the Negro Kingdoms of the White Nile* appeared in August 1854; *The Lands of the Saracen: or Pictures of Palestine, Asia Minor, Sicily, and Spain* appeared in October 1855;* and *A Visit to India, China, and Japan in the Year 1853* appeared in September 1855. They

*In that month also James T. Fields brought out his *Poems of the Orient,* a collection that proved to be the most popular of his books of verse.

were published by Sampson Low in London as well as Putnam in New York and went through edition after edition.

Since Taylor initially undertook his travels for his own pleasure the books' narratives are structured by his own interests rather than by any obligation to report on specific matters. Taking their tone and shape from his personality they possess the kind of distinctive identity that *Eldorado* did not have. To be sure, in them Taylor still resorts to guide-book filler from time to time, compelled either by the *Tribune* or his own streak of didacticism, but his sense of himself as the ultimate subject of his writing now assumes confident authority over the simulated objectivity of the reporter. The resulting books contain a goodly number of interesting episodes spiced with the discerning observations of one adept at yielding to the ways of the societies he visited. They also provide a fascinatingly fateful illustration of the relation of the literary representation of alien cultures to the assumption of cultural superiority transmitted to the reader.

The personal note that is to hold sway is sounded at the outset. "I determined to penetrate as far into the interior of Africa as the time would allow, attracted less by the historical and geographical interest of those regions than by the desire to participate in the free, vigorous, semi-barbaric life."[9] But although it occurs at the start of the narrative, the remark is shaped by the wisdom of hindsight. Far from being "semi-barbaric" the initial ascent of the Nile was made in the company of a new acquaintance, a wealthy German, Count Bufleb,* who before the journey was several days long became an intimate friend. They had all the luxurious, indeed effete, comforts that could be provided by Egyptian hoteliers, porters, guides, donkey boys, camel drivers, and boatmen who in the wake of the heavy invasion of wealthy tourists that had commenced some twenty years earlier now constituted a somewhat uncoordinated tourist industry dependent upon the annual flood of

*Count Bufleb was to remain a lifelong friend. He accompanied Taylor on his later travels in Scandinavia, bought him a house near his own estate in Germany, and introduced him to Marie Hansen of Schleswig-Holstein, who was to become Taylor's second wife and the caretaker of his posthumous reputation.

"Franks," as all tourists were called in memory of the earlier Napoleonic invasion of the land. Their boat had a spacious cabin with beds and divans and a covered area on deck with cushioned seats on which they sat to smoke their water pipes in the twilight. Little wonder that Taylor assigned the craft the trite name of *Cleopatra*. "Into the heart of a barbarous continent and a barbarous land, we carry with us every desirable comfort and luxury" (*Central Africa*, p. 96), he wrote.

As Taylor said at the beginning, he intended to "penetrate" Africa. But what he had thus far carried to its "heart" served principally to maintain his distance from it. His "comfort and luxury" intensified the contrast between the peasant life he observed and the life he lived as he observed it. Witnessing scenes first-hand, he was, uncannily, as detached from them by the frame of his gliding boat as is his reader by the frame of the printed page. But at Aswan Bufleb reluctantly parted with Taylor to return to obligations at home, having already delayed beyond his original plans because of the delight he took in Taylor's company. Taylor went on to Khartoum alone, and after some ten days there "began to think of penetrating further into the interior" (p. 315). With four weeks to spare before beginning his return from the Sudan to Egypt, he decided to go further up the White Nile. The *Cleopatra* returned to Cairo without him and his conversion from tourist to traveler was signalled when he christened the craft that would carry him beyond Khartoum: "I named the boat the *John Ledyard,* in memory of the first American traveller in Africa" (p. 317).

It is on the White Nile that Taylor begins to become a participant in the life that surrounds him, drawn first by the stunning sensory assault of existence on the river where swarms of wild birds fill the air, a prolonged snarling roar sounds from a beast invisible on the bank, light flashes from the silver wing of an alighting heron, hippopotami surface, splashing and grunting. The intensity of his youthful experience on the Rhine had been mediated by the readings he carried in his memory, but the powerful effect of his experience on the White Nile emanated from responsive sources that lay more deeply within him than the memory of books: "This was Central Africa as I had dreamed it—a grand though

This picture of Bayard Taylor illustrating "Oriental Costume" was taken in the Mathew Brady studio and used as the frontispiece to some editions of *A Journey to Central Africa* (Reprinted by permission of the National Portrait Gallery, Smithsonian Institution).

savage picture, full of life, and heat, and with a barbaric splendor even in the forms of Nature" (p. 328). Heat especially came to figure for Taylor as the physical manifestation of the barbarism he had been seeking. To yield totally to the searing sun was to reach the self beneath.

At Merowe in the Sudan the Nile curved southward to Ed Debba before resuming its twisting northward descent to the Egyptian plain. To travel on it from Merowe to Wadi Halfa was to go some 400 miles along a crooked course that began by dipping down before taking its wriggling way upward. The overland route directly northward from Merowe to Wadi Halfa was shorter by some 200 miles, but it lay across the Nubian Desert, a barrier to all save the native traders who ventured across in camel caravans, not uncommonly with loss of animal and human life. But infatuated with the strength of the African sun Taylor resolved to submerge himself completely in its rays. With a quick ear for languages he had been daily improving the little Arabic with which he began his travel in Alexandria and now with sufficient command of the language to be able to travel in the company of those who spoke no other tongue he joined a caravan.

Taylor's record of his journey by camel across the Nubian Desert, an ordeal of heat, thirst, and physical suffering, is also the record of an ecstasy, albeit one sometimes veiled by the gentility of literary convention. When the pain in his eyes became insufferable he resorted to hashish to alleviate the symptoms and wrote vividly about its effects, alterations of perception that in a glaring desert were heightened by the absence of any of the physical coordinates that had previously established his reality. The desert enthralled him. After his return to Cairo in April 1852—he had been out five months—Taylor, preparing for his journey to Palestine (and the second volume of his Oriental travels) noted the way other tourists

> prepared themselves for the journey across the Desert, by purchasing broad-brimmed hats, green veils, double-lined umbrellas, and blue spectacles. These may be all very good, but I have never seen the sun nor felt the heat which could induce me to adopt them. I would not exchange my recollections of the fierce red Desert, blazing all over with intense light, for any amount of green, gauzy, sky and blue sand. And as for an umbrella, the Desert with a continual shade around you, is no desert at all. You must let the Sun lay his sceptre on your head, if you want to know his power. (pp. 521–22)

The travels to Palestine, Syria, Asia Minor, Sicily, and Spain that followed directly after the Egyptian sojourn are chronicled in *Lands of the*

Saracen. It is a curiously mixed work. On one hand, Taylor wanted, as he said, to provide the "many thousands who can only travel by their firesides" with "cosmoramic views" of such standard sites as the hills of Palestine, the minarets of Damascus, and the pine forests of Phrygia.[10] The more such sites had been described by previous travelers the more, it seems, succeeding travelers were obligated to visit and again describe them. Otherwise the reader would have felt cheated. After all, what was a book about Palestine if the holy places were not included? A thoroughly professional travel writer, Taylor met this obligation, at times with some freshness but at a good many others with a generous amount of the wholly predictable.

On the other hand, the Oriental life into which Taylor had first waded on the White Nile and into which he plunged more fully in the Nubian Desert drew him powerfully and he wanted his book to convey what he called the "inspiration and the indolence of the Orient" (p. vi). The latter term, he recognized, was a pejorative in his hustling America, and he devoted his literary energy to dramatizing the positive value of yielding to "annoyance without anger, delay without vexation, indolence without ennui, endurance without fatigue, appetite without intemperance, enjoyment without gall" (p. 357). In illustration he did not merely retail the pleasures of Turkish bath, water pipe, and flowing trousers, although his descriptions of these are sensuously tempting, but insisted that to enter into Oriental life was to rediscover the pleasures of pure "animal existence"—another conventionally pejorative term that he sought to recuperate—and recognize that Western progress was a nervousness that destroyed the healthy physical development at the core of life fully lived.

Previously Taylor had taken hashish medicinally, in Damascus he tried it for the experience itself and smoked what proved to be a highly potent dose. There followed hallucinations which he described in detail, and even after these passed the drug's effects lingered on and for days he found himself falling into unanticipated stupors. He assured the reader that he had thus learned the lesson of the majesty of human reason and will "and the awful peril of tampering with that which assails their integrity." But he did so only after having reported on what it feels like to slip their fetters and experience "deeps of rapture and of suffering which my natural faculties could never have sounded" (p. 133).

"Were I cast here," Taylor wrote of Jerusalem, "ignorant of any religion, and were I to compare the lives and practices of different sects as the means of making my choice—in short to judge of each faith by the conduct of its professors—I should at once turn Mussulman" (p. 79). The conditional into which his sentence was cast deflected accusations of heterodoxy but his intention was clear. As his Arabic improved he was able to pass as an Arab and took pride at his ability to enter mosques unchallenged. The term that he came to oppose to "Oriental" was not "Occidental" or "European" but "Christian," and in Spain he said that "In Granada, as in Seville and Cordova, one's sympathies are wholly with the Moors" (p. 425).

Far from a scholarly observer—"The man of science, may complain with reason that I have neglected valuable opportunities for adding something to the stock of human knowledge" (p. vi)—Taylor was, nevertheless, America's first great popular Orientalist, bringing to his country the glamour of the exotic East. He emphasized his Orientalism with an illustration of himself in native costume. Edward W. Said writes that to the European traveler the Orient suggested "sexual promise (and threat), unstinting sensuality, unlimited desire, deep generative energies" (*Orientalism,* p. 188). John Lloyd Stephens reflected this suggestion, albeit cautiously, but Taylor steered clear of explicit sexuality, as others did not, tiptoeing into its remote vicinity only once in an uneasy description of the performance of two belly dancers he had hired. But the intensity of his submissions to practices not in themselves sexual resonate with erotic overtones. Even his worship of the sun moves in that direction: as he proclaimed, he exposed himself to the sun's "scepter" in the Nubian Desert; and in another place he speaks of turning his face "from side to side that I might feel his touch on my cheek" (p. 390). That the subsurface eroticism is gendered male while his physical descriptions of men and boys are generally more detailed than those of women suggest also that Taylor may have been experiencing a release from more than the institutionalized confinement of heterosexuality in his homeland.

Taylor's love of Eastern life is genuine and his convincing rendering of an immersion in it remarkable in view of his having spent months not years there. Yet the Orient he evokes and commends in his pages is, finally, not the opposite of his and his readers' America even though he represents it as such; it is, rather, America's complement. Eastern physical contentment may show up Western moral nervousness, Eastern pleasures show up Western guilt, but Taylor's very ability to assert this stems from his retention of his sense of the enclosing superiority of Western culture that permits his excursions into the exotic. Even as he indulges himself in different practices he conveys an awareness of himself as a participant in a performance that he can end whenever he wishes although the other actors cannot. Disguised as a Moslem he enters a mosque with pleasure at the success of his masquerade but also with the confidence that if he is detected all that can happen is that the worshippers there will be outraged; he, after all, will remain what he is, an outsider who only wanted to have a look. The same may be conjectured about the many readers who followed Taylor out of Western garb into Eastern, out of Christian culture into Moslem, out of the dominion of the will into that of vision. They only wanted to have a look, to supplement, as it were, their own cultural baggage.

If there was something worth the taking in Oriental culture however, Taylor made it clear that this did not extend to what he called African, meaning Negro, culture. He hailed with triumph archaeological findings that overthrew the theory that the grandeur of Egyptian Memphis and Thebes followed from that of Ethiopian Merowe,* because they confirmed what he had observed: "There is no evidence in all the valley of the Nile that the Negro Race ever attained a higher degree of civilization

---

*Now within the nation of Sudan, Merowe, spelled Meröe by Taylor, was in his day considered to be in Ethiopia. This emphasized the blackness of its natives, Ethiopian being in the United States a synonym for Negro regardless of the country of the person's origin. So, for example, one could attend the "Ethiopian Minstrels" and there hear "Ethiopian melodies."

than is at present exhibited in Congo and Ashantee," so that "those friends of the African race, who point to Egypt as a proof of what the race has accomplished are wholly mistaken" (*Central Africa,* p. 158). When he took to the lecture circuit upon his return, speaking to packed houses, Taylor offered his visits to the habitats of other races to authenticate such contentions as, "Moral and mental traits are almost uniformly revealed in the physical appearance of a race. The African negro is tall, but absolutely without grace or beauty. Correspondingly, he has no significant art. The bodies of the Chinese lack *harmony*. Moreover, their crooked eyes are typical of their crooked moral vision" (Beatty, p. 150).

Bayard Taylor was opposed to the institution of slavery. The Quaker ambience of his upbringing, his close association with Greeley's politics, and the sense of pained frustration he felt together with other Americans abroad when slavery was cited to them as a justification for dismissing everything worthy about American life all combined to lead him to abolitionism. In the early months of the Civil War he feared nothing so much as the possibility that some compromise would be reached and the war would end without the abolition of slavery. If slavery was abhorrent to all that was civilized, however, civilization itself was for him a function of race and "the highest Civilization, in every age of the world, has been developed by the race to which we belong" (*Central Africa*, p. 237). To be sure, civilizations like individuals could become fatigued. Even as he recovered from the exhaustion brought on by his life in America through imbibing a dose of "semi-barbarism," so civilization would benefit from a similar renewal from time to time. But he was locked in a circle: the ultimate mark of the superiority of Western civilization was its production of significant art; art was significant to the degree that it reflected Western civilization. Although he traveled widely over the world he always traveled within this mental circle and the message the famous traveler conveyed to his stay-at-home countrymen was that their cultural/racial superiority was confirmed by the ways of the world.

The acquisition of California at the close of the Mexican War suggested that direct trade from the West Coast was an inevitable and desirable development for an expanding United States.[11] American mercantile houses had been established on the China coast for some decades, serviced by the famous China clippers making long and perilous voyages from the Atlantic seaboard around the African or South American capes, but the advent of steam—still in the 1850s a supplemental means of locomotion with side paddle wheels installed on sailing ships—combined with the possession of California opened a new avenue to Asia. European nations shared the China trade with America, one or another European nation had commercial colonies in Southeast Asia, and Britain prominently held sway over South Africa and India. But save for limited intercourse with Holland, Japan remained apart from the Western economies, its market scarcely touched by foreigners. It loomed as a tempting arena for the enactment of America's new sense of itself as a transcontinental nation poised to push westward across the Pacific.

In December 1852 a naval squadron under the command of Commodore Matthew C. Perry, a proven veteran of the Mexican War, embarked from the east coast, charged by the Fillmore administration with opening relations with Japan. Little was known about that nation save that it maintained a policy of exclusion. What license did the United States have to force a door that the rightful owners desired to keep shut? Perry characterized his goal as an "attempt to bring a singular and isolated people into the family of civilized nations," but ominously concluded his sentence by hoping that his attempt "might succeed without bloodshed" (Hawks, 1:236). The Japanese should be persuaded to join "civilization." If, however, they preferred to remain apart from it then civilization just might have to fire some guns to punctuate the benefits of civility.

The news of a planned expedition to Japan excited enormous interest. Political analysts were eager to learn about a form of government that could sustain what seemed so refined a state of society while maintaining isolation from other nations; ethnologists sought details on the physical appearance, language, history, and racial affiliations of the inhabitants; and physical geographers, naturalists, and scholars of the arts each had questions they felt justified attempting the locked gates. Patriots with fewer intellectual interests could support the expedition on the ground of what was due "the dignity of the American flag." In 1837 an American sailing ship, the *Morrison,* had attempted to enter Tokyo Bay in order to search for shipwrecked American sailors only to be fired upon and retreat without injury; was it not time to teach Japan a lesson? And missionary zeal, ever the companion of imperial ambition, endorsed the enterprise: "The Christian desires to know the varied phases of their superstitions and idolatry; and longs for the dawn of that day when a purer faith and more enlightened worship shall bring them within the circles of Christianity" (1:3).

Many reasons, then, to visit Japan. But most pressing was the knowledge that Japan possessed valuable productions and the consequent conviction that it ought to be brought into a trading relationship; indeed, some even avowed "that Japan had no right thus to cut herself off from the community of nations; and that what she would not yield to national comity should be wrested from her by force" (1:76). So crass a proposition, however, was not official policy. The letter from President Fillmore and Secretary of State Edward Everett that Perry finally placed in the hands of the emperor's representatives asked for friendship, commerce, provisions, protection for shipwrecked Americans—principally from the whale fishery—and a supply of coal for American ships.

As soon as the expedition was announced applications poured in from literary and scientific men who wanted to accompany it. Powerful political influences were brought to bear on the secretary of the navy, John Pendleton Kennedy, himself a literary man of note,* not the least of which came from Greeley as he exerted pressure to have Bayard Taylor accepted into the expedition. But although Kennedy seconded this and several other petitions, Perry remained firm and rejected all such applications. When Greeley reached Taylor in Constantinople and directed

*His *Swallow Barn* (1832) was the best novel of antebellum plantation life published in the actual antebellum period and remains superior to the novelistic idealizations of that life that sprang up after the Civil War.

him to China to meet Perry he was relying on Taylor himself to persuade Perry as no one had yet been able to do.

Commodore Perry was a martinet who wanted no one aboard who was not under military discipline and so before sailing rigidly barred civilians. If he succeeded in his diplomatic mission, he reasonably argued, then scientific and literary visits could follow, but the success of the primary mission depended upon secrecy, the withholding of information from powers that might employ it to impair the mission's success. Accordingly, in addition to excluding any not under naval command he insisted upon reviewing and approving all communications sent during the expedition. He also made clear that all notes, journals, and data gathered by members of the expedition were the property of the United States Navy and were to be delivered into his hands at the conclusion of the voyage. Stuffed shirt though he may have been—a midshipman observed that no one appreciated a joke less than the commodore, and others who sailed with him found him eminently unlikable—Perry, nevertheless, had an enlightened vision of his profession. He noted with envy the accomplished scientific reports and the literate narratives produced by members of the British naval service and to his other reasons for excluding scientific and literary men he added that this provided an opening for his officers to exercise themselves in those fields. He requested that they employ whatever spare time they might have by contributing to the general mass of information, asking them to choose according to their interests from a list that ran from hydrography to religion, terrestrial magnetism to philology and ethnology, ichthyology to artistic matters. Adhering to the letter of naval regulations, as was his wont, he added that his was not an *official* request, although it is difficult to imagine how an officer could sail with him and comfortably ignore it. The information thus gathered eventually made up the latter two volumes of the large, folio-sized, official *Narrative,* volume one being the narrative account itself.

On December 14, 1852, outward bound to the Indian Ocean, Perry wrote Secretary Kennedy about the need to secure safe harbors along the western Pacific route to Asia, the British having locked up all such ports from Africa east to the Pacific. He proposed establishing a major coal depot at an island in the Loo Choo group (so little was known of Japan and Japanese that he thus employed the Chinese term for Okinawa).

While Perry was calling attention to British control of the route to Asia east of Africa, Bayard Taylor was traveling along that route in order to rendezvous in China with the American squadron. With several months to spare after receiving Greeley's instructions in Constantinople, he went to London before reversing and visiting Spain, another "Saracen Land," en route to Gibraltar. There he boarded a British mail steamer on which he rounded Africa, stopped at Aden, and then proceeded to Bombay. He crossed India to Calcutta, the first 375 miles to Indore by banghy-cart, a two-wheeled, hooded buggy (American buggies were four-wheeled and open),* and the remainder by mail cart. At Calcutta he took a steamer to Hong Kong, stopping off at Pinang—"I thought then, and I think so still, that Penang [sic] is the most beautiful island in the world"[12]—thence to Singapore and Hong Kong where he intersected with Perry and received the permission to accompany the fleet that had been denied all others.

Why Taylor so uniquely succeeded is a matter of conjecture. In his abridged edition of the expedition's *Narrative,* Sidney Wallach says it was because Taylor made "so gracious an impression" on Perry (p. 297n) and this is highly plausible. It is well documented that once he was a member of the squadron the convivial, knowledgeable, and highly adaptable Taylor was very popular with both officers and men. Since he could only be admitted under naval discipline he was given the nominal rank of master's mate and assigned to mess with the other master's mates: Heine, the artist, Draper, the telegraphist, and Brown, the daguerreotypist. Amused by his insertion into the naval hierarchy, albeit at a rather junior level, he wryly observed that according to regulations he was supposed to have "unlimited respect for my superiors,

---

*The *Oxford English Dictionary* lists the origin of the word "buggy" as unknown. That the vehicle in India is called a "banghy-cart" might suggest otherwise.

and the reverse for my inferiors" (*Japan,* p. 361). But the ease with which he made friends, the facility with which he adjusted to novel circumstances, and the quick eye for detail he had developed in his travels elevated his duties beyond that of an observer. When the squadron touched at the Bonin Islands, for example, he was put in charge of a shore party sent on a two-day exploration.

In September 1853, when the squadron returned to China after its four-month visit to Okinawa, the Bonin Islands, and Japan, Taylor received his discharge together with a nominal fee for his services as master's mate. After several weeks of waiting, he found a ship homeward bound and arrived in New York on December 20th, 101 days out from China. He had been absent for two years and four months.

Knowing that he would have to surrender his journal at the conclusion of his voyage to Japan, Taylor closed the account he had kept to the date of his enlistment so as to exempt it from this requirement and started a new journal just for the Japanese venture. This he did surrender assuming it would eventually be returned after the navy made use of it in the official *Narrative.* Perry, characteristically unaware of how others regarded him, asked Taylor if he would serve as compiler of the official account, but Taylor who with many another on the expedition had come to dislike Perry turned down the offer.* A more pressing reason for his refusal was the large public he quite unexpectedly found awaiting him on his return and his wish to capitalize upon it by publishing his books of travel quickly and in advance of the authorized account, even if his report on Japan would have to depend on his memory rather than his journal.

"The portions of the book devoted to India and China are as complete as the length of my stay in those countries allowed me to make them," Taylor explained. But because he could not consult notes, "The account of my visit to Loo-Choo and Japan . . . is less full and detailed than I could have wished." So, "like John Ledyard, in a precisely similar case,

*Perry's first choice was the American consul whom he had met at Liverpool, Nathaniel Hawthorne, son of a ship's captain, but Hawthorne declined.

I shall have the alternative of an unusually tenacious memory" (p. vi). The account he dredged from his memory during the long voyage home in the South Atlantic, however, is inferior to the official *Narrative* not just in details but in the actualization of the principal scenes in the drama. Taylor provided an American public hungry for a first-hand report food with which to indulge its patriotic appetite. To his credit, the accounts he wrote and dutifully submitted to Perry—one, for instance of an exploration of Okinawa by a small party of which he was a member— were so precise and fluent they were copied verbatim into the authorized *Narrative*.* But the sense of the unique mixture of diplomatic skill and racial arrogance, professionalism and naivete, genuine wonder and blinkered vision that richly arises from an attentive reading of the *Narrative* is missing from Taylor's account. Some scenes are artfully painted, some characters artfully etched, but without journal entries to assist him and with an eager America wanting good news about itself, he offered his narrative as a display of triumphant diplomacy, without providing the range of observations that would permit his reader to gauge the price of that conquest.

Taylor had participated in an astounding display of bullish diplomacy. When the squadron called in at Naha in Okinawa in order to establish a coaling station for future voyages Perry secluded himself from the official visitors who came off to greet his ship because he did not wish to appear common in their eyes. Only after the regent of the island's royal family made a formal call did he emerge and then, to that dignitary's consternation, announced that in a few days he would pay a visit to the royal palace. The regent protested that such a visit would be inconvenient and offered instead to receive Perry at his residence but Perry replied that he was fully determined to go to the palace and expected such a reception as befitted his rank and position as commander of the squadron and diplomatic representative of the United States.

*To his disgust, Taylor never could recover the reports he thought he had only temporarily surrendered to the navy. After their use in the official *Narrative* they were deposited in the naval archives and now repose in the Special Collections of the Rutgers University Libraries.

Meanwhile, brushing aside requests that they not do so, the officers he had dispatched to make hydrographic surveys spent their nights on shore and the marines were landed to drill there.

When Perry made his promised visit he did so in a sedan chair that had been constructed in haste by the ship's carpenter. Hung about with red and blue cloths, it was carried by two four-man relays of Chinese "coolies" and was preceded by a company of marines, a marching band, and a contingent of naval officers. Taylor had his modest place in the procession. At the palace, however, the commodore was told the royal family's ill health did not permit them to receive him and the reception would have to be held at the regent's. Perry had made his point and the Okinawans had made theirs.

The conduct at Loo Choo, as the Americans termed the island, was a rehearsal for the procedure followed when the squadron arrived at the entrance to Yedo (Tokyo) Bay. Again Perry refused to meet with the first contingent that came off in boats to greet him and when the vice-governor of Uraga arrived to open official negotiations, aimed principally at getting the Americans to leave the bay and sail to Nagasaki, the only port designated to receive foreigners, Perry communicated with him through an aide, insisting that he himself would meet only with an ambassador who came directly from the emperor. In the words of the narrative he authorized, "He was resolved to adopt a course entirely contrary to that of all others who had hitherto visited Japan on a similar errand—to demand as a right, and not to solicit as a favor, those acts of courtesy which are due from one civilized nation to another; to allow none of those petty annoyances which had been unsparingly visited upon those who had preceded him, and to disregard the acts as well as the threats of the authorities, if they in the least conflicted with his own sense of what was due the dignity of the American flag" (Hawks: 1,235).

Putting aside the repeated requests that he proceed to Nagasaki, Perry continued a slow progress up the bay, making hydrographic surveys as he advanced, and came to anchor on July 8, 1853. There he remained until he had received visits from emissaries whom he deemed were sufficiently close to the emperor that he could deal with them di

Commodore Perry attending a reception in his honor as drawn by the expedition's artists; Taylor was probably in the contingent (Francis L. Hawks, *The Expedition of An American Squadron to the China Seas and Japan,* 1856; Amherst College Archives and Special Collections).

rectly without compromising his dignity. To them he delivered the president's letter, suitably enclosed in an elaborate casket, and then on July 17th weighed anchor and departed. He felt victorious: "The vigorous grasp of the hand of America which was proffered in a friendly spirit, but thrust forward with an energy that proved the power to strike, as well as the disposition to embrace, had stirred Japanese isolation into a sensibility of its relationship to the rest of the world. Japan had broken its own code of selfish exclusiveness to obey the universal law of hospitality" (Hawks, 1:273). Taylor's narrative mixture of superiority toward, and sympathetic interest in, the Japanese exactly paralleled Perry's diplomatic mixture of a power to compel and a disposition to conciliate.

The major portion of *A Visit to India, China and Japan,* however— more than 300 pages—is based on the journals Taylor secured before

Reception for the Japanese emissaries under canvas on the deck of the *Powhatan,* Perry's flagship, as drawn by the expedition's artists (Hawks, *Expedition,* Amherst College Archives and Special Collections).

joining Perry and is lively, crammed with novel scenes and confident opinions. What might have weakened the account of a less experienced traveler—the speed with which he whirled past sites as he crossed half the world in order to catch up with the American squadron—actually strengthens his book. His narrative acquires something of the dash of the journey itself, confining his observations to what is most salient and preventing excursions into guidebook information (although he does, reluctantly he says, meet the reader's expectations and describe the Taj Mahal at length). Because he is only in India in order to leave it he is emboldened to strike off one quick portrait after another and they succeed in capturing life in a way that some of his more leisurely efforts did not. He offered a not too guarded critique of Christian missionizing and a sprightly defense of Indian "idolatries," including the worship of *lingam,* the phallic symbol: "There is a profound philosophical truth hidden under the singular forms of this worship, if men would divest themselves for a moment of prudery with regard to such subjects, which seems to be the affectation of the present age" (p. 247). Yet for all his sympathy with Indian ways, he said, "I can . . . feel neither the same interest in nor respect for the natives of India, as for the Arab races of Africa and Syria. The lower castes are too servile, too vilely the slaves of degrading superstition, and too much given to cheating and lying. One cannot use familiarity towards them, without encouraging them to impertinence. How different from my humble companions of the Nubian Desert!" (p. 210).

The thematic core of a narrative that eventuates in Japan is not a journey into the exotic but a journey into colonialism. Taylor could very aptly have given it the subtitle that he had earlier bestowed on *Eldorado*, "Adventures in the Path of Empire." Moving toward Perry and America's attempt to establish a commercial foothold in Japan and secure the way stations this necessitated, his attention was fixed on the way the British were managing India and maintaining their roadway to it. He admitted to an American dislike for the English class system which he anticipated he would find in its extremest form in the British colonies. He was not disappointed; there was a lot to disapprove of. And yet he was also drawn into admiration for the efficient ease with which the British subjugated alien peoples, regarding their success not so much as the result of national character as of racial superiority, and he was beguiled by the generous hospitality he received throughout India, one British host after another providing him with letters that assured a warm reception all along the line of his travels.

The mixed lesson on imperial rule that he never succeeded in untangling began when his steamer stopped for refueling at Aden, where, devotee of civilization that he was, he

> never felt more forcibly the power of that civilization which follows the Anglo-Saxon race in all its conquests, and takes root in whatever corner of the earth that race sets foot. Here, on the farthest Arabian shore, facing the most savage and inhospitable re-

gions of Africa, were Law, Order, Security, Freedom of Conscience and of Speech, and all the material advantages which
are inseparable from these. Herein consists the true power and
grandeur of the race, and the assurance of its final supremacy.
(p. 30)

This flush of racial pleasure, however, was quickly followed by the
chill of racial arrogance as his steamer prepared to depart Aden and
fired its signal gun for the passengers to come off and rejoin it:

One young lady remained . . . remained nearly two hours longer,
the steamer waiting solely on her account. Less consideration
was shown to a luckless native, who had fallen asleep in one of
the boats and was not observed until we were under way. He
was immediately thrown overboard in spite of his entreaties,
and left to take his chance of reaching the shore which was half
a mile distant. There was a collier lying about a hundred yards
off, but he would not be able to get on board of her so late
at night, and the forcing of him into the sea, under the circumstances, showed a most criminal disregard of human life.
(pp. 30–31)

And so the thermometer of civilized behavior rose and fell throughout his crossing of India. The country was well regulated and his travel
was made smooth by the splendid hospitality of the colonial community
and the well-tended roads over which his buggy wheels rolled. Yet the
man who prided himself on his sympathetic association with Islam and
his ability to enter a mosque in native garb was piqued to find "In India
all places of worship, except the inner shrines—the holy of holies—are
open to the conquerors, who walk in, booted and spurred, where the
Hindoo and Moslem put their shoes from off their feet, as I did in other
Moslem countries, but was told it was now never expected of a European, and would be in fact a depreciation of his dignity" (p. 102).

At his departure from India, Taylor attempted an evaluation of British rule there. Comparing it with governance by the rajahs he found it

better; India was benefitting from the law, order, and security brought by civilization. Still, he was "disgusted and indignant" at

> "the contemptuous manner in which the natives, even those of the best and most intelligent classes, are almost invariably spoken of and treated. Social equality, except in some rare instances, is utterly out of the question. The tone adopted towards the lower classes is one of lofty arrogance; towards the rich and enlightened, one of condescension and patronage. I have heard the term 'niggers' applied to the whole race by those high in office; with the lower orders of English it is the designation in general use. (p. 273)

Although he found the Arab character more attractive than the Indian, Taylor nevertheless retained his strong American conviction that "social equality" was a desirable goal of the colonial process, at least as it applied to races, such as those of India, that appeared capable of civilization. Those that appeared incapable were best left outside the pale rather than coerced into it only to be treated with contempt.

Up until he encountered the Chinese, Taylor had in his travels always, albeit in varying degrees, succeeded in obtaining an inside view of the life of the peoples he visited, succeeded, as he was fond of saying, in "penetrating" their society. He was aided in this by the enviable facility with which he acquired new languages. Even in India, thanks to an educated, English-speaking, native class, he had been able to gain some glimpse of the way of others. But the instant aversion he felt when in Singapore he first saw a large Chinese community prevented him from wanting to look further. If, on one hand, the Chinese were inscrutable, he, on the other, felt so immediate a repulsion that he did not care to scrutinize.

The repulsion Taylor felt amounted, in effect, to a horror. In Shanghai he uncharacteristically remained within the foreign sector, venturing into the city only once and that in order to meet his responsibility as a travel writer rather than to satisfy his own curiosity. Offering his observations of that walk into the streets of Shanghai he said, "Superficial as they were, I found nothing in the subject sufficient to tempt me into a further endurance of the disgusting annoyance of a Chinese city. I shall ask the reader's patience during the promenade on which I propose to take him, since it is for the first and last time" (p. 322). What follows is not so much a succession of disgusting sights, although there is nothing pleasant about them, as of tediously ugly ones reported by a surly pedestrian.

Taylor came to Shanghai on the *Susquehanna,* one of the warships of the Perry squadron, dispatched there to signify to the warring factions upriver that like the other members of the foreign community America too would retaliate with force should its nationals and their establishments be endangered by the forces threatening to descend upon the city. He was there when rumors of attack swept over the city and was caught up in the fearful and precautionary reaction. But unlike Stephens, who, when he found his trail following the path of a war, then intertwined his private history with that public event and incisively set forth the political and economic conditions that had led to war, Taylor offers no explanation of what the war is about. The concern of the foreign community in Shanghai was not so much for its physical safety as it was a concern that the rebellion was taking place in the silk district of Suzhou, centering on a struggle over control of Nanjing. Taylor, however, reported uneasiness at rumors and the responding movements of the *Susquehanna* without offering any sense of what was at stake and who was involved. He was a good reporter, but his loathing for China led him to rant rather than describe: the Chinese are morally the most debased people on earth; they have deeps on deeps of depravity, so shocking and horrible that they cannot even be hinted at on the printed page; the only taste they possess is for the monstrous and they admire whatever is distorted and unnatural. The crescendo of Taylor's compulsive excoriation reaches its climax in a stern admonition as horror turns into terror: "Their touch is pollution, and harsh as the opinion may seem, justice to our own race demands that they should not be allowed to settle on our soil" (p. 336).

In Asia Taylor had finally come up against a people who shook his racial theories. Civilization, as he conceived it, could not affect the Chinese
either in the complementary relationship of superior to inferior that
civilized persons enjoyed in the Middle East or the imperial relationship
of conqueror to subject they exerted in India. His physical description of
the Chinese is not so much that of an inferior race as it is of aliens so
different from all other humans as to exist on a separate planetary level:
"Dull faces without expression, unless a coarse glimmering of sensuality may be called such, and their half-naked unsymmetrical bodies,
more like figures of yellow clay than warm flesh and blood" (p. 285).
Nonhuman rather than subhuman, these are the monsters of a science
fiction that had not yet been born. If superior means the capacity to
prevail in a confrontation, then Taylor's horror at the Chinese stemmed
finally from an unconscious realization that once drawn closely into
their sphere the presumably superior race would prove powerless to
prevent its own transformation into otherness.

It was with relief that Taylor when in Japan was able to return to the
familiar racial scale and note "the regular, compact, files of our men,
and their vigorous, muscular figures, and the straggling ranks of the
mild, effeminate-featured Japanese" (p. 429). The sense of superiority
that had prevailed throughout his two previous books and for almost all
of this third one thus reappeared to close his account of more than two
years of wandering the world. He had met the challenge of the Shanghai
nightmare by urging the exclusion of the Chinese from the United States
yet concluded his book with a laudatory account of how the Japanese
insistence upon the exclusion of Americans had been disregarded.

Bayard Taylor returned to a nation of people eager to see and hear
as well as read him. In the winter lecture season of 1853–54 he gave
130 lectures, all of them to packed houses, and on the platform as in
print his chief aim was to bring the sights he had seen to those who
would otherwise never see them. Inevitably in so doing he also educated
Americans about their place on a racial map of the world: "every important triumph which man has achieved since his creation belongs to the

Caucasian race. Our mental and moral superiority is self evident," he announced (Beatty, p. 151).

But because he had become "familiarly acquainted with all the civilized races of the earth" (Beatty, p. 154) he believed he had acquired a comparative base from which also to point out to his countrymen America's shortcomings—the drive toward material acquisition, for example, which destroyed even among the wealthy the easeful pleasures of everyday life as they were enjoyed in the average, humble German household. Although he had never visited the American South, he took his license to criticize its mentality from the way in which the institution of slavery and its apologists so maddeningly led Europeans to an easy dismissal of everything American. With the courage of his convictions he took this message to audiences he knew might be hostile; in Philadelphia, on one occasion, the police accompanied him to the platform to keep watch over a restive, vocal crowd.

Taylor both made money from lecturing and found the activity quite dreadful. To meet his fellow Americans in railway carriages, hotels, dining salons, and lecture halls from Maine to Wisconsin was to wince at how uncultured they were compared with their European counterparts and how tedious their daily reality was compared with the people of the desert. Grace Greenwood (poet, essayist, editor, and author of *Haps and Mishaps of a Tour in Europe*—her actual name was Sarah Jane Lippincott) remembered meeting Taylor in Boston's Old Corner Bookstore and being advised by him against lecturing. It was, he told her, "an occupation full of misery, that he himself detested it, and that an audience seemed to him no other thing than a collection of cabbageheads." Her bookstore visit continued to be lively because "a few minutes later Mr. Emerson congratulated her upon the thought of lecturing, saying that there was recompense for all the hardships of the work in the kind words and the smiling faces and the bright eyes of the audience" (Smyth, p. 103). Emerson was a thinker for whom lecturing was a vital step toward the plateau of a finished essay; a platform appearance was completely coherent with his sense of himself as a man of letters. But Taylor wished to be something other than the kind of traveler his audience came to see. In a light verse, sent to a friend but kept from print, he mimicked that audience: "Ain't you now the greatest/Traveler alive?/ What's the land where turnips/Seem the best to thrive?" (Beatty, p. 212).

The larger part of Taylor's irritation with his lecturing, however, arose not from a distaste for the public but from a newly acquired sense of the true value of travel and what it meant to be a "great traveler." Each time he went before an audience this title was reconferred upon him by his listeners, and impelled by a reputation he had not sought he began after his return from Asia to think seriously about the question of what kind of travel could validly be called "great." His, he knew, had been more or less accidental, motivated by circumstances rather than design. As a boy of nineteen he had gone to Europe in search of the education he was unable to receive at home. Quite unexpectedly his account of his wanderings had become famous not for its literary merit (it had little), nor for any new discoveries, but simply because he had shown that one need not have much money to do what he did. His subsequent journey to California and Mexico came from no roving propensity but from a professional assignment, and his third journey, to Egypt and the Middle East, had started as a personal pilgrimage to the "cradle of civilization" in an attempt to ease his bereavement. At its outset, he believed that once he made that visit his interest in foreign lands would be satisfied: he would have no need for further travel; he certainly was not a professional traveler. He continued on to Asia only because he was charged to do so and the alternative was less agreeable: "It was not the sphere of activity which I should have chosen, but it was a grateful release from the drudgery of the editorial room."[13]

Now when he paused to think more deliberately about the nature of travel Taylor came to feel his own insignificance as a traveler. Commissioned by a Cincinnati publisher to compile a *Cyclopaedia of Modern Travel* (first edition 1856, enlarged two-volume edition 1859) he studied explorers from Herodotus to Humboldt, envying those of the Classical and Middle Ages for a frankness of speech permitted them in their times that more than compensated for their naïveté. As his study advanced to the modern period and its reigning genius, Humboldt, it became embarrassingly clear to Taylor that the great travelers had brought to their enterprises a scientific knowledge he sorely lacked—Ledyard before him had expressed a similar concern. The more he looked the more he saw that "Man" was more important than "Nature," and ethnology and anthropology were fields a traveler must master if he meant to make a meaningful contribution. And he began to consider that maybe, after all, it was not too late to earn through actual accomplishment the title that had been undeservedly thrust upon him.

Accordingly, when Taylor left home in 1856 for another visit to Europe he did so with the design of combining a trip to the Arctic Zone with a plan to study the Scandinavian "races and languages." This counterpart to his previous experience in southern lands would form the groundwork for the construction of the "human cosmos" he envisaged. Then if at some future time he was able to visit the Caucasus and South America he would have acquired all the necessary materials for a representation of the human race, its grand divisions, and the relation of differences in moral and mental development to differences in soil and climate. He set off filled with ambition, but early into his Scandinavian visit he found that his "former enjoyment of new scenes, and the zest of getting knowledge at first-hand, were sensibly diminished by regret for the lack of the preparatory studies which would have enabled me to see and learn so much more" (*By-Ways*, p. 13). He knew he didn't know, and that it was too late to undertake repair. All that remained to him was the familiar pattern of firsthand reports offered with no further pretension than bringing home to the American fireside a picture of remote regions. The two books that resulted from the 1856–58 travels, *Northern Travel* (1859) and *Travels in Greece and Russia, with an Excursion to Crete* (1859), were the last book-length narratives of travel he was to publish, although he continued to write essays and compile them into volumes that subsequently appeared in the collection, *Bayard Taylor's Travels*. If together the two narratives constitute Taylor's farewell to the genre that had made him famous and the profession that he had, in effect, invented, singly they represent a distinct high and a distinct low point in his practice.

The high is reached in *Northern Travel,* a book that unlike any of his others results from Taylor's purposely setting a specific adventure for himself that compelled him to a degree of subjectivity beyond that of his other books. Earlier travels, as he claimed, came about rather accidentally. His accounts commanded interest to the extent that interesting things were seen and done. But the heart of *Northern Travel* is a journey into blankness, the account of which depends for its interest not on the repetitive starkness of the landscape but on the shifting effects of cold and light on the mind of the narrator. It is the most literary of Taylor's travel books. Like the others it was materially constructed by cutting and pasting a number of previously published reports but since it lacked the exotic content provided by the scenes and societies of the Near East and Asia it was not so well regarded by a public who preferred to see him in Arab garb when they pictured him. Even his widow wrote rather dismissively of it: "The narrative of the excursion leaves upon the reader's mind the impression that it was a feat performed rather than a pleasure enjoyed" (*Life and Letters,* 1:329). The "feat" referred to was a winter journey to the far North, but remarkable as this may have been, the more remarkable feat was the literary one.

Tennyson once told Taylor, who longed for poetic distinction, that "A book of travels may be so written that it should be as immortal as a great poem" (*By-Ways,* p. 16). Taylor had his doubts and *Northern Travel* is far from the kind of book Tennyson envisioned. But it is worth noting that the Duke of Argyll later told Taylor that "he was the cause of Tennyson's visit to Norway; after reading 'Northern Travel' Tennyson was determined to see the Northern lands" (Smyth, p. 97).

In Stockholm in preparation for his journey Taylor took a week of intensive Swedish lessons, employing two teachers in double daily sessions. A week, even an intense one, was, he knew, a ludicrously brief time, but he was fluent in English and German and with his gift for linguistic acquisition felt ready to set out on his route without that "most inconvenient and expensive of persons," an interpreter.[14]

With a companion, Taylor left for Katukeino in Finland (at about the latitude of Murmansk) in the dead of the winter of 1856–57. They began

in a horse-drawn sleigh and when they reached Lapp country transferred to pulkas, single-occupant canoe-shaped sleds pulled by reindeer. Always a good handler of horses (and passably of camels) Taylor
started off clumsily behind a reindeer but persevered and continued
northward with increasing skill. When he reached the country of the
Lapps he was accompanied by one guide after another as he moved in
and out of a given guide's region. Despite the sparse population of the
subarctic wastes, at the end of most days' journeys he managed to reach
manmade shelter, and he rarely wanted for food. At Stockholm he had
found no useful guidebooks and had to listen to the dolefully reiterated
advice that he was in for hardships and privations and must carry an
abundance of provisions because nothing was to be had along his route.
"This prospect," he said, "was not at all alarming, for I remembered
that I had heard much worse accounts of Ethiopia while making similar
preparations in Cairo, and have learned that all such bugbears cease to
exist when they are boldly faced" (p. 25). He was not posturing. For him
the master key of travel was the ability to communicate with, and learn
from, the native inhabitants who were to be found in all regions, even
those most remote from civilization. This applied on a tundra as it did in
a desert. Where a native could survive so should a traveler be able to do.

Taylor's description of his northward journey from muted colors to
colorlessness, from settlements to isolation, from frozen light to numb-
ing darkness is interwoven with extended observations on the societies—Swedish, Lapp, Finnish—he encountered. At this first stage of his
journey his tone is that of a self-assured observer:

The sun rose a little after ten, and I have never seen anything
finer than the spectacle which we then saw for the first time, but
which was afterwards almost daily repeated—the illuminations
of the forests and snow-fields in his level orange beams, for even
at midday he was not more than eight degrees above the horizon. The tops of the trees only, were touched: still and solid as
iron, and covered with sparkling frost-crystals, their trunks
were changed to blazing gold, and their foliage to a fiery orange-

Bayard Taylor, northern traveler, in a studio photo, probably by Napoleon Sarony
(Reprinted by permission of the National Portrait Gallery, Smithsonian Institution).

brown. . . . There is nothing equal to this in the South—nothing
so transcendentally rich, dazzling, and glorious. (p. 53)

The exhilaration felt then continued as he proceeded northward toward
a treeless dark and crossed the Arctic Circle: "I had thought to find the
winter landscape of the far North a sublimity of death and desolation—a
wild, dark, dreary monotony of expression—but I had, in reality, the
constant enjoyment of the rarest, the tenderest, the most enchanting
beauty" (p. 54).

When Taylor and his companion turned southward, however, the
cold that had always been with them as a stimulant now stalked them as
a predator creeping closer and closer. The temperature dropped to a

steady forty below zero after they left the barren snowfields to arrive at a landscape that might have been imagined by Poe: "We again entered the snowy woods, which were dimly lighted up by an aurora behind us— a strange, mysterious, ghastly illumination, like the phosphorescent glow of a putrefying world." Hopelessly cold, their limbs numb and tor-pid, they found it impossible to keep entirely awake but in a comatose state talked incessantly to keep from lapsing into mortal slumber, "mak-ing random answers, as continual fleeting dreams crossed the current of our consciousness" (p. 166). Surviving this stage they proceeded, and the cold resumed its attack: "The air was hazy with the fine, frozen atoms of moisture, a raw wind blew from the north, the sky was like steel which has been breathed upon—in short, the cold was visible to the naked eye." Although they managed to reach shelter, since they were without food they could not remain but were forced outdoors again into the paralyzing cold. "The smoke was white and dense, like steam; the wind was a blast from the Norseman's hell, and the touch of it on your face almost made you scream . . . flaying, branding with a hot iron, cutting with a dull knife . . . may be something like it, but no worse" (p. 172).

When the latitude of daylight was reached at last and an illuminated world burst forth in visual splendor, that splendor no longer enchanted but was seen for what it really was, the decor of the house of death:

The twigs of the birch and the needles of the fir were coated with crystal, and sparkled like jets of jewels sprouted up from the im-maculate snow. The clumps of birches can be compared to nothing but frozen fountains—frozen in full action, with their showery sheaves of spray arrested before they fell. It was a won-derful, a fairy world we beheld—too beautiful to be lifeless, but every face we met reminded us the more that this was the chill beauty of Death—of dead Nature. Death was in the sparkling air, in the jewelled trees, in the spotless snow. Take off your mitten, and his hand will grasp yours like a vice; uncover your mouth, and your frozen lips will soon acknowledge his kiss. (pp. 173–74)

Taylor's description of his travel to and from the Arctic Circle is a literary achievement unmatched in his other books. Lucid and pliant though his prose usually is, nowhere else is subjectivity so powerfully forced upon him and nowhere else does he respond to it so effectively. The change from a traveler confidently observing the outer world to a concerned narrator anxiously watching himself parallels his gathering realization that beauty and death are not antagonists but partners.

Like Taylor's other travel narratives, *Northern Travel* is some 400 pages long. Included in it is an account of a later summer trip made to Norway and observations on the manners and morals of Lapps, Finns, Swedes, and Norwegians. The length of these disquisitions is apparently a vestige of his original intention to make his research part of a magisterial "human cosmos." If he was not a trained ethnologist at least he was a keen observer and emboldened by his recent studies in travel literature he discussed the sexual mores of the societies he visited in order to demonstrate to his readers that their own moral code was arbitrary, no more natural than that of others. At the same time, he was forced to admit that the very standards he wished to interrogate through applying his experience hindered his ability to deal frankly with them, pulling him short of the full effect he sought: "It is a pity that many traits which are really characteristic and interesting in a people cannot be mentioned on account of the morbid prudery prevalent in our day, which insults the unconscious innocence of nature. Oh, that one could imitate the honest unreserve of the old travellers!" (p. 152). In an age when an American woman requires that certain parts of the body and articles of clothing be referred to in delicate circumlocutions, Swedish women, unconscious of any impropriety, enter his room as he is dressing in order to bring the morning's coffee and make up his fire: "This is modesty in its healthy and natural development, not in those morbid forms which suggest an imagination ever on the alert for prurient images" (p. 74). As a poet Taylor showed little inclination to depart from the moral zone of Whittier and none whatsoever to approach that of Whitman, nor as a traveler did he seem to take significant advantage of his distance from his homeland's physical boundaries to transgress its moral boundaries. But on his return to America he did attempt to redraw those boundaries.

Even within the customary frame of his travel narratives Taylor's awakened interest in the nature of travel, combined with his deepened awareness that the impression he could make upon his readers was directly proportionate to its degree of strength upon his own mind, promised to elevate his work to a higher level than that on which it had previously rested. *Northern Travel* shows this potential. But its immediate successor, *Travels in Greece and Russia*, erases it. A lackluster trudge through sites familiar to readers of travel literature, it is his dullest work. Taylor lived in Athens for months in order to learn the Greek language but could not disguise his gloom during that period. The view from his windows was "almost disgusting," the winter weather abominable. Once the winter ended and he was on his way he seemed to wander from place to place with no clear objective and rather than enriching his work his new interest in political and economic analyses weakens it. Chapters with such titles as "People and Government" and "Agriculture and Resources" interrupt the pedestrian narrative but are equally lifeless. In his preface, signed July 1859, Taylor said the volume had been "too rapidly prepared for the press to allow me to add a special chapter on the Ethnology of Greece" (p. iii). In view of the set pieces that form a parallel with this missing chapter, the reader has had a lucky escape.

Ten years later Taylor confessed that while engaged in the travel that led to this book he found himself bored. *Travels in Greece and Russia* is leaden, weighed down by the author's realization that he no longer values the narrative of personal experience he once wrote yet is incapable of composing the kinds of social scientific analyses he wishes to write. It is a pity he did not stop with the achievement of *Northern Travel,* but it is to his credit at least that he saw himself in the dull mirror of his next book and abandoned the genre.

When Bayard Taylor returned to America in October 1858 he was accompanied by Marie Hansen-Taylor, the niece of the wife of his friend Count Bufleb whom he had married in Gotha in the previous year. The couple set about building a house on land Taylor had purchased in his native Kennett Square where his parents still lived. The $15,000 for the construction of the house, named Cedarcroft, came from book royalties, lecture fees, and compensation paid by magazines happy to print his poems, sketches, and reviews. A well-known author—to his eminent American friends he had added acquaintanceships with Tennyson, Carlyle, the Brownings, and other British literati—he sought the solidity of reputation brought by making his name synonymous with a place, as Irving had famously done at Sunnyside or Hawthorne at the Old Manse. The linkage also served to counter notions of him as a wanderer.

At Cedarcroft Taylor continued his prolific output, compiling the two books based on his 1856–58 journey, putting together a book of sketches of "life, scenery, and men," publishing collections of poetry, and contributing work to periodicals. The high-principled, temperance, Quaker community around his home rather disapproved of the good times that seemed to echo from Cedarcroft where guests were frequent and meals were served with wine. But they had a celebrity in their midst, and he was a native son at that.

As the decade drew to a close, however, so did the days of Taylor's greatest prosperity. The effects of the financial depression of 1857 reached his investments, and his generosity toward his siblings—on the eve of the Civil War, for example, he gave $1,000 to buy an army commission for his brother Fred—further drained his resources. It was necessary for him to go back to work for the *Tribune*. In 1862 he was in Washington as the *Tribune*'s war correspondent when Senator Simon Cameron of his home state of Pennsylvania, who had just been appointed American minister to Russia, offered him the post of secretary of legation. The remuneration, $6,000 per annum, was not terribly attractive, but Cameron also said that he would be leaving his ambassadorship within the year and Taylor's chances for succeeding him, at a salary of $12,000, were excellent. Acceptance of the position also opened to Taylor a prospect that he had for so long thought closed that he had just about abandoned it, the opportunity finally to visit Central Asia and the Caucasus and to do so under the protection of the Russian government. Perhaps a memory of the resistance Ledyard met in his attempt to cross greater Russia increased his interest in such a journey.

Taylor arrived in St. Petersburg in May 1862 and true to his word Cameron departed for home in September, leaving Taylor as chargé d'affaires. His chief diplomatic task in a period when the Union appeared to be unable to check Confederate victories was to dissuade Russia from regarding the Civil War as anything other than an internal matter. European powers seemed to be moving toward diplomatic recognition of the Confederacy and Taylor was pleased with his success at keeping Russia from any such gesture, but Secretary of State Seward found fault with his approach to the matter, believing that in his letters to the Russian government Taylor seemed to imply that there was reason to doubt Northern military success. Political favoritism back home, however, was probably the stronger reason why Cassius M. Clay who had preceded Cameron in the post was appointed to succeed him despite Cameron's best efforts on Taylor's behalf. A bitter Taylor returned home in September 1863 and indignantly called upon Seward for an explanation only to become further embittered by Seward's evasiveness. In his sonnet, "A Statesman," Taylor rendered his impression of the secretary. It begins

> He knew the mark of principle to wear
> And power accept while seeming to decline:
> So cunningly he wrought, with tools so fine,
> Setting his course with so frank an air,
> (Yet most secure when seeming most to dare.)[15]

Taylor also called upon the president for an explanation only to find that his reputation as the great traveler eclipsed the reality of his diplomatic service: "Hell," said a surprised Lincoln, "I thought you were in Persia" (Beatty, p. 228).

For the next decade and a half Taylor combined his various assignments for the *Tribune* with a prodigious literary output: books of poetry, three novels, collected travel sketches, and revisions of his more popular travel books climaxed by the collection, *Bayard Taylor's Travels,* published in 1874. But by the end of the 1860s his greatest commitment was to German literary studies. He gave lectures on German literature at Cornell and his translation of Goethe's *Faust* appeared in parts in 1870 and 1871. He also worked on a history of Germany, and was concentrating especially on a joint biography of Schiller and Goethe when he finally received handsome reparation for his earlier diplomatic disappointment. In 1878 the Hayes administration named him its minister to the Germany of Bismarck.

Taylor arrived in Berlin in May, warmly received by a nation that knew of his devotion to German literature as well as his storied travels. But he arrived ill. Stomach troubles that the doctors never managed to diagnose worsened with each succeeding month until, since he insisted on carrying on with his official rounds, the traveler who had eaten sparse fare in the Nubian desert and sparser in the subarctic wild sat in pain at lavish diplomatic dinners unable to eat at all. Surgery was recommended but failed to relieve him. By early winter he was in a bed from which he knew he would never rise, regarding his life as incomplete because his life of Goethe was incomplete. Bayard Taylor died in Berlin in December 1878, a month shy of his fifty-fourth birthday.

In the volatile New York literary world of Taylor's day, periodicals constantly warred, rival salons zealously excommunicated each other's members, and cynical, pay-per-word hack writers gathered in beer parlors to exchange tips on who was buying what kind of pieces at what prices. It was an environment in which literary gossip—the more disparaging the better—moved freely among all camps, and no tidbit was more widely circulated and more gleefully repeated than Humboldt's remark about Bayard Taylor: "He has travelled more and seen less than any man living."

Actually, Humboldt never said any such thing. The anecdote was invented by Park Benjamin, the day's master at vituperative, personal journalism—he was once sued for libel by James Fenimore Cooper—who in 1864 made a deathbed confession of his authorship, not, in all likelihood, because he wanted to do justice to Taylor but rather because he did not want to lose credit for so telling a witticism. Nevertheless, even after the confession the anecdote lived on; it just fit both Humboldt and Taylor too well to be discarded.

No one knew better than did Bayard Taylor himself why the anecdote was so popular. At its core was a kernel of truth. With his sense of what travel writing should contribute to human knowledge and his consequent dislike of a reputation that falsely implied he had made such a contribution, he wrote that if Humboldt had actually said " 'No man who has published so many volumes of travel has contributed so little to positive science'—he would have spoken the truth and I should have agreed with him" (By-Ways, pp. 13–14). What, apparently, Humboldt had actually responded when Taylor told him that he would find nothing in his books that contained the special knowledge a scientist needed was that the unscientific traveler who knows the use of his eyes in effect observes for the scientist without being aware of it. It was a kind remark, gratefully received.

If the fictional Humboldt comment is unfair to Taylor, however, the actual comment is more benign than accurate. Taylor did know the use of his eyes but his observations were of no particular use to science. As their popularity indicated, however, they were of considerable consequence in shaping the views literate, white Americans held about other peoples, other lands. His represented world was their real world; his represented Egypt, for example, what Egypt really was to them. For thousands upon thousands Taylor constructed not just a world but a world view. It saw white racial superiority as definitively validated by comparative experience. It saw primitive peoples as picturesque in the savage peculiarities that made them distinctively different from the civilized reader but uninteresting or repulsive in their shared resemblances with the reader. And it saw the arts that had evolved in Europe as the universally applicable definition of civilization. In sum, even while broadening provincial Americans' frame of reference, Bayard Taylor's travels confirmed them in their provincial sense of superiority.

From Jefferson to Emerson, American thinkers urged young Americans to stay at home and in the free air of their new world form them-

selves in response to the needs of their society. But the United States had
not long been a political fact before this good sense was countered by a
deeper longing. Most immigrants had found in America the material
advantages and social dignity denied them in their homelands, but by
the third generation their well-fed descendants found that their imagi-
nations remained starved. Europe was the home of the poetry, folklore,
and rich historical associations that were lacking in their muddy little
towns and unshingled backwoods settlements. It was not the United
States but Europe that was, as Washington Irving said, the "promised
land," because there was the milk and honey that could feed the hunger
for a culture larger than political rallies and spelling bees. Irving, and
after him Longfellow, served as messengers who in their books brought
the riches of the promised land home to America.

Bayard Taylor revolutionized this situation when in a youthful, often
amateurish, travel book he demonstrated that Europe was available to
many more young Americans than the rich or especially talented. After
the flood he thus turned loose it would no longer be possible to write
about a visit to Europe simply because one had made that visit. Too
many had made it also. To be of interest travel books would have either
to take their readers to more exotic scenes, or, if to familiar ones, then to
conduct that visit with a superior degree of aesthetic tact (as would
Henry James) or from a very novel viewpoint (as would Mark Twain).

If Taylor, however reluctantly, invented the profession of travel writing he did so not just by traveling widely but by working conscientiously
as a writer. With regard to the perilous enterprises necessary for his
kind of travel narrative, he said "Danger is oftener a condition of one's
own mind than an absolute fact, and I presume that my share of personal adventure was no more than would fall to the lot of any man" (*By-
Ways,* pp. 17–18). Ultimately his narratives had to depend for their
effect not upon the adventures themselves, however daring, but upon
the skill with which he could convey to his reader the impressions made
upon his mind. His travel books were thus the beneficiaries of his constant practice as a poet and an essayist, but were also the casualties of
his journalistic commitment to meeting readers in terms of interests

and attitudes they already possessed. Their prejudices could, from time to time, be challenged, but in a journalistic format could hardly be undermined. As a consequence, like the proverbial newspaper of yesterday, *Bayard Taylor's Travels* no longer has readers. But the attitudes he shaped when he brought the world to the American fireside have had an afterlife beyond the books themselves. And the practitioners of the profession he invented continue to follow his pattern in their search for more and more exotic places about which to write and stranger and stranger ways of reaching them.

CHAPTER 4

Mark Twain

————⟫•⟪————

The Innocents Abroad (1869)
Roughing It (1872)
A Tramp Abroad (1880)
Life on the Mississippi (1883)
Following the Equator (1897)

Accompanied by his family, Mark Twain sailed from New York for Hamburg in April 1878. He went abroad to save money. The cost of living in Germany, even of luxurious living, was well below that in his native land. And he went abroad to make money. Faced with declining sales for his recent works he intended to tour European sites in order to return to the genre in which he had scored his initial literary triumph—the travel book. His *Innocents Abroad* (1869) had been an instant popular success and although he had published a great deal of fiction since then (including *Tom Sawyer*) and was now America's most celebrated author, that early travel book continued to be his best-selling work.

The *Holsatia* that carried Twain to Germany also carried Bayard Taylor, the newly appointed American minister to the court at Berlin. Well before their shipboard meeting Taylor had acknowledged that the romantic curiosity and unqualified enthusiasms that marked his own travel writing had been driven out of fashion by the kind of debunking reportage made popular by Twain. In a letter to the *Tribune* written during a return visit to Egypt in 1874, he had self-consciously remarked, "Well, I meant to send you practical, realistic reports of Egypt, and this letter will be sure to bring down upon me the wrath of Mark Twain, and all others who distrust earnest impressions."[1]

But on the *Holsatia* there were no hard feelings: indeed, Taylor on his way to an important diplomatic post and resources for the completion of his intended study of Goethe and Schiller was happy to escape a literary routine that now struck him as drudgery undiluted. And Twain, if he did not yet have that sense of the matter while on board with Taylor, arrived at it very quickly thereafter. The writing of travel sketches, he was soon to say, is a "sterile obligation,"[2] and as he worked to complete *A Tramp Abroad* he declared that he despised the book. The depression he felt as he coped with his work deepened in January 1879 when word of the death of Taylor reached him in Munich. "It is too sad to talk about" (Kaplan, p. 220), was all he could bring himself to say.

Yet as hateful as he insisted that he found the genre, Twain was to return to the travel book again and again after the 1880 publication of *A Tramp Abroad*. Most obviously he did so because unlike fiction, the rewards of which were never certain, his travel writing could, conservatively, be expected to produce a profit and, optimistically, to generate large earnings. Risk was all but eliminated by the fact that a travel book was made up in great part of letters that had been contracted and remunerated in advance by newspapers and magazines. Revenues from book sales, therefore, were in addition to income already realized from the work, albeit it was necessary to revise and supplement the journalistic letters before they found book form: they needed, as Twain said, "to have some of the wind and water squeezed out of them."[3] Those contracted letters, however, also obligated Twain to produce on schedule week after week for months at a stretch and he was a lazy man, or at least a man who forever called himself lazy because he did his best work at unanticipated hours and in unexpected seasons rather than within any regimen. He loathed the travel-letter arrangement as an affront to his constitution even as he abominated the sheer physical exertion and petty mental calculations connected with leaving one place only to set up in another which would soon be left. Characteristically he appears at his happiest—and his narratives are often at their best—not when he is at a site but when he has nothing to do but lie back in stagecoach or steamship and drawl on as he awaits an arrival he more than half-wishes will never come.

It is, nevertheless, a mistake to understand Twain's repeated return to the travel narrative as primarily linked to his financial circumstances. There is a deeper, more literary, connection. Twain was a master at revealing character through dialogue and capturing in the printed marks on the page the pitch and stress of the spoken American tongue—to read his work is to hear it. He could deploy the vocabularies and rhythms of a range of dialects, and tell a comic story past its climax but to the wistful, softly expressed afterthought that undermined that climax and brought the story tumbling down under its own weight; which is to say not only were his content and manner comic but so was his form. Twain, however, was not an accomplished maker of extended plots. He is at his best in his short pieces or in the incidents within his novels, while the plots of the novels as a whole rely upon coincidence and mistaken identities and often evoke the tedium of a good joke that goes on too long. Even *Huckleberry Finn,* his masterpiece, is weakened by the incongruity of the final episodes.

Rather than linking incidents into the complex network of cause and effect that is a plot, Twain manages a sequence of events most tellingly when he allows them to follow his mind's meanderings, as one thing reminds him of another which leads to yet another it is associated with in his mind. The incidents are knit together psychologically rather than causally or chronologically.

Strolling in the Neckar hills not far from his hotel, for example, Twain became lost in the woods. His disorientation opened his imagination to what he had read about the presence in the German forests of gnomes and fairies, and he "fell into a train of dreamy thought about animals which talk, and kobolds, and enchanted folk, and the rest of the pleasant legendary stuff; and so, by stimulating my fancy, I finally got to imagining I glimpsed small flitting shapes here and there down the columned aisles of the forest."[4] The gauzy fabric of this magic, pine-woody mood—sunlight without, twilight within—was suddenly torn by the raucous croak of a raven. Startled, Twain glanced up to have his surprise turn to embarrassment when the challenging bird summoned a second raven and the two, calling in yet a third, proceeded to talk him over in a distinctly insulting fashion. "They were nothing but ravens—I knew that,—what they thought about me could be a matter of no consequence—and yet when a raven shouts at you, 'What a hat!' 'O, pull down your vest,' and that sort of thing, it hurts you and humiliates you, and there is no getting around it with fine reasoning and petty arguments" (p. 35).

"Animals talk to each other, of course" (p. 36), Twain insists. He learned this in his days in California where he knew a simple-hearted miner, the sole inhabitant of a forsaken corner of the Sierras, who understood the language of the birds. In a section ostensibly about Heidelberg and its environs there then follows one of Twain's greatest stories, "Jim Baker's Blue-Jay Yarn." Disconnected times (fifteen years ago and yesterday), places (California and Germany), and experiences (imagined and immediate) have melded together to inspire a masterpiece of American humor.

In his last years, lying abed and dictating what he called his "Autobiography," Twain refused to proceed chronologically but insisted on jumping from the memory of a given event to the memory of another that his unreined mind associated with it even though the remembered events occurred decades apart and sometimes were further disconnected by one having been a personal experience and the other an item he had read in the newspaper. He justified this erratic—yet always traceable—course by claiming he had invented "a form and method whereby the past and the present are constantly brought face to face, resulting in contrasts which newly fire up the interest all along like contact of flint with steel" (*Autobiography,* 2:245). This seems a somewhat overstated justification for garrulous rambling, but, then, Twain at his best always rambled and to recognize this is to identify a fundamental

connection between his mental and his physical wanderings.[5] A journey's serial progress from place to place stimulated his mind's parallel
excursion along a path of linked memories. Far from being antipathetic
to his literary practice as he often proclaimed it to be, travel writing was
a perfect vehicle for Twain's imagination.*

Twenty-six years of age, Sam Clemens in 1861 headed for the Nevada Territory in flight from the Civil War and in pursuit of he knew not
quite what. After the war had disrupted traffic on the Mississippi and
put a halt to his budding career as a steamboat pilot on that river, he
spent several weeks with a band of fellow Missouri townsmen who had
formed themselves into a troop of Confederate irregulars. But not much
time was needed to show him his essential inability to participate in the
rituals of military discipline with a straight face—it seemed to be such
playacting. When, moreover, the playacting turned grim with a shooting
that led Clemens to fear that he may actually have participated in a
killing he was ready to make a rapid exit from the stage. His brother
Orion was leaving for the West to take up the post of secretary to the
governor of the Territory of Nevada and Sam set out with him. There he
would do what just about every other man, young, old, and in-between
was doing, try his hand at mining.

The flush times of Nevada silver and California gold were to find their
most enduring image in the picture of them Clemens eventually drew
after he became the author, Mark Twain. But for some four years following his arrival in the Washoe in 1861 he worked and loafed with miners,
exploding the charges that laid bare the vitals of the Nevada mountains,
and skimming the skin off the California earth to sift through the beds
of her hillside streams. More than once he thought sudden wealth was
his, but the mineral fortune at his fingers' ends always managed to
wriggle into the palm of another. Together with miners, vagabonds,

---

*This extends to some of his fiction also, most notably *Huckleberry Finn,* which arranges
its incidents along the line of a journey down the Mississippi and contains descriptions of
the different kinds of communities and types of characters encountered along the way—a
travelogue through Mississippi River society, circa 1845.

speculators, horse traders, and courtroom hangers-on he played crude
and often violent practical jokes upon newly arrived greenhorns, but
from these Westerners he also learned the subtle art of the vernacular
comic story—to tell it with a straight-faced seriousness that grew longer
and graver in direct ratio to the outrageous improbability of what was
being said.

Some seven years after he left the West, Twain told the story of his
mining ventures in *Roughing It* (1872). When all of his attempts at working mines and trading in mine stocks had brought him up against the
blank wall of failure, he said, a partner stirred him to make one last try
at working their claim. Accordingly, armed with a long-handled shovel
he descended into an eight-foot shaft in order to clear it of loose rocks
and dirt: "You must brace the shovel forward with the side of your knees
till it is full, and then, with a skilful toss, throw it backward over your left
shoulder. I made the toss and landed the mess just on the edge of the
shaft and it all came back on my head and down the back of my neck. I
never said a word, but climbed out and walked home. I inwardly resolved that I would starve before I would make a target of myself and
shoot rubbish at it with a long-handled shovel. I sat down and gave
myself up to solid misery—so to speak."[6] "So to speak" qualifies the desperation considerably because it is at this point in his account that the
failed miner reveals that he had earlier amused himself with writing letters to the Virginia City (Nevada) *Daily Territorial Enterprise* which had
printed them. Now returning to his cabin from his defeat at the end of a
shovel he found a letter inviting him to become city editor of the *Enterprise* at a salary of twenty-five dollars a week. Although Sam Clemens
did not then realize it, he had finally hit pay dirt. From that time forward he was to write for a living and refine the ore within himself into
Mark Twain.

From Nevada Twain eventually drifted into California and continuing newspaper work which in March 1866 eventuated in his stepping
aboard the *Ajax* to sail to the Hawaiian (Sandwich) Islands in order to
furnish letters to the *Sacramento Union*. He spent four months and a
day there, wrote twenty-five letters to the *Union* about the islands, and

after his return to San Francisco, on the basis of the local fame his letters had earned he announced a public lecture on his experiences. He thus launched the platform career he was to continue to pursue throughout his working life, locked in the cycle of travel leading to writing leading to lecturing, which, of course, involved further travel that led to further writing, and so forth.

The Hawaiian letters were revised six years later to form the final chapters of *Roughing It* although they are rather disconnected from the pictures of the West that make up the greater part of the book. By that time Twain, an established author living in the East, had a national audience that consisted of *all* members of the average reading family—women and men, girls and boys—an uncommon phenomenon for an American author. His books were sold by subscription rather than in bookstores, the publisher's agent calling door-to-door with sample pages brimming with illustrations, and, equally important, sample bindings from cloth to hand-tooled Morocco, with which to entice a householder who in most cases purchased but one or two books a year into putting his name on the subscription list. The buyer, as Justin Kaplan writes "was typically rural, a farmer or small tradesman with little education, for whom bulk was an index of value" (p. 62); hence Twain's filling out a book about the continental West with the Hawaiian letters. Subscription books ran over 600 pages. George Ade who grew up with such books called them "front-room literature." They were not to be read from cover to cover any more than the front room itself was to be occupied on weekdays.

Twain changed all that. "His books," Ade recalled, "looked at a distance, just like the other distended, diluted, and altogether tasteless volumes that had been used for several decades to balance the ends of the center table . . . so thick and heavily emblazoned with gold that [they] could keep company with the bulky and high-priced Bible." Remembering his childhood in rural Indiana, Ade asked, "Can you see the boy, Sunday morning prisoner, approach the book with a dull sense of foreboding, expecting a dose of Tupper's *Proverbial Philosophy?*" And then can you see how enthralled he is when he finds that into the company of the other ponderous volumes crowded with wood-cuts, stuffed with commonplace pieties, and varnished with lachrymose sentiment has crept a comic narrative peppered with zany incidents involving a range of characters whose ignorance and sublimely idiotic behavior were both intensely familiar to any common American yet had never before been displayed on the printed page?[7] For the provincial American, to read Twain was, among other delights, to enter into the thrill of realizing that the pompous bores and inspired fools he met in his everyday life were as much the stuff of literature as were exemplary children and monitory elders.

Mark Twain's travel narratives combined into one audience readers customarily divided by different interests. It included not only women, the conventional readers of novels, and boys and young men, the conventional readers of sensational journal tales, but men who usually read nothing at all save the newspaper, the ledger, and the Bible. No American author of his time attracted so many male readers, and this massive quantitative addition to the limited reading public enjoyed by other authors early established and long maintained his celebrity. As the St. Louis *Republican* said of Twain's Sandwich Island lecture, delivered there in March 1867, "He succeeded in doing what we have seen Emerson and other literary men fail in attempting—he interested and amused a large and promiscuous audience."[8]

The distinctive approach that attracted male readers was developed in the days of Twain's Western journalism when he had no readership other than the kind of men with whom he had worked, drunk, and played in Virginia City, Angel's Camp, and San Francisco. The nature of such an audience may readily be inferred from a reading of the original travel letters from Hawaii. Although literate its members are distrustful of the literary and welcome an outlook that validates their suspicion that diction is polished in direct proportion to its detachment from the actual—truth needs only plain talk. They are curious about the way other men in other places go about making a living and keen to improve the opportunities this may suggest to them, but they are proud to be Americans and savagely defensive in the face of older and more cultured societies. Willing to learn and even sympathize with the viewpoint of nonwhites they nevertheless equate being American with being white and however sympathetic they may be to others are not so to the point of relinquishing their feeling of superiority to them. Over the course of his career Twain came to disagree with many of the convictions held by such readers, but he never lost his sense of who they were and how their attention was to be held, even when he intended to laugh them out of their views and shame them into his.

Earlier, however, the author of the Hawaiian letters was very much one of the boys—booted, tobacco-chewing, westerners who are confident they are the true representatives of the national character. And, indeed, as with the addition of new states the nation became more western in the second half of the nineteenth century, so the national tone also became more western. Even easterners acknowledged there was something more American about a region that had never been under what Hawthorne called "the damned shadow of Europe." Learning his craft by addressing westerners, Mark Twain was, in effect, learning how to address a nation; William Dean Howells was to call him the "Lincoln of our literature."

The letters from Hawaii are a mix of keen observations that seek to inform and gross distortions that seek to amuse. In them Twain experiments with ways in which he can provide his readers with accurate physical descriptions of the islands, speculate on their potential value to the United States, and explain the nature of their government and society, yet keep those readers' attention with laughter. One solution was to provide himself with an invented companion who could stand in for the uneducated, rough-and-ready reader, rooted in the particulars of physical life and distrustful of idealization. This companion, Mr. Brown, can be relied upon to bring any excursion into the literary ether back to earth with a thump. He will respond to Twain's praise of the superior warmth of the Hawaiian climate and the superior cleanliness of the houses and streets of Honolulu when compared with San Francisco by complaining about the heat and detailing the awesome array of insects that annoy during the day and make sleep impossible at night. Both commentators invite laughter: the narrator Twain who has allowed himself to soar too far from the plane of actuality in his enthusiastic descriptions, and his pedestrian companion Brown who cannot grasp the larger implications of what he sees because of the flea bite on his hand. Twain is thus able to fulfill the travel narrative's obligation to provide description and information while also carrying on a comic critique of the travel form.

Brown is an amusing prop and he or his equivalents were to reappear in later travel narratives. But the more challenging task was to develop a single authorial voice that could be both funny yet listened to on serious matters, convey a sense of an ambience larger than the sum of particulars yet avoid the bookishness of what Bayard Taylor would call "earnest impressions." Even as Twain employed Brown he was moving to replace him by incorporating his outlook into a first-person account that could also see beyond the details. Most commonly he combined the two—the literary observer and the horse-sense commentator—by following up descriptions that might appear to be echoes of nineteenth-century parlor literature with a comment that undercut without quite disabling them. In *Innocents Abroad,* for example, he writes, "Toward nightfall, the next evening, we steamed into the great artificial harbor of the noble city of Marseilles, and saw the dying sunlight gild its clustering spires and ramparts, and flood its leagues of environing verdure with a mellow radiance that touched with an added charm the white villas that flecked the landscape far and near." Immediately after which he adds, the brackets are his, "[Copyright secured according to law.]"[9] If Twain thus satirizes conventional travel literature, he is having his cake as well as eating it: he does not mock the literary until he has shown that he can be literary if he so chooses. The laugh comes only after he has displayed what he can do. When he really wishes to marshall an all-out assault on descriptive twaddle he most frequently does so by carrying a passage to absurdity: "The table d'hote was served by waitresses dressed in the quaint and comely costume of the Swiss peasants. This consists of a simple gros de laine, trimmed with ashes of roses, with overskirt of sacre bleu ventre sans gris, cut bias on the off side, with facings of petit polonaise and narrow insertions of pate de fois gras backstitched to the mise en scene in the form of a jeu d'esprit" (*Tramp Abroad,* p. 340).

As early as the Hawaiian letters Twain evinced a stunning ability to use similes drawn from the banal, even vulgar, experience of his readers with which to picture with exactness the exotic. His taste was not always impeccable: "The red sun looked across the placid ocean through the tall, clean stems of the coconut trees," he told his California readers, "like a blooming whiskey bloat through the bars of a city prison."[10] An arrestingly precise picture, but one so coarse in tone it destroys what it achieves. More often than not, however, even while still addressing a California audience Twain was emerging from such slips in taste while retaining his striking eye for the simile that was both unexpected yet just right. The top of a coconut palm looks like "a feather duster struck by lightning" (p. 229); that's dead accurate.

En route to the islands Twain started his letters with the comment that despite its name the Pacific was not calm at all. The observation was trite, just the kind he would soon strive to avoid, and aware of its staleness even at this early stage he moved to enliven it with an insertion of brash irreverence: "All the days of our boyhood we read how that infatuated old ass, Balboa, looked out from the top of a high rock upon a broad sea as calm and peaceful as a sylvan lake, and went into an ecstasy of delight, like any other greaser over any other trifle, and shouted in his foreign tongue and waved his country's banner, and named his great discovery 'Pacific' " (p. 10). The assertion is tasteless at the very least, in tone very much like the "whiskey bloat" simile. Twain is reaching for effect and allowing the worst part of his anticipated readership to dictate an adolescent mockery of school-learning and a chauvinistic, not to say racialist, mockery of Spaniards and their California descendants. But he is also opening a theme that will develop into one of the distinguishing characteristics of his best work, an insistence upon measuring history in terms of his direct experience rather than the reverse, and over the course of his career such questioning of history almost uniformly led him to a sympathetic defense of peoples who were marked as inferior if not despicable by European and American historians who thereby established the cultural climate that justified the masses to think in terms of "greasers." The Hawaiian letters get past the puerile observation on Balboa to take the part of the islanders against Cook, who Twain says, abused them although they treated him well. Further to his distrust of official history, he insists that Ledyard's journal "is the most just and reliable account of this eventful period of the voyage" and does so because "Ledyard's account and that of the natives vary in no important particulars" (p. 219).

Twain's siding with the islanders against Cook foreshadows the anti-imperialism of his mature career. The thirty-year-old reporter, however, is more ambivalent. He sees foreign control of the islands to be inevitable and so welcomes the advent of the steamship as the improvement that will guarantee American dominance: "If California can send capitalists down here in seven or eight days time and take them back in nine or ten, she can fill these islands full of Americans and regain her lost foothold" (p. 12). Missionaries he both satirizes and praises in reflection of his uncertain feelings about the so-called civilizing of the native population. On one hand he deplores the systematic reduction of beauty, grace, and guiltlessness as the islanders become church-going Protestants, but on the other reveals a horror of what he sees as savagery. Another factor dictating this ambivalence may well be his newspaper audience; ruder than that back East it nevertheless has its proprieties and so only a limited capacity for criticism of religion. But Twain's capacity was to grow steadily.

The principal end of the Hawaiian letters is to portray a place and its way of life to those who have never been there and Twain's success is evident. Lively vignettes concerned with the particulars of his lodgings, his laundry, his food, and his drink convey a strong sense of place, and if particular anecdotes about the scrapes into which he gets and the blunders he commits are to be suspected as fictional they nevertheless serve the larger purpose of letting us know what his Hawaii was like, giving us a feel for it, as it were. Here as in all the travel writing that followed Twain displays an uncanny skill at claiming as factual personal incidents that are manifestly invented, yet in so doing heightening his readers' sense of the reality of the world depicted rather than undermining it. What Russell Banks writes of *A Tramp Abroad* applies to Twain's other travel writing as well; in spite of digressions, exaggerations, and omissions, "there is an implicit, underlying contract with the reader, an assurance that this journey actually took place and that it went approximately as described."[11]

Having, in a manner of speaking, conquered the West, Mark Twain, an author of popular stories,—"The Jumping Frog of Calaveras County" had been reprinted in newspapers throughout the country—a lecturer who found eager audiences, and a reporter who had proved his proficiency as a travel writer, backtrailed to the East: by sea down the coast to the Isthmus, across Nicaragua to the Gulf, and thence to the United States where, lecturing as he went, he proceeded to New York by way of his native Missouri. Along the way he sent sketches of his travels back to the San Francisco *Alta California*. As he had reported to Californians on Hawaii now he was to tell them about the state of things back in the regions whence they had originated and in the nation's burgeoning metropolis, New York. He was fascinated by a new-fangled heater that he encountered in Quincy, Illinois: "I don't take any interest in prize bulls, astonishing jackasses and prodigious crops, but I took a strong fancy to that gas apparatus" (*Travels with Mr. Brown,* p. 136), and in addition to reporting from New York on omnibuses, horse cars, the Russian Bath, and Barnum's Museum, he described women's fashions, gazed at women who wore far less than was decorous (in the melodrama, *The Black Crook*), and attended Anna Dickinson's feminist lecture which, he said, was worth listening to.

At an exhibition at the Academy of Design in New York, Mark Twain made the first of the sojourns into art criticism that later, when he reported from Europe, were to mark him as either an uncultivated buffoon, a sharp-eyed pragmatist, or, possibly, something of each since in go-getting America ignorance and astuteness were not mutually exclusive. "I know," he wrote, "I ought to have admired that picture by one of the old masters, where six bearded faces without any bodies to them were glaring out of Egyptian darkness and glowering upon a naked infant that was not built like any infant that ever I saw, nor colored like it either. I am glad the old masters are all dead, and I only wish they had died sooner" (p. 239). With such remarks Twain, addressing readers who have had as little experience of art as he has had, chooses the shabbier course of playing up to that ignorance rather than informing it.

If this is reprehensible, however, there is something sanative in his bringing a sense of the essential America of commerce and accelerating industrialization to his criticism of an American art that, in effect, avoids America in its adulation of foreign models:

> The Academy people call their costly stack of architectural devil-
> try 'the Moorish style'—as if the atmosphere of antiquity and po-
> etry and romance, that cast a charm around that style in its
> ancient home beyond the seas could be reproduced here in the
> midst of railroads and steamboats and business rush and
> clamor, and acres of brownstone fronts—and as if it could be
> anything but clownish and repulsive without that atmosphere.
> They might as well have put a wigwam there and expected it to
> be romantic and picturesque without its natural surroundings of
> flowers and grass and brooks, and the solemn silence of dim old
> forests. (p. 242)

Such an outlook foreshadows the work of Louis Sullivan at century's end and the architects of the twentieth century who were to build in America buildings that connected to the living American scene.

In one of the letters to the *Alta California,* Twain wrote on March 2, 1867 that "Prominent Brooklynites are getting up a great European pleasure excursion for the coming summer, which promises a vast amount of enjoyment for a very reasonable outlay" (p. 111). Originating among members of Henry Ward Beecher's Pilgrim Church, the leisurely excursion to the Holy Land by way of Europe would be made in a ship exclusively devoted to that purpose—no venture in group tourism on so extended a scale had ever before been undertaken. With the fare fixed at $1,250 in American currency and passengers advised to carry $500 in gold for further expenses, the *Quaker City* was to be equipped with a library, musical instruments, and a printing press for the production of a daily newspaper. The Reverend Henry Ward Beecher and General William Tecumseh Sherman were advertised to be among the 110 passengers the steamer would be accommodating on a voyage scheduled to last from June to November although the possibility of its being extended if the passengers so desired was held open. "Isn't it an attractive scheme?" Twain wrote. "Five months of utter freedom from care and anxiety of every kind, and in company with a set of people who will go only to enjoy themselves, and will never mention a word about business during the voyage" (p. 113). His letter was both a report to the readers of the *Alta California* and a petition to its management to underwrite the cost of his participation.

The company who went "only to enjoy themselves" proved, on the whole, to be a dreary, hymn-singing lot of "venerable fossils." They duplicated on a large scale the characteristics of a devout believer Twain had observed on board the ship that had carried him from San Francisco to the Isthmus. During a storm when the sea flowed into the forward cabin and washed the carpet bags aft this pattern of devotion had clasped a stanchion with one arm and held it firmly as he prayed, while with the other arm he grabbed each carpet bag as it floated past, making sure it was not his before he reached out for another. "Any man of judgment cannot but think well of his modesty," Twain wrote, "in only relying on Providence to save the ship but looking out for his carpet sack himself" (*Travels with Mr. Brown,* p. 17).

In the event, neither the Reverend Beecher nor General Sherman could make it—indeed even a well-advertised actress found she had other commitments. But if the celebrities could not make the voyage Mark Twain could and the voyage gained him a celebrity to rival Beecher and Sherman. He wrote fifty-eight letters about the tour to the *Alta California* as well as six for the New York *Tribune,* and one each for two other newspapers, but reprinted none verbatim when he assembled them into *The Innocents Abroad*. Published in July 1869, it "has been the most popular book of foreign travel ever written by an American."[12]

When he reported on Hawaii and his journey from California to New York, Twain described places about which a relatively scant literature existed. But he was keenly aware of the vast amount of writing that existed on France, Italy, and the Holy Land, and that his readers were, on the whole, familiar with it. "I make small pretence," he wrote at the outset, "of showing any one how he *ought* to look at objects of interest" (*Innocents,* p. v); that's what other books do. Rather he will suggest to the reader how he would see Europe if he looked with his own eyes rather than those of previous travelers.

This outlook led him to two bold, not to say outrageous, commitments: he would ignore sites that bored him, regardless of how famous they might be; and he would pit his opinions against the standing truths, however uncouth this might reveal him to be. Although he meant to be scornful of the Moors he observed in North Africa when he wrote that they "like other savages, learn by what they see; not what they hear or read" (p. 86); that was very much the kind of "savagery" to which he himself adhered in both his finest moments of comic deflation of the pompous and his worst moments of adolescent mockery of the cultivated.

The Innocents Abroad is a book about touring, not traveling, and that is its strength. The tour was laid out in advance and Twain embarked on it because everything had been prepared for him. He didn't know the language of any country he visited and his foreign acquaintanceship was limited to guides, hoteliers, waiters, and shopkeepers. At no point did he pretend otherwise or wish to alter this condition—to imagine he was a traveler rather than a mere tourist—because he brilliantly perceived that the originality of his work compared with other books of travel would reside in his paying closer attention to the tourist experience and to tourists themselves than to the places visited. *Innocents Abroad* is a book about the comic adventures of a group of tourists far more than it is about the places they visit. They are, indeed, innocents

A wary, semisavage, New World "innocent," Mark Twain prepared to depart for the Old World (From an advertising prospectus for *Innocents Abroad*, reprinted with kind permission of The Mark Twain Project, The Bancroft Library).

abroad, clueless as to where to go and how to react except as steered by guides and prompted by travel books and they are marvelously fit subjects for the comic art.

Although by dint of being their observer Twain separates himself from his fellows he does not absolve himself from being a tourist. In an echo of Bayard Taylor's refusal to wear the customary protections donned by tourists against the desert sun he remarks that "No Arab wears a brim to his fez, or uses an umbrella, or any thing to shade his eyes or his face," but unlike Taylor he spurns these not because he wishes to be like an Arab but because he sees what the others look like and doesn't want to look like them: "They travel single file; they all wear the endless white rag of Constantinople wrapped round their hats, and dangling down their backs; they all hold white umbrellas, lined with green, over their heads" (p. 466), and so costumed they ride bouncing along, knees up, elbows out, umbrellas popping up and down. "It will be bad enough to get sun-struck, without looking ridiculous into the bargain" (p. 467).

Unlike Taylor, too, is his opinion of foreigners. On Fayal in the Azores "The community is eminently Portuguese—that is to say, it is slow, poor, shiftless, sleepy, and lazy" (p. 55). Italians are a happy, cheerful, contented, superstitious, poverty-stricken, indolent, and worthless lot. The "priestcraft" to which they submit "suits these people precisely; let them enjoy it, along with the rest of the animals" (p. 209). Arabs are filthy, squalid, simple, superstitious, disease-tortured creatures and are by nature a thankless and impassive race who possess all the distempers that are born of indolence and iniquity.

Such unqualified ridicule of other peoples is slightly leavened by the absoluteness with which it is affirmed, as if in being so sweeping Twain relies upon the reader's sense that these generalizations are completely subjective, offered as examples of his comic irascibility rather than as objective truths. Yet even granting this somewhat doubtful contention, the heaped-up diction of derision goes beyond comic intent or even scorn to convey an almost violent abhorrence of other peoples because they are not clean, not sensible, not industrious, not modern—not, in a word, American. His fellow tourists "entered the country [of the Bible] with their verdict already prepared, and they could no more write dispassionately and impartially about it than they could about their own wives and children" (p. 511). In opposition to such passionate partiality, however, Twain's authorial position was not one of dispassionate objectivity. Rather, he offered a different but equally passionate partiality. The comic corollary of seeing with one's own eyes demanded that conventional observations be contradicted, and so at times he not so much saw with his own eyes as with the eyes of others and then inverted the view.

At its best Twain's commitment to taking a position opposed to that of the most prominent travel books on the Holy Land results in sharp-eyed observations such as those on the Sea of Galilee, the oft-described "beauty" of which he exposes as a fiction, first by comparing it with the true beauty of Lake Tahoe, which is fresh in his memory, and then by quoting and analyzing the descriptions of the Sea of Galilee in revered texts (such as *The Crescent and the Cross* and *Tent Life in the Holy Land*) to show that those books actually unsay what they claim to say: "Nearly every book concerning Galilee and its lake describes the scenery as beautiful. No—not always straightforward as that. Sometimes the *impression* intentionally conveyed is that it is beautiful, at the same time that the author is careful not to *say* that it is in plain Saxon. But a careful analysis of these descriptions will show that the materials of which they are formed are not beautiful and can not be wrought into combinations that are beautiful" (pp. 510–11). Such close reading plays a significant part in all of Twain's writing because he believes, in effect, that deceptions, even authorial self-deceptions, will be betrayed by the very language in which they are presented. Ultimately his view of language is nominalistic; he does not believe in any reality that is larger than the sum of the observed details. At its worst such nominalism prevents the possibility of seeing a truth that may transcend the particulars of a scene. A group of Arabs lounging about a well, for example, reminds him of the biblical illustrations he had "worshipped" as a child except that in the pictures there was no dirt, desolation, ugly features, sore eyes, or raw-backed donkeys; no "disagreeable jabbering in unknown tongues; no stench of camels; no suggestion that a couple of tons of powder placed under the party and touched off would heighten the effect and give to the scene a genuine interest and a charm which it would always be pleasant to recall, even though a man lived a thousand years" (p. 544). When the crescendo of dislikes finally erupts into a fantasy of destruction we understand this is only comic exaggeration; what is actually being exploded are not real Arabs but the meretricious generalizations about life in the Holy Land (and by implication in the Bible) that run completely counter to observed details. And yet we may still remain disturbed. Must a keen eye for details necessarily blow to bits the possibility of seeing beyond them to a larger verity? The question applies to more than literary technique; it applies to how people whose everyday life differs radically in its details from those of the observer are to be understood by that observer.

"Travel and experience mar the grandest pictures and rob us of the most cherished traditions of our boyhood" (p. 597), Twain writes. What, then, do they supply? Why do tourists tour? Twain answers: "We wish to learn all the curious, outlandish ways of all the different countries, so that we can 'show off' and astonish people when we get home. We wish to excite the envy of our untraveled friends with our strange foreign fashions which we can't shake off. All our passengers are paying strict attention to this thing, with the end in view I have mentioned" (p. 233).

This adolescent desire to be envied, prominently on display in *Tom Sawyer*, for example, was a constant motivating factor in Twain's life. He went upon the river, he said, because of the distinction it would bring him in the eyes of the boys back home. "I first wanted to be a cabin-boy, so that I could come out with a white apron on and shake a table-cloth over the side, where all my old comrades could see me; later I thought I would rather be the deck-hand who stood on the end of the stage-plank with a coil of rope in his hand because he was particularly conspicuous,"[13] and finally, of course, he decided upon the most enviable position of all, steamboat pilot.

Similarly, when the war closed river traffic and he headed for the

West, he did so, he said, because he envied his brother the glory he would acquire back home because of his travels, and he deliberately expressed this envy in terms of the comically naive wonder of an adolescent, even though he was at the time of going West twenty-six, and at the time of writing about it thirty-two: "Pretty soon he would be hundreds and hundreds of miles away on the great plains and deserts, and among the mountains of the Far West, and would see buffaloes and Indians, and prairie dogs, and antelopes, and have all kinds of adventures, and may be get hanged or scalped, and have ever such a fine time, and write home and tell us all about it, and be a hero" (*Roughing It,* p. 19). Reason enough, then, to accompany his brother and gain his share of the envy of those back home.[14]

This, however, is but half of the matter. In the sentences that follow his description of himself and his fellow tourists as traveling in order to be able to "astonish people when we get home," Twain writes: "The gentle reader will never, never know what a consummate ass he can become, until he goes abroad. I speak now, of course, in the supposition that the gentle reader has not been abroad, and therefore is not already a consummate ass" (p. 233), and therein resides the power of Twain's travel writing and the persisting appeal of *Innocents Abroad*. He is, as the other great nineteenth-century common man of American literature, Walt Whitman, said of himself, both in and out of the game. He can exploit the comic potential of his fellow tourists because he recognizes his share in their aspirations. His frequent reversion to an adolescent outlook is a constant reminder of his participation in the national naivete—the unsophistication of the plush-parlor, church-going, unliterary, provincial, flag-waving, American middle class—even while he satirizes it.

In the face of Old World civilization Twain's characteristic response is to bring to the monuments of European art an unabashedly materialistic yardstick and an aggressively patriotic political outlook. There is, doubtless, a good deal that is defensive about this. Unable to appreciate the aesthetics of masterpieces he is expected to admire he changes the frame of reference from art to politics and considers them in terms that permit him to reject them. So in Paris, "miles" of paintings by the old masters lead him to say: "Some of them were beautiful, but at the same time they carried such evidences about them of the cringing spirit of those great men that we found small pleasure in examining them. Their nauseous adulation of princely patrons was more prominent to me and chained my attention more surely than the charms of color and expression which are claimed to be in the pictures" (p. 137). If this is vulgar in the sense of lacking in refinement, it is vulgar also in the sense of being representative of ordinary people. Twain, too, had patrons, and patrons he could identify almost as precisely as could a painter employed by a nobleman, because his books were sold by subscription. He did not "cringe" to his patrons but he certainly spoke to them in terms of values he shared with them, and these were a respect for material attainment as a measure of worth and the belief that American democracy was the best political system in the world.

"Medicis are good enough for Florence," Twain writes. "Let her plant Medicis and build grand monuments over them to testify how gratefully she was wont to lick the hand that scourged her" (p. 245). His friends abuse him, he says, because he fails to see the beauty in the productions of the old masters. He cannot help but see it now and then, he admits, "but I keep on protesting against the groveling spirit that could persuade those masters to prostitute their noble talents to the adulation of such monsters as the French, Venetian and Florentine Princes of two and three hundred years ago" (p. 260). Whatever the shortcoming of his aesthetic sensibility his reaction carries the doughty strain of republicanism that may be viewed, for example, in John Adams's remark to Jefferson that "Every one of the fine Arts from the earliest times have been enlisted in the service of Superstition and Despotism."[15] Yet it also points to the feeling of inadequacy that arose within him when he confronted the civilizations of the Old World. Although he was able to cite his democratic instincts in defense of his uneasiness in the presence of the fine arts he was unable to bring the same impulses to bear upon his reaction to the degradation he saw in the streets. Rather than regarding filth and poverty as the effect of the same political conditions that had reserved to a few the capacity to patronize art, he recoiled in disgust as if the condition of the poor was a natural consequence of their racial identity. In effect, Twain aestheticized the life of the common people whose lands he visited, finding it repellently ugly, even as he politicized the monuments of art, finding them socially oppressive. Underlying his shifting criteria was a desire to provide a rationale for his sorely challenged sense of American superiority.

The mechanical arts are the American arts, Twain asserts. Just as the popes have patronized and preserved art so "our new, practical Republic is the encourager and upholder of mechanics. In their Vatican is stored up all that is curious and beautiful in art; in our Patent Office is hoarded all that is curious or useful in mechanics" (p. 305). The imbalance of the comparison is glaring and the implication that fine arts and mechanical arts cannot coexist is faulty, but in this rambling giant of a book in which themes disappear to reemerge again, Twain can also be compelling when comparing European culture with American. He says of his inability to write about Rome: "What is there in Rome for me to see that others have not seen before me? What is there for me to touch that others have not touched? What is there for me to feel, to learn, to know, that shall thrill me before it pass to others? Nothing whatsoever" (p. 267). The series of questions is almost wistful, coming as it does from a writer who has most to say when a site has acquired a history of commentaries which he can proceed to demolish as he gets at the details before him. Twain's restraint appears to proceed from genuine awe. The overwhelming presence of Rome cannot be laughed away. With nothing left for him as a writer to discover, he turns the tables and in the pages following talks of what a resident of the Campagna would discover in America: people without a mother church; no foreign soldiers to protect the government; common literacy; glass windows; wooden houses; fire companies; insurance companies; newspapers; printing presses; Jews treated just like human beings; people who can complain about the government and take hold of it themselves; people who know more than their grandfathers and employ modern mechanical methods. In its way this is, after all, a description of Rome.

The *Quaker City* called at the Azores, Gibraltar, Marseilles, Genoa, Leghorn, Civita Vecchia, Naples, Athens, Constantinople, Sebasatapol, Odessa, Yalta, and Smyrna, remaining at some ports long enough for the tourists to make extended excursions to inland cities or take overland routes and meet it at a further port of call. "Such was our daily life on board the ship—" Twain wrote after returning home, "solemnity, decorum, dinner, dominoes, devotion, slander. It was not lively enough for a pleasure trip; but if we had only had a corpse it would have made a noble funeral excursion" (p. 645). Yet traveling without the constant care of changes of vehicle, lodgings, and diet, without the problem of baggage transport and the nuisance of dealing with servants and officials suited him extremely well.

When the *Quaker City* stopped at Odessa for recoaling Twain was relieved to learn from his guidebooks that there were no sights to see in the city "and so we had one good, untrammeled holyday on our hands" (p. 388). Nothing so sets the tourist off from the traveler as does such an attitude which, until Twain converted it into comic art, was precisely what travel literature strove to avoid. "The voices raised against 'mere tourism,'" James Buzzard has written, "were often those raised also against the spread of technology and machinery" (p. 32); so that, for example, travel by rail was decried as antitravel. John Ruskin said that it was like being sent as a package. Mark Twain, however, reveled in the luxury of steamships and the speed of fast trains and constantly measured foreign life against the material standard achieved in America. Insofar as travel is seen as necessitating work for its results he emerges in *Innocents Abroad* as the consummate antitraveler even as his account of such antitravel endures as the most popular travel book ever written by an American.

Elisha Bliss, proprietor of the American Publishing Company, which had published *Innocents Abroad,* urged Twain to supply an account of his Western experiences to follow upon the great success of that book. Twain started on it in 1870, the year after *Innocents* was published, and *Roughing It* appeared in 1872. Like its predecessor it too was sold by subscription and it too contained more than 600 heavily illustrated pages. It did not, however, sell nearly so well. Considered as a physical object "the finished book showed too many seams, betraying its origin as a cut-and-paste operation with inconsistent text and careless drawings"[16] that placed it visually in the company of comic monthlies, editorial cartoons, and dime novels.

Yet with this said, *Roughing It* is clearly superior to *Innocents Abroad* as a literary work, and since Twain's day has been far more frequently reprinted. Its picture of the American West in the boom times that followed the gold rush and the unearthing of the Comstock Lode continues to be the classic portrait of that era and its comic episodes—the purchase of the genuine Mexican plug, the great landslide case, Buck Fanshaw's funeral, or the cat who didn't like quartz mining, to name a few—are fresh at each rereading because unlike jokes that climax in a punch line the joy they provide is embedded in the telling. *Innocents Abroad* was written unit by unit as the travels described were taking place, but *Roughing It* is a retrospective work. Although it too is largely episodic and often follows the path of associations rather than the track of travel it has a theme that underlies the separate incidents and provides a unity lacking in *Innocents Abroad*. *Roughing It* is a narrative of travels that changed the traveler from an innocent into a veteran, in Western terms, from a greenhorn into an old settler—one great difference from the East being that in the West becoming an old settler is a matter of acquiring a set of habit-changing experiences rather than accumulating years of residence. And it is a narrative of the scenes and adventures that changed the bumptious young fool who piled into the stagecoach at St. Joseph and journeyed across the continent to Fort Laramie, South Pass, Salt Lake City, Carson City, and the California gold fields into a master storyteller. Significantly, although less apparently, it is also a view of the American West that for all the youthful naïveté of its protagonist is informed by the maturity of an author who has traveled abroad and brings that knowledge to his sense of what is uniquely American.

Some seventy hours out of St. Joe and rolling along in a stagecoach, Twain saw his first coyote (which he consistently spelled "cayote") and

The author of *Roughing It,* photographed by Jeremiah Gurney, c. 1873 (Reprinted by permission of the National Portrait Gallery, Smithsonian Institution).

described him thus: "The cayote is a long, slim, sick and sorry-looking skeleton, with a gray wolf-skin stretched over it, a tolerably bushy tail that forever sags down with a despairing expression of forsakenness and misery, a furtive and evil eye, and a long, sharp face, with slightly lifted lip and exposed teeth. He has a general slinking expression all over" (*Roughing It,* pp. 48–49). In fuller illustration of the coyote's manner, he describes what happens when a swift-footed dog, especially one that has a good opinion of himself, sets out to chase the coyote. The pursued coyote begins at a trot with a fraudful smile that encourages the dog who speeds up and, panting fiercely, approaches to within twenty feet of the coyote only to find that however great his exertion he cannot close that distance even though the mangy coyote still is going at a soft trot and, indeed, seems even to be slackening speed so as not to run away from him. Maddened the dog gives a last desperate burst, when in an instant there is a rushing sound and "behold that dog is solitary and alone in the midst of a vast solitude!" (p. 51). The dog recognizes too late that he has been fooled by the coyote's seeming shiftlessness into believing in his own superiority. He is taught differently through humiliation.

Many a reader of Twain has recognized in that anecdote a parable of Twain's Western experience. The trim and natty townsman looks at the shabby settler and is confident of his superiority. The shabby settler encourages him in this belief, indeed seems in effect to admit his inferiority. Yet somehow the dandy can never quite overtake the rustic in whatever dealing they have although not until the rustic decides the deception has gone on long enough and in an instant speeds away does it dawn upon him that instead of outsmarting the country yokel he has been taken in by him. In a series of early incidents in *Roughing It,* Twain is like the town dog—purchasing an uncontrollable nag under the impression that "genuine Mexican plug" is the name of a choice breed, giving himself up for dead in a blizzard when he is but fifteen steps from a station house as even his horse knows—ignorant of the ways of the West and confident in his eastern ways. But through a series of humiliations he learns to put on a face that no longer mirrors his mind, and like the coyote he takes on the coloration of his environment. The comic narrator who emerges does not betray any consciousness that the tale he tells is funny—the town dog would be chuckling in advance, approach his punch line with guffaws, and even repeat it a few times—but seems dead serious about his story and apparently puzzled by the laughter it evokes.

When after crossing Scott's Bluff Pass Twain first saw alkali water lying in the road, he recalls, it excited him because he could add it to the list of things which he had seen and many other people had not: it was "a thing to be mentioned with eclat in letters to the ignorant at home." But Twain the writer of this account is no longer the young fool who first saw alkali water, no longer, that is, a tourist, and he goes on to reflect that his brother and he were "the same sort of simpletons as those who climb unnecessarily the perilous peaks of Mont Blanc and the Matterhorn, and derive no pleasure from it except the reflection that it isn't a common experience" (pp. 72–73). Looking back on his Western experience through the lens of his more recent pilgrimage to Europe and the lands of the Bible, he saw that the value of travel resided in the shedding of false ideas of the world and the acquisition of self-knowledge rather than in the collection of sights to be displayed back home as tokens of one's superiority. Through travel Twain learned to unlearn sham beliefs and *Innocents Abroad* is full of the fun of such unlearning. What might be called the greenhorn chapters of *Roughing It* play further variations on the theme, but in the latter work one sees this negative process accompanied by the positive emergence of the man who was always there.

"Every now and then, in these days, the boys used to tell me I ought to get one Jim Blaine to tell me the stirring story of his grandfather's old ram—but they always added that I must not mention the matter unless Jim was drunk at the time—just comfortably and sociably drunk" (p. 383); so begins the fifty-third chapter of *Roughing It*. What follows is a small masterpiece that is not just Mark Twain in his prime but American humor at its best. Blaine gets drunk in the right degree one night, the boys summon Twain, they all crowd into the miner's small, candle-lit cabin, seat themselves on empty powder kegs, and Jim Blaine commences the story of the old ram: "There never was a more bullier old ram than what he was. Grandfather fetched him from Illinois—got him from a man by the name of Yates—Bill Yates—maybe you might have heard of him; his father was a deacon—Baptist—and he was a rustler, too; a man had to get up ruther early to get the start of old Thankful Yates; it was him put the Greens up to jining teams with my grandfather when he moved west" (p. 384). That first is the last mention of the celebrated ram. Mention of the Greens leads to Sarah Wilkerson whom Seth Green married which brings up Sile Hawkins who wanted to court her and so one name continues to lead to another, each attached to an incident or detail that vividly renders the person that bears the name: old Miss Wagner had to borrow a glass eye to receive company in but more often than not the glass eye dropped out without her noticing it, "being blind on that side you see;" Uncle Lem, standing under a scaffold, had his back broken in two places when a bricklayer with a hod full of bricks fell on him. That was no accident; divine providence had appointed him to be under the scaffold in order to break the bricklayer's fall. His dog was with him but was not appointed because he would have seen the man falling and stood from under: "A dog can't be depended on to carry out a special providence." And so Blaine's tale proceeds in a crescendo of violent yet harmless incidents, much in the manner of the maiming explosions that cheerfully occur in animated cartoons. Extraordinary as they are, the incidents are nevertheless grounded in the culture of rural, midwestern America. Although Blaine never gets back to the ram, his string of associations coheres into an indelible picture of a people and their ways: election day shenanigans, quiltings, Dorcas Society meetings, westward migrations, church affiliations. Moreover as one name reminds Blaine of another and he connects them through courtships, marriages, and deaths, despite the violence contained in almost every incident his discourse comes to resemble nothing so much as the talk at a family gathering, say at Thanksgiving, that is overheard by a curious child. As the elders catch up on family and neighborhood news, mention of one person leading to gossip about another, through their talk they in effect build the community into which the eavesdropping child is socialized.

Blaine's story is an ingeniously packed example of the larger coherence that can arise from an artful pursuit of associations. In his books, to be sure, Twain never followed his associative rambling in a direct line away from the starting point without once looking back. For example, a description of sagebrush as useful as a fuel but useless as a vegetable leads him to say that only mules and jackasses eat it, because, he muses, they and camels "have appetites that anything will relieve temporarily but nothing satisfy." When he was traveling in Syria, for example, a camel ate his overcoat and the contents of its pockets—percussion caps, cough candy, and fig paste—but choked to death on the manuscript letters he was writing for the home papers. Finally though, unlike Jim Blaine he does circle back: "I was about to say, when diverted from my subject, that occasionally one finds sage-brushes five or six feet high, and with a spread of branch and foliage in proportion" (p. 36). What the reader remembers, however is the camel not the sagebrush. The story of the old ram is both a conscious expansion into irresistible absurdity of an important structural element in all of Twain's travel writing and a breathtaking demonstration of the patterns of coherence that emerge when the mind is let loose to ramble. "Since I digress constantly," Twain finally tells himself, "perhaps it is as well to eschew apologies altogether and thus prevent their growing irksome" (p. 352). He's right.

The Indians in *Roughing It* are targets of Twain's not-so-funny irascibility as most foreign peoples were in *Innocents Abroad,* principally because he is intent on debunking the noble savages of Fenimore Cooper, Emerson Bennett, and the melodramas of the popular stage. Romance quickly falls away once an actual Indian is encountered, he says, and what one sees is treacherous, filthy, and repulsive. Where a literature exists Twain continues to seek originality in contradicting it, which is not, as has been observed of similar passages of *Innocents Abroad,* seeing with one's own eyes so much as it is seeing with the eyes of others but reversing the image they see.

Twain, however, looks more closely at the Chinese in the West than he does at the Indians. What had been written about them was, in the main, negative; Bayard Taylor's absolute terror at the idea of Chinese immigration into the country is an example. But Twain's positive view comes not so much from an automatic reversal of such literature as it does from personal observation of the Chinese community and a scorn for the kind of humanity represented by those who persecute the Chinese. In his comments on the subject he sounds a note that will grow stronger in each succeeding decade of his life as he increasingly attacks the ignorance and hypocrisy on which the complacencies of American social, political, and religious life are based, using his observations of other people to drive this message home. "All Chinamen can read, write and cipher with easy facility—pity but all our petted *voters* could"

(p. 392), he writes with special reference to laws that discriminate against the Chinese. He characterizes the Chinese as industrious and quick to learn, sympathetically discusses their desire to be interred in China and the burial societies that exist for this purpose, and concludes:

> They are a kindly disposed, well-meaning race, and are respected and well treated by the upper classes all over the Pacific coast. No Californian *gentleman or lady* ever abuses or oppresses a Chinaman under any circumstances, an explanation that seems to be much needed in the East. Only the scum of the population do it—they and their children; they, and naturally and consistently, the policemen and politicians, likewise, for they're the dust-licking pimps and slaves of the scum, there as elsewhere in America. (p. 397)

Henceforth he was to use exotic cultures to expose the hollow core of American self-satisfaction rather than to find those cultures wanting by American standards.

In *Roughing It* we are told of John Smith, a Nevada hay rancher, who becoming suddenly rich through his interest in a mine was able to travel in Europe. "When he came back he was never tired of telling about the fine hogs he had seen in England, and the gorgeous sheep he had seen in Spain, and the fine cattle he had noticed in the vicinity of Rome" (p. 321). John Smith advised everybody to travel because one could never imagine what surprising things there were in the world unless one did so. His story is offered as amusement, but there is a subtext. The hay rancher's failure to have had Westminster Abbey, the Escorial, or the Coliseum register upon his imagination while his mind remained, as it were, in the barnyard, may cause a laugh, but the burden of his tale is that he used his travel to reassess the value of what he knew best back home. On the larger scale of manners and morals this was how Mark Twain would come to approach his travel.

The disappointing sales of *Roughing It* and *Tom Sawyer* (1876) put Twain's financial returns into a slowly descending spiral which his departure for Europe on the *Holsatia* was designed to arrest. And *A Tramp Abroad* (1880) did succeed in reversing the downward drift, achieving a popularity greater than the books that immediately preceded it. It has not, however, survived the test of time very well. To be sure, there are some striking moments in its 631 pages, such as Jim Baker's blue jay yarn, but these are fewer than in his other travel works. Throughout one witnesses Twain straining to produce copy to meet the demands of the format his earlier works had established. Comic fantasies that are at best one-paragraph jokes are spun out into tedious chapters and although in his other travel books Twain had borrowed material from earlier authors to blend into his own observations in *A Tramp Abroad* such borrowings are lengthy and extrusive. So, for example, the ascent from Zermatt to the Riffleberg Hotel, a well-marked walk of three hours, is seized by Twain as the occasion for a labored lampoon of the literature of exploration wherein he leads an expedition of 134 men and 51 animals outfitted with lavish rations and elaborate equipment on this pretendedly perilous route, which takes them seven days to accomplish, and during which they have a number of presumably comic misadventures. The descent is accomplished by riding the Gorner glacier down as if it were a moving train, another joke rather feeble to begin with and quickly tiresome when extended. The glacier leads Twain to give, one after another, quoted or paraphrased accounts of avalanches and other Alpine catastrophes. The whole consumes more than seventy pages and reveals nothing so much as it does that Mark Twain had little to say about his actual experience at Zermatt.

The *Holsatia* had arrived in Hamburg in late April of 1878 and Twain and his family proceeded to Heidelberg by way of Frankfurt. In early August Twain's close Hartford friend and fellow yarn spinner, the Reverend Joseph Twichell, joined him, Twain paying his expenses, and the two toured Germany and Switzerland for six weeks. Aside from the genuine pleasure he took in Twichell's company, a pleasure increased by his manifest boredom with those he met in Germany, Twain had a literary use for Twichell. In his pages he transformed him into Mr. Harris, a relatively humorless traveling companion who supplies deflating details about, or satirizable reactions to, the places they visit as Twain in search of material resurrects the device represented by the Mr. Brown of his first travel letters. One of the running gags in *A Tramp Abroad* is the determination of the two to make theirs a walking tour. With apparent allusion to Bayard Taylor's *Views A-foot,* Twain wrote, "One day it occurred to me that it had been many years since the world had been afforded the spectacle of a man adventurous enough to undertake a journey through Europe on foot" (p. 17). Predictably, he then develops one excuse after another to take trains, boats, and carriages on his tour of Europe "on foot."

In *Innocents Abroad* Twain was following an itinerary prepared for him and was further equipped with a band of tourists whom he could observe as amusingly as he did the sites visited. In *Roughing It* Twain reconstructed the life he had led in a world of violent wonders, enriching his account with the perspective upon his youthful self gained from his subsequent experiences. But there was no goal that unified *A Tramp Abroad* other than the search for subjects to write about, no reason to start from one place rather than another or visit one site rather than another, and no perspective other than a palpable uneasiness at having to do it at all.

"Without a courier," Twain writes, travel "hasn't a ray of pleasure in it, anywhere; but with him it is a continuous and unruffled delight" (p. 351). He then details a courier's services—making bookings, assuring that hotel servants do their jobs, arranging baggage transfers—all of which afford him the further satisfaction of witnessing the agonies of travelers who do not have couriers and so stand in the rain for a cab, rush for railway seats, wrestle with trunks, and go from hotel to hotel seeking a room. The twin pleasures of travel offered here, comfortable accommodations and the entertainment to be derived from witnessing those who don't possess them, are hardly the stuff of good travel writing, even good comic travel writing.

There is one moment during his travels, however, when Twain does lash out effectively in favor of his kind of touring, doing so, characteristically, by satirizing the traveler who is above being a tourist rather than by offering a positive defense of tourism. At a Swiss hotel he meets a young American, scion of an eminent Boston family, and fixes his character in a sentence: "His hair was short and parted accurately in the middle, and he had the look of an American person who would be likely to begin his signature with an initial, and spell his middle name out" (p. 440). Although but twenty-three, this young man refers to himself as an "old traveler" and a "man of the world," and looks back at, and down on, his native Boston as narrow. He explains:

> I flit-and-flit,—for I am ever on the wing—but I avoid the herd. To-day I am in Paris, to-morrow in Berlin, anon in Rome; but you would look for me in vain in the galleries of the Louvre or the common reports of the gazers in those other capitals. If you would find me, you must look in the unvisited nooks and corners where others never think of going. One day you will find me making myself at home in some obscure peasant's cabin, another day you will find me in some forgotten castle worshipping some little gem of art which the careless eye has overlooked and which the unexperienced would despise; again you will find me a guest in the inner sanctuaries of palaces while the herd is content to get a hurried glimpse of the unused chambers by feeing a servant. (p. 442)

It seems very probable that Twain drew closely upon an actual person for this characterization; in the pages devoted to him there is an unusual specificity of detail and Twain was not above paying off those who irked him by displaying their idiocy in print for those who might recognize them. But he was also defending his anti-aesthetic by going on the offensive against those who traveled to refine their sensibilities. Many travel works were centrally devoted to a form of art appreciation that bored Twain and that, he suspected, was based upon social snobbery far more than superior taste.

Halfway through his sixteen-month European stay, Twain wrote to William Dean Howells: "I wish I *could* give those sharp satires on European life which you mention, but of course a man can't write successful satire except he be in a calm judicial good humor—whereas I *hate* travel, & I *hate* hotels, & I *hate* the opera, & I *hate* the Old Masters—in truth I don't ever seem to be enough in a good humor with anything to *satirize* it; no, I want to stand up before it & *curse* it, & foam at the mouth—or take a club & pound it to rags & pulp."[17] There is no reason to believe that Twain had read the *Transatlantic Sketches* (1875) of Henry James, another friend of Howells's and, like Twain, a contributor to his *Atlantic Monthly,* but James's travel writing may be taken as representative of the kind of travel that Twain self-consciously realized would be weighed against his in cultural centers such as Boston, home of the pompous puppy he skewered in his pages. When in his letter to Howells Twain concluded his tirade against European life, and especially European art, by saying he wanted to pound it to "rags and pulp," consciously or not he was talking about the two main ingredients of paper. The pages of *A Tramp Abroad* are the rags and pulp to which he reduced European life.

"I wonder why things are?" Twain wrote. "For instance, Art is allowed as much indecent license to-day as in earlier times—but the privileges of Literature in this respect have been sharply curtailed" (p. 577). This is not, however, a claim that the writer should be as free to portray the sexual as is the painter the nude, but rather a wish that the painter too be reined in. The proper father of three daughters wholeheartedly subscribed to the proposition that in the enlightened second half of the nineteenth century the only standard for exhibited art or published literature (as opposed to smoking-car exchanges) should be its fitness for the eyes of the American girl. Titian's nude Venus in the Uffizi with her hand extended down toward her—no, it is unmentionable—is "the foulest, the obscenest picture the world possesses" (p. 578), and yet that is what they call "Art," Twain fumed.

At the opera and again at the theater Twain was made uneasy by the German custom of withholding applause until the end of an act. In America a more boisterous custom was still followed, the audience bursting into applause (or boos) in instant response to what was going forth on the stage. Twain loved it that way: "I don't see how an actor can forget himself and portray hot passion before a cold still audience. . . . It is a pain to me to this day, to remember how that old German Lear raged and wept and howled around the stage, with never a response from that hushed house, never a single outburst till the act ended" (p. 95). His preference for spontaneous applause and his resistance to Wagner—he lampooned a performance of *Lohengrin*—and the notion that in opera there could be music throughout rather than in a series of set pieces parallel the rambling, anecdotal structure of his writing with its preference for laughter at point after point over the cumulative response gathered by a sustained plot. At work as well in Twain's preference for audience intrusion into the performance is his democratic instinct and his sense that the stage is being taken away from the people when they are required to sit in respectful silence before spectacles that are presumably so sacred they are not to be interrupted by reflexive responses.[18] Although his squeamishness in the Uffizi arose from the prim proprieties of America's cultural commitment to the mental condition of the young girl, beneath his priggishness there resided a sense that European art as it was presented to American aspirants depended for its appeal not so much on its inclusionary as on its exclusionary force, not so much on the way it brought Americans into a culture far richer than that available back home as on the way it conferred a social superiority on those who had seen and claimed to have appreciated it.

Speaking about classical music Twain spoke, in effect, about all high art: "We want it because the higher and better like it. But we want it without giving it the necessary time and trouble, so we climb into that upper tier, that dress circle by a lie: we *pretend* we like it. I know several of that sort of people,—and I propose to be one of them myself when I get home with my fine European education" (p. 237). Even as he thus satirizes the cultural pretensions of the returned tourist, however, he recognizes there is something more rewarding than such meretriciousness; but it will take work.

So home Twain goes to breakfasts of beefsteak with yellow fat at its margins and coffee with cream clotting it, instead of the European fare he called insipid. The pleasure of getting back was manifestly greater than any pleasure he had experienced on his travels, and the book that grew from such feelings could not disguise the fact that it had become a chore. Strikingly, two of the six appendices that were added to make up the book's required length are actually better reading than any section of comparable length within the narrative proper: "The Awful German Language" is an amusing yet perspicacious account of the perplexities that language presents to the eager learner, and "German Journals" is a lively and informative analysis of German newspapers by a writer who had known journalism as a reporter, editor, and publisher.

Yet for all its faults *A Tramp Abroad* sold better than *Roughing It* and at some level of consciousness Twain's awareness of its inferiority must have given him a contempt for his European experience even deeper than the ridicule he displayed in his pages.

"After twenty-one years' absence, I felt a very strong desire to see the river again, and the steamboats, and such of the boys as might be left; so I resolved to go out there";[19] so reads Mark Twain's account of why in April 1882 he was once again on the Mississippi. With him were James Osgood, the Boston publisher with whom earlier that month he had signed a contract to produce a history of the Mississippi River, a subject he had long contemplated, and a stenographer who was to record his reminiscences and his opinions as they were stimulated by his return to scenes where he had once practiced the profession he said he loved "far better than any I have followed since" (p. 166). The contracted book was again to be sold by subscription and so again would be more than 600 pages in length.

Five years earlier, before his departure for Europe and the travels that led to *A Tramp Abroad,* Twain had written a series of seven sketches about his apprenticeship and practice as a riverboat pilot. Titled *Old Times on the Mississippi* they ran from January to August 1875 in the *Atlantic Monthly* and were the stimulus for Osgood's seeking to contract a full-length book about the river from Twain. Broken into smaller units, the sketches in *Old Times* became chapters four to seventeen of *Life on the Mississippi* which in total consisted of sixty chapters and the custom-

ary appendices. Introductory to the *Old Times* chapters and then intermittently throughout the remainder of *Life on the Mississippi* Twain
discussed the history of the river as he took it from various sources and
also discussed in some detail the famous—and to almost all Americans
notorious—reactions to the river of English visitors such as Frances
Trollope, Charles Dickens, and Captain Basil Hall. He did so, however,
with a rather unexpected understanding of their points of view even
while disagreeing with their opinions. But the backbone of the book
is Twain's return to the Mississippi in 1882 and his journey down it from
St. Louis to New Orleans then up it to St. Paul. To this journey are hinged
historical summaries, reminiscences, tall tales, anecdotes, and social
commentaries. As a whole, *Life on the Mississippi* is a shaggy conglom-
erate of genres—journal, autobiography, history, fiction, and travel—
and as such it has troubled those critics who despite their knowledge of
Twain's usual habits of composition nevertheless complain that it lacks
unity, as if this were a new phenomenon. Actually the book holds together rather splendidly because it is illuminated throughout by Twain's
evident delight at being back on the river. His first sentence is "The
Mississippi is well worth reading about" (p. 21) and the many pages that
follow make good this proposition. They are marked throughout by the
sharpness of observation and confidence of a man who knows what he is
talking about, as contrasted with the frequently uneasy defensiveness of
his European observations. Twain's intimate connection with the river
from infancy through early manhood provided a lens through which to
view the panorama of the present, and the relative cosmopolitanism he
had acquired from his foreign travels and his fame as a writer—"I became a scribbler of books and an immovable fixture among the other
rocks of New England" (p. 246), he explained—provided him with just
the right degree of detachment. There is in *Life on the Mississippi* a
nostalgia for what has departed but no sentimentality. While adhering
to his belief that there never was and never could be anything so colorful
and pleasurable as steamboating, Twain nevertheless accepted the railroad and barge traffic that replaced the paddle-wheelers as improvements in time, money, and safety. Noting that even after a crippling civil

war Southern society still clung to the empty platitudes of its pre-war days—belief in the literal truth of Bible stories and attachment to the chivalric idealizations of romantic literature—he deplored the stagnant culture that resulted but did so without the derisive scorn he applied to foreign cultures he disliked. Rather, his censure was on behalf of, rather than against, Southern society, which, in his view, not having outgrown its primitive convictions continued in a state of stunted development when it had so much that deserved enhancement.

Life on the Mississippi is not a travel narrative as were *Innocents Abroad* and *A Tramp Abroad*. And yet no discrete unit of travel writing Twain previously wrote is comparable in sharpness of observation and good-humored (if critical) tone to his description of the graduated changes in the culture of his fellow Americans as he journeys by rail from New York to St. Louis then downriver to New Orleans. His details are of physical appearances yet they are so keenly realized they add up to a social geography of the American hinterlands. Soon after leaving New York a change in picturesqueness becomes apparent, arising not so much from the actual clothing, the same being available in the provinces, as in the carriage of the local inhabitants, the absence in them of the "godless grace, and snap, and style" (p. 248) of New Yorkers. Another day out on rail and the region of the goatee worn without accompanying moustache is struck: "The goatee extends over a wide extent of country; and is accompanied by an iron-clad belief in Adam and the biblical history of creation." Further into the Midwest the character of railway-station loafers changes. Now they carry *both* hands in their breeches pockets; "it was observable, heretofore, that one hand was sometimes out of doors." Moreover, "Heretofore, all along, the station-loafer has been often observed to scratch one shin with the other foot; here these remains of activity are wanting. This has an ominous look." By and by the tobacco-chewing region is entered and next boots begin to appear; "not in strong force, however. Later—away down the Mississippi—they became the rule. They disappeared from other sections of the Union with the mud" (p. 249). It is a pleasure to travel with someone who has an eye for such matters.

In the *Old Times* section of *Life on the Mississippi* Twain included in his account of his ascent from naive ambition through perplexities and humiliations to knowledge of the river and the achievement of the rank of pilot a consideration of what he had lost as well as gained by learning his craft: "Now when I had mastered the language of this water and had come to know every trifling feature that bordered the great river as familiarly as I knew the letters of the alphabet, I had made a valuable acquisition. But I had lost something which could never be restored to me while I lived. All the grace, the beauty, the poetry had gone out of the majestic river!" (p. 119). In illustration he described a wonderful sunset he remembered from the days when steamboating was new to him: the river turned red and gold, a solitary log floating past, a long sparkling mark across the river, opal-tinted tumbling rings of water, the broken shadow of the forest on the surface. After he had mastered the water's language, however, he could see no beauty in the scene: the sun meant wind tomorrow, the floating log meant the river was rising, the slanting mark indicated a bluff reef that could tear the bottom out of a boat, the tumbling rings told that a bar was dissolving and the channel was changing, and the break in the shadow warned that a tree had fallen into the river, presenting a threat to navigation. To the eye of experience "the romance and the beauty were all gone from the river" (p. 120).

The sense of gain and loss thus described extends beyond the craft of piloting to that of writing. Significantly, looking back twenty years later Twain thought of the knowledge of the river he had acquired as the mastery of a language. His subsequent career as a writer with his consequent mastery of language itself was always to carry with it a distrust of diction that asserted value beyond the observed details—that spoke in terms of majestic, enchanting, romantic. From his Hawaiian letters through to his more mature travel writing he was always uneasy with the description of landscapes he could not read, undercutting himself, as has been seen, when he drifted toward picturesque effects, seeking the similes that would bring the exotic into the frame of the everyday rather than elevate it into a supernal realm. Knowledge of details led to mastery of language; knowledge of language led to mastery of details.

As a consequence of this nominalistic view—the view, that is, that there is no reality other than the sum of its particulars—Twain was a wary depicter of natural landscapes, save for the river, because the constituents of such landscapes did not signify to him beyond such blurry terms as "beauty." He said of a travel writer who praised one site after another in such a vocabulary, "The man has got the panegyrics,"[20] and that was a disease he did not wish to contract. On the other hand, he was a master at rendering the details of a social landscape so that they signified an entire way of life. The brilliance which he exhibited in observing the changes in American character as he journeyed westward simply by registering differences in dress and physical carriage reached its zenith in the thirty-eighth chapter of *Life on the Mississippi,* titled "The House Beautiful." "Every town and village along that vast stretch of double river-frontage had a best dwelling, finest dwelling, mansion— the home of its wealthiest and most conspicuous citizen" (p. 400), he begins, and then from the grassy yard with its white paling fence "in fair repair" he views the facade, enters the door, and proceeds in a paragraph that runs for more than four pages to provide an unrivaled anatomy of the opinions, sentiments, aspirations, and sorrows of the residents in that vast region simply by passing the reader's eye over one after another of the furnishings of the house: planed wood floors, ingrain carpets, the scenes in the framed lithographs, airtight stove, closed fireplace, two shells, the Lord's Prayer carved on one, portrait of Washington on another (missing the mouth)—these the memorials of a wedding trip to New Orleans and the French Market—the crayon drawings of the young ladies of the house, the titles of the books arranged on the center-table of the parlor with a cast-iron exactness, and so on through a range of precisely observed actualizing details to the concluding observation, "not a bathroom in the house; and no visitor likely to come along who had seen one" (p. 406).

"The House Beautiful" is the work of a great social artist. It takes *Life on the Mississippi* from the realm of history and travel, which it occupied only sporadically, into the world of fiction; from the reporting of what lies before the eye to the evocation, in all its triviality and all its

The best room in the best house of a riverfront village; one of the more than 300 illustrations in the first edition of *Life on the Mississippi,* 1883.

wonder, of the way an entire society met the problems of living the everyday life.

When Twain went back to the Mississippi in 1882, he left the manuscript of a stalled novel on his desk in Hartford. The scenes he revisited and the memories they released unlocked that frozen fiction. Two years after the publication of *Life on the Mississippi* (1883), *Huckleberry Finn,* a novel about a boy who journeyed down the Mississippi and through the subtle changes of the society along its banks, was completed.

The evident pleasure Mark Twain took in his literary venture on the Mississippi seemed to provide a corollary to the unmistakable dislike for foreign travel he displayed in *A Tramp Abroad.* Indeed, in the final pages of that narrative he wrote of his return from Europe in 1879, "I was glad to get home—immeasurably glad; so glad, in fact, that it did not seem possible that anything could ever get me out of the country again" (p. 580). Vain prophecy! On the sixth of June, 1891, the Clemens family— husband, wife, and three daughters—sailed for France, and for eight of the next nine years remained abroad, while in the four years from 1891 to 1895 the head of the family made twelve Atlantic crossings. Although Mark Twain's literary earnings would have been adequate to support his family in the bounteous life centered in their Hartford mansion, his investments in his own failing publishing house together with his copious financial support for the development of an automatic typesetter that promised astronomical profits if only one more costly adjustment could be paid for, then just one other, and then maybe another, *ad infinitum,* drove him to the relative economy of life in Europe—an economy he had tested during the residence that led to *A Tramp Abroad*—while at the same time his frantic efforts to remain afloat financially required he shuttle back and forth across the Atlantic. In 1895, however, all attempts to retain solvency failed and he was bankrupt.

Forced, at last, to recognize his financial incompetence, Twain agreed to place his business affairs in the hands of his Hartford friend, Henry H. Rogers, a vice-president of Standard Oil skilled in the ways of a financial world ruled by robber barons. Although the wealthy and

powerful Rogers well knew that was not the way one did things in the
business world he nevertheless acquiesced in Twain's insistence upon
paying his debts in full rather than coming to terms with his creditors
for a percentage of them, because he realized, as Fred Kaplan in his
review of the matter observes, "America's most famous writer would be
an even more valuable market property if he epitomized the lie that
nineteenth-century Americans liked to believe about their great men:
they always paid their debts in full. In such matters Rogers was even
shrewder than Twain, and each by his own reasoning reached the same
conclusion."[21] To raise the money, then, at the age of sixty the marketable Mark Twain, physically spent and morally disheartened, once
again entered upon the activities he had repeatedly said he detested
and wished never again to undertake, and traveled in order to lecture
and in order to write another travel book. He did so, moreover, on a
scale that dwarfed the journeys of his younger self, visiting almost every
country in which an English-speaking audience could be expected to
welcome him. Thanks to the British Empire, this meant a journey round
the world.

Accompanied by his wife and his daughter Clara, Twain left Elmira,
New York, in July 1895, lectured across the Midwest and West to Vancouver, sailed from there in late August, and read from his work and
lectured some one-hundred times in Australia, New Zealand, Ceylon,
India, and South Africa; his public appearances stretched from Cleve-
land to Cape Town. In July 1896, a year after he set out, his tour ended in
England and there he settled to write *Following the Equator*. He spoke
of the work in a letter to Howells: "I wrote my last travel-book in hell; but
I let on, the best I could, that it was an excursion through heaven. Some
day I will read it, & if its lying cheerfulness fools me then I shall believe it
fooled the reader. How I did loathe that journey round the world!—
except the sea-part & India" (Bridgman, p. 132).

The hell Twain lived in while writing was that of a tortured father and
husband. When in England he went about his task word arrived that his
daughter Susy, who had remained with family in Elmira, was seriously
ill. His wife and daughter Clara set sail for America to be with Susy but

The Clemens family on board ship in British Columbia setting forth to follow the equator. The inscription appears to be in Twain's hand (Yale Collection of American literature, Beinecke Rare Book and Manuscript Library).

while they were still at sea news of Susy's death from spinal meningitis reached Twain by cable. To his desolate realization that he was never to see Susy again and his anguished sense that in undertaking his global tour he had somehow abandoned her was added the unbearable anticipation of his wife's landing in New York unaware of the dreadful news that awaited her. Yet *Following the Equator* while frequently a serious book does not, save in one extrusive moment when Twain speaks bitterly of Nature's capacity to maim and torture its creatures,[22] give itself over to the hellfire that was to smolder in his late essays and in fictions such as "The Mysterious Stranger."

There is anger aplenty at the colonial treatment of the native populations in the countries he visits but it is vented in passages of outright satire or sarcasm, social criticism that implies better ways of behavior are possible. Of the Australian system whereby labor for the plantations is supplied by recruiters who transport boys from South Sea islands, Twain writes, for example, "But for the meddling philanthropists, the native fathers and mothers would be fond of seeing their children carted into exile and now and then the grave, instead of weeping about it and trying to kill the kind recruiters" (p. 82). Writing ostensibly about the dingo, he says: "He has been sentenced to extermination, and the sentence will be carried out. This is all right, and not objectionable. The world was made for man—the white man" (p. 186). The accompanying illustration, by Dan Beard, makes the point less subtly: a bearded and monocled white hunter, cartridge belts around his waist and across his chest, cigarette dangling from his lips, stands jauntily with one leg flexed, doffing his pith helmet with his left hand while in his right he holds the gun that accounts for the bodies, animal and native human, lying at his feet; behind him stands a skeleton wielding a scythe that cuts across a full moon around which is arched the legend, "Thou Shalt Not Kill."

Twenty-five years earlier, in *Roughing It* Twain had treated American Indians with contempt; they were scarcely human. Now touring a museum in Australia he is struck by the absence of any aboriginal artifacts and, with his customary attention to linguistic precision, grimly amused at the fact that the word "native" is applied to Australian-born whites only, the true native population being demoted to the classification "blackfellows." The home lesson about the mental annihilation of a native population is not lost on him. Abroad he carps at the true natives being unrepresented in the museum but in America, he now realizes, the same is true; "it never struck me before" (p. 155), he admits.

The outrage the treatment of the aboriginal population of Australia invoked was increased tenfold when he visited Africa. After detailing the way in which whole populations there are tricked, robbed, and impressed into labor under conditions worse even than those that existed under American slavery, Twain launches his peroration:

We humanely reduce an overplus of dogs by swift chloroform;
the Boer humanley reduced an overplus of blacks by swift suf-
focation; the nameless but right-hearted Australian pioneer humanely reduced his overplus of aboriginal neighbors by a
sweetened swift death concealed in a poisoned pudding. All of
these are admirable and worthy of praise; you and I would
rather suffer either of these deaths thirty times over in thirty
successive days than linger out one of the Rhodesian twenty-
year deaths with its daily burden of insult, humiliation, and
forced labor for a man whose entire race the victim hates. Rho-
desia is a happy name for that land of piracy and pillage, and
puts the right stain upon it. (p. 691)

In pointed opposition to his contempt for the ways of the white settlers, throughout *Following the Equator* Twain is enthralled by people of
color. Earlier when he had come up against the difference, the otherness, of European and Near Eastern cultures, his customary response
had been to see their divergence as a sign of their inferiority, at times
even, of a kind of willed stupidity as they lagged behind the technological advances of the nineteenth century. As such, he was the tourist par
excellence. But as he wearily set out to circle the globe after the collapse
of his business enterprises the exotic cultures he encountered spoke to
him of other and better ways of conducting one's daily life. "There is
probably not one person whose reverence rose higher than respect for
his own things; and therefore, it is not a thing to boast about and be
proud of" (pp. 514–15), he wrote.

Accordingly, instead of the gleeful narrator who made joke after joke
after joke about Mormon polygamy in *Roughing It,* or scorned Italian
"priestcraft" in *Innocents Abroad,* the Twain of *Following the Equator* is
keenly interested in understanding the kinds of alien behavior he once
seized upon to raise a laugh. For example, he observes a Parsee funeral
with its termination in the placement of the corpse on a "tower of silence," there to be wasted by the elements and consumed by birds of
prey, and explains the way in which every aspect of the funeral is con-

nected to a principle of purity. When on the hot plain outside Allahabad
he comes upon roads crowded with pilgrims who "had come from all
over India; some of them had been months on the way, plodding pa-
tiently along in the heat and dust, worn, poor, hungry, but sustained
by an unwavering faith and belief," he notes that they are supremely
happy and content because upon reaching the Ganges they will be
cleansed from every vestige of sin. The notion that thenceforth whatsoever thing they touch, even the dead and rotten, will be made pure is
not treated as explodable superstition but as awe-inspiring belief: "It is
wonderful, the power of faith like that, that can make multitudes upon
multitudes of the old and weak and the young and frail enter without
hesitation or complaint upon such incredible journeys and endure the
resultant miseries without repining. It is done in love, or it is done in
fear; I do not know which it is. No matter what the impulse is, the act
born of it is beyond imagination marvelous to our kind of people, the
cold whites" (p. 469).

"The cold whites"—in Ceylon and again in India Twain is forcibly attracted to color, the color of skin, the color of garments, and the warm
vitality they signify. Walking groups of Ceylonese are clad in "thin, soft,
delicate clinging" silks, "a splendid green, a splendid blue, a splendid yellow, a splendid purple, a splendid ruby" which as they sweep by
him make him catch his breath with joy. "I looked at my women-folk's
clothes," he says, to recognize them as the dreary Sunday clothes of
England and America, "and was ashamed to be seen in the street with
them. Then I looked at my own clothes and was ashamed to be seen on
the street with myself" (p. 343). As is characteristically the case when
Twain fixes on the details of appearance, more than physical description is involved. The clothes of American men and women in their drab
propriety suppress the human instinct for color, grace, and harmony:
"Yes, our clothes are a lie, and have been nothing short of that these
hundred years. They are insincere, they are the ugly and appropriate
outward exposure of an inward sham and a moral decay" (p. 344).

Skin color also signifies more than meets the eye immediately:
"Nearly all black and brown skins are beautiful, but a beautiful white

skin is rare. . . . Where dark complexions are massed, they make the whites look bleached-out, unwholesome, and sometimes frankly ghastly. I could notice this as a boy down South in the slavery days before the war" (p. 381). As this passage suggests, at the heart of Twain's remarkable surrender to color is the mechanism of his extraordinary memory and the manner in which it could erase time and instantly invoke a past experience when prompted by an incident in the present. And the past to which he was returned time and again by the brown bodies in the lands he visited was his boyhood in the days of slavery.

When the German proprietor of his Bombay hotel showed Twain to his room, a native was there working on his knees to adjust the glazed door that opened onto the balcony. The proprietor walked over to the native and before stating what he wanted done gave him a brisk cuff on the face. "I had not seen the like of this for fifty years. It carried me back to my boyhood, and flashed upon me the forgotten fact that this was the *usual* way of explaining one's desires to a slave" (p. 351). Thus transported to the past Twain remembers his father, a kindly man, who nevertheless treated Lewis, "our harmless slave boy," in such a fashion, and then relives the moment when at the age of ten he witnessed a man fling a lump of iron ore at a slave in anger, killing him:

> Nobody in the village approved of that murder, but of course no one said much about it.
>
> It is curious—the space annihilating power of thought. For just one second, all that goes to make the *me* in me was in a Missourian village, on the other side of the globe, vividly seeing again those forgotten pictures of fifty years ago, and wholly unconscious of all things but just those; and in the next second I was back in Bombay, and the kneeling native's smitten cheek was not done tingling yet! (p. 352)

The injustices of the prewar South were so constantly present to Twain as he traveled, especially in India and Africa, that he registered the value of the peoples whose lands he visited with a sympathy, indeed an advocacy, that was new to his travel writing. His pages dealing with the dignity of native peoples and the cruel mendacity of their colonial exploiters foreshadow the social critic who was to become increasingly vehement in his attacks on imperialism as in the year after the publication of *Following the Equator* the United States launched its colonial career by going to war with Spain. Twain's celebrated attacks on the hypocrisy, cruelty, and greed of imperialism in writings such as "To the Person Sitting in Darkness" (1901) and "King Leopold's Soliloquy" (1905) are certainly more relentless than any social criticism in *Following the Equator*, but, by the same token, they are not so generously informed by a sense of the corporeal reality of native peoples. Awakened by his travel round the world, there emerged from beneath the surface of his consciousness a mixture of loving memories of the gait, the voices, and the physical aura of slaves he had known and gnawing memories of the everyday exercises of inhumanity toward them to which he was a youthful and uncomplaining witness.

Although the use of memory as an exercise in contrition and the consequent yearning toward the worlds of brown-skinned peoples marks *Following the Equator* off from earlier travel books it too has its share of comic incidents, passages from other works paraphrased or quoted at length, and funny stories remembered. One such story, built up from Twain's inappropriate response while witnessing a fox hunt in England—when asked by the Master of the Hunt whether he has seen the fox, he asks "Which fox?"—is constructed with a mastery that indicates he had lost none of his great skill as the straight-faced teller of a comic tale on whom the humor of what he tells is entirely lost. Mature in years as he then was, in *Following the Equator* as in his previous works Twain nevertheless persisted in the adolescent habit of relishing the physical comforts of his travel arrangements most when he saw less comfortable travelers envying him, and again he was at his happiest, and quite engagingly so, when traveling in a comfortable conveyance with nothing to do but lounge lazily between sites. The ship from India to Mauritius lulled him into so easy a tropical routine he hoped it would never arrive. Always the tourist, Twain might alter his outlook as the result of his experiences but his daily habits remained as unchanged as circumstances permitted. The nearest he approached experimentation was in a daring trial of pyjamas in place of his usual nightshirt, but it proved too close to day-gear and so failed: "I missed the refreshing and luxurious sense, induced by the night-gown, of being undressed, emancipated, set free from restraints and trammels" (p. 459). And as a travel writer he continued artfully to evade the conventional set pieces called for at famous sites. Whereas Bayard Taylor gamely took up the task of describing the Taj Mahal even though, he ruefully realized, it had been accomplished a hundred times before and he had nothing to add, Twain in a resourceful move reminiscent of the way he dealt with the problem of describing a Rome that had been described a thousand times before, dealt with the Taj Mahal by explaining why it was impossible for him to see it save through the mass of words already expended on it, then proceeded to describe at length a New England ice-storm, a marvel of nature as the Taj Mahal was a model of human art, he claimed, but a marvel that had never before been described.

Yet despite all its compliance with the characteristic structures of his other travel narratives, Twain's longing for the worlds of color—those he visited and those he retained from his infancy—sets *Following the Equator* apart. In the nearly thirty years since he was an innocent abroad the tourist who had responded to his difference from other peoples with a scorn for their inadequacies had developed into an advocate for the kinship of all peoples and a severe critic of the inadequacies of his own people. Twain's mood of enchantment with everything that he and his go-getting America were not reached a climax in India where the sheer density of humanity magnetized him, drawing him out of his skeptical self to seek merger. No longer the querulously impatient traveler, he finds even a two-hour delay in an Indian railway station to be over too soon. There is so much to see in the thronged humanity there "the charms of it are beyond speech" (p. 475). Remembering Bombay he remembers the "delirium" he felt the entire time he was there and hopes it will never leave him.

When we realize that soon after *Following the Equator* Twain was to arrive at a view of all mankind as "the damned human race," his immersion in the massed humanity of India seems magical. For all his nominalistic skepticism this great practitioner of horse sense did for an exalted moment before his final plunge into colorless nihilism achieve transcendence. Almost in spite of his intentions travel had, in the best sense of the word, "civilized" Mark Twain.

This last of Twain's travel works was his least successful commercially, but together with the income from his worldwide lecture tour it returned him to solvency and, with H. H. Rogers's help, to affluence soon after. His expatriation had served its purpose. "On October 15, 1900," Justin Kaplan writes, "after an exile of nearly ten years and an unbroken absence of over five, Mark Twain returned to America and to an ovation that went on for the rest of his life" (p. 358). He no longer had to travel to gather material for his books; he no longer had to take to the road in order to give lectures. Yet between his return to Manhattan in 1900 and his death in 1910, Twain went to Saranac Lake, Nova Scotia, the West Indies, Missouri, and Maine, then to Genoa and Florence, back across the Atlantic to Elmira, over to Massachusetts, down to Manhattan, up to New Hampshire, over to Bermuda, London, and Oxford, back to New York, and then again to Bermuda before returning to Connecticut. His days of travel writing had ended but the psychological link between his mind's rambling along the route of associations and his need to journey from place to place continued to his death.

CHAPTER 5

Henry James

—————»•0•«—————

Transatlantic Sketches (1875)
Portraits of Places (1883)
A Little Tour in France (1884)
English Hours (1905)
The American Scene (1907)
Italian Hours (1909)

Quite literally, Henry James was born to travel. His parents delayed their planned departure to Europe because his mother was pregnant with him, and within a year of his birth on April 15, 1843, they took him and his brother William, older by a year, to England and then France. Years later he astounded his parents by describing to them an early memory of being on the lap of some person seated opposite them in a moving carriage. "I had been impressed with the view," he told them, "framed by the clear window of the vehicle as we passed, of a great stately square surrounded by high-roofed houses and having at its cen-tre a tall and glorious column." As his parents sought to match this description with an actual moment in the family's history, they could only conclude that their son was, remarkably, recalling an impression made upon him when he was not yet two years old: "I had naturally caused them to marvel, but I had also, under cross-questioning forced them to compare notes, as it were, and reconstitute the miracle. . . .

Conveyed along the Rue St-Honoré while I waggled my small feet, as I definitely remember doing under my flowing robe, I had crossed the Rue de Castiglione and taken in, for all my time, the admirable aspect of the Place and the Colonne Vendôme."[1] His perception of Paris had, as he expressed it in the elaborate embroidery of his late style, awakened "a vibration of my very most infantine sensibility," and he was able to preserve that impression for subsequent reference as an adult. Clearly, Henry James was born equipped to record travels as well as to travel.

In 1870, James's first travel sketches began appearing in the *Nation*. He was then living in Cambridge and having already contributed stories and book reviews to American magazines he was adding the travel report to his repertoire as he pursued the possibility of supporting himself through his writings. His first sketches dealt with a journey to upstate New York, Vermont, and Quebec, and included, among other topics, a consideration of the tone of social life in Saratoga, which he compared unfavorably with that of Newport, a place he knew well from his family's having lived there, and a description of a visit to Niagara. When he returned to Europe in 1872–74 for his second visit as an adult—as a child he had visited Europe, lived, and been schooled there in two separate periods, 1855–58 and 1859–60, after his initial "infantine" journey, and in 1869–70 he had made his first adult visit, unaccompanied by family—he began sending back travel sketches on England, France, Italy, and Switzerland, at first to the *Nation* and then to other magazines, most notably the *Atlantic Monthly*, as editors such as William Dean Howells, responding to the attractive force of his confident, witty, and open-eyed depictions of European sites and his extraordinary skill at capturing in sentence or paragraph the nuances that set foreign society off from American, solicited his work.

In late 1875 James returned to Europe yet again, but this time, in a manner of speaking, for the last time because he took lodgings in London's Mayfair at the close of 1876 and began a lifelong residence in England. Until 1876 one may speak of the young James's Atlantic crossings in terms of returns to Europe—there were six of them; after that

year, however, it is more accurate to speak of the crossings as returns to
America—there were four of them, the third resulting in *The American
Scene* (1907), the most remarkable of all his travel works as well as one
of the most distinguished analyses of American culture ever written by
any author.

Throughout the 1870s, both before and after his settling in London,
James published more than fifty travel sketches. The number seems
extraordinary since in the same period he also produced seven books of
fiction and two of literary criticism. But as Leon Edel pointed out,[2] this
relatively easy form of writing—compared, that is, with the fiction with
which he was struggling to establish his reputation—in effect paid for
the travels that nourished his fiction. In the 1870s, characters such as
Roderick Hudson, Christopher Newman, and, most famously, Daisy Miller, opened his lifelong theme of the American in Europe and the moral
implications of cultural difference.

But attractive as the travel sketches were to magazine editors, James
Osgood, the Boston publisher, was reluctant to undertake a book-length
collection of them without a financial subsidy. Mark Twain was then
setting the tone for popular travel writing, his *Innocents Abroad* had
appeared in 1869, the year of James's first adult visit to Europe, one he
thought of as a "passionate pilgrimage." In its joyous embrace of the
uncultured American's reaction to foreign parts, Twain's book, humorous where James was witty, rambunctiously parochial where James
was confidently cosmopolitan, could hardly have been more different
from the collection James was proposing. Osgood, moreover, had been
reading Twain's Mississippi pieces in the *Atlantic Monthly* and had his
eye on persuading Twain, as he eventually did, to expand them into the
work that became *Life on the Mississippi*. But with underwriting from
James's father, Henry James, Sr., Osgood did bring out *Transatlantic
Sketches* in 1875 and the book soon repaid the subsidy, went on into a
number of editions, and in 1883, under the title *Foreign Parts,* Tauch-
nitz, the Leipzig publisher, brought out a revised edition formatted for
English-speaking travelers in Europe.

The success of *Transatlantic Sketches* led Osgood in 1884 to publish

another gathering of James's travel pieces, *Portraits of Places*. All save
one of the pieces in that collection dated from the previous decade,
among them James's 1870 contributions to the *Nation* on his visit to
upstate New York and Canada. James thus managed to reprint in book
form, with some revisions, usually slight, just about nine-tenths of the
large journalistic output of the 1870s. Moreover, his adept recycling did
not end there. When in 1905 he published a collection of his English
sketches under the title *English Hours,* all but two of the pieces included
there had previously appeared in either *Transatlantic Sketches* or *Portraits of Places*. Similarly, most of the items that made up *Italian Hours*
(1909) dated from the journalism of the 1870s and had subsequently
appeared in one or the other of the two earlier collections. So, to se-
lect one example, the sketch, "A Roman Holiday," written in February
1873, appeared in the *Atlantic Monthly* in July of that year, was put into
Transatlantic Sketches in 1875 (and thus also appeared in *Foreign
Parts* in 1883), and then reappeared in *Italian Hours* in 1909.[3] James
was not only a great man of letters, he was also a practiced business-
man of letters.

After the 1870s the pace of James's travel writing dropped off
sharply. He wrote but four or five such pieces in the 1880s while publishing twelve books of fiction in that decade, almost all of which had European settings. *The Portrait of A Lady,* for example, opened in the English
countryside then moved to Florence and Rome, and *The Princess Casamassima* centered in London with a momentous excursion to Paris. But
while he turned away from shorter pieces he did in his middle and then
in his late period produce the two of his travel books that were written as
entire works rather than gathered from separated sketches. *A Little
Tour in France,* serialized in the *Atlantic Monthly* in 1883–84 and within
months published in book form by Osgood, was a straightforward (if
such a word can ever be applied to James) travel narrative, and *The
American Scene,* published in January 1907 after ten of its fourteen
chapters had appeared in magazines in preceding months, was fully
developed as a coherent social analysis shaped on the frame of travel
through the eastern part of the United States.

The backward view from 1909 when *Italian Hours*, the last of James's travel books, was published, is of a young but rapidly maturing author who sold a large number of travel pieces to journals in the decade of the 1870s but as he entered into international eminence as a novelist and critic only rarely after 1880 wrote travel sketches although he assiduously mined those he had written for collections published in 1875, 1883, 1905, and 1909. Having in effect abandoned the genre of the periodical travel piece, however, in 1885 and again in 1907, he produced the two of his travel books that were conceived as coherent entities.

At the outset of his literary career in the 1830s, Nathaniel Hawthorne contributed travel sketches to the *New-England Magazine* and the *American Monthly Magazine*, periodicals that, unlike the *Nation*, the *North American Review*, and the *Atlantic Monthly* to which James contributed at the outset of his career four decades later, play no significant part in American literary culture beyond the fact of their existence and the archival interest of a few pieces such as Hawthorne's. After the 1837 publication of his *Twice-Told Tales*—he was then thirty four—Hawthorne in effect stopped writing travel pieces and the attention his slight, early efforts command today is principally biographical: they were written by the man who was later to produce great fiction. In them one sees a shy and solitary young provincial seeking his way into the world of letters from a society in which no models for such an entry existed. Practicing his craft in solitude he had to acquire his literary culture without access to living writers and develop his aesthetic sensibility in a nation in which there were no great works of art or architecture to excite his imagination. In 1879, when James wrote his monograph on Hawthorne for the "English Men of Letters" series—the first book ever in that series to be devoted to an American author—he defined the young Hawthorne's cultural situation as one in which there was "a vivacity of desire and poverty of knowledge."[4]

That was hardly the situation of the young James who three and a half decades after Hawthorne's travel sketches were published himself set out to travel in the same region Hawthorne had visited for his sketches. He was then living in Cambridge, the home of Longfellow, Lowell, and other members of a professoriate who had lived and studied in Europe. From his extended study years abroad, Longfellow had brought back a fluency in both Romance and Germanic languages and had translated into his own amiable, easy-paced, and popular verse the literature and lore of those languages, bringing to Americans' firesides a sense of culture and civility larger than the seasonal rounds of their village life. Volumes of his poems traveled west on the covered wagons and together with the Bible formed the pioneer mother's principal weapon in her battle to keep her children from savagery in a savage country. Emerson, now at the start of a long sunny decline from the fullness of his powers, was a familiar friend of the James family, and James Russell Lowell, founding editor of the *Atlantic Monthly*, subsequently editor of the *North American Review*, successor to Longfellow in the Smith Professorship at Harvard, and a prolific literary and political essayist as well as noted poet, served as the local model of a universal man of letters. In their determined translation of the literature and ideas of other lands to an America sadly in need of some leavening of its provincial rusticity, the Cambridge-Boston thinkers and writers may at times have appeared to confuse the genteel with the intellectual. But if not cosmopolitan—and Henry James was fast concluding it was not— the society in which he lived in 1870 strove at least to maintain a sense of itself as participant in the ideals of high European culture.

For all that, however, it was Hawthorne, who had died in 1864 and had never been a part of the Cambridge milieu (although he was a college friend of Longfellow's), whose presence James most strongly felt as in the 1860s he began his career as a professional writer. Of all Americans it was Hawthorne whose achievement in fiction he most greatly admired, and so it was Hawthorne with whom he came most consciously to compete as he sought to establish his own literary identity. The ghost of Hawthorne was to appear, fade, and reappear throughout James's career: his early Italian travels were informed by a sense of Hawthorne's *Marble Faun* (1860), a novel American travelers frequently used as a guide to Italian sites, and his late novel, *The Golden Bowl* (1904), resembled in plot the way in which sets of paired Hawthorne characters in the intensity of their relationships exhausted the social atmosphere that surrounded them. Additionally, in his monograph on Hawthorne, James came both to praise his predecessor and to bury him.

In his 1870 northern travels James visited and wrote about some of the same places Hawthorne had sketched. That he was aware of this is most strongly evidenced by what appears to be a deliberate effort on his part to say something completely different. At times this could even mean saying nothing at all about a site Hawthorne had described although the place was standard tourist fare. Fort Ticonderoga, for example, was one such place, the site of the revolutionary victory of that American Achilles, Ethan Allen, and before then of the French presence in New England. When Hawthorne visited in 1835 the fort was already a ruin, and after doing his best with a literal description of a scene that resisted the picturesque, he sat down in one of the roofless barracks and permitted what he called his "fancy" to provide the description. Then he saw a war party from the old French war moving about a bustling fort and he proceeded to describe a scene that existed only in his imagination.[5]

The ruin was even more ruinous when James passed in 1870, and cooly remarked to readers of the *Nation:* "Of the fort I shall not speak: I dined, perforce, in the half-hour during which I might fastingly have explored it. I saw it only from the top of the coach as we passed. It seemed to me in quite the perfection of decay—of stony decrepitude and verduous overgrowth—and to exhale with sufficient force a meagre historic melancholy. I prefer to speak of the lake" (CTWAm, p. 748).

There is more than a touch of defiance, even a flavor of arrogance, in preferring dinner to a sacred historic site, but there is also a deliberate decision not to compensate for a lack of picturesqueness by providing, as did Hawthorne, an account drawn from its history. James chose not to speak at all if history was all that could be recounted. This tactic, first announced in his American sketches, was one he continued to employ in his later pieces on European sites. At Poitiers in 1883, for example, he

spent a second or two wondering where the famous battle fought by the
Black Prince took place, but quickly regained his indifference to military
topography, content to recognize that a great victory took place there
without attempting its revivification. After all, the most charming thing
in Poitiers is the Promenade de Blossac, he says, well worth walking and
well worth describing. Its attractiveness does not, however, mask the
"groveling vision which, on such a spot as the ramparts of Poitiers,
peoples itself with carrots and cabbages rather than with images of the
Black Prince and the captive king."[6]

Unlike the eminent American writers of travel who had preceded
him, James never visited exotic places and so could place no reliance on
mere description of the unfamiliar to hold his reader's interest. Dealing
always with what was to a degree known to his readers, he unerringly
moved in his travel writing toward a reliance upon his sensibility, upon
the representation of the impression a site made upon him. Regardless,
on one hand, of how trivial an incident might appear in itself, or, on the
other, of the readerly expectations a famous site might arouse, he was
primarily if not exclusively concerned with the sensitive rendering of his
affective response to it. When celebrated places failed to set off the vibration he required—negative or positive—he did not write about them.
By the same token, when slight sights—a child in a restaurant, hay-
stacks in a flood—made their impress he described them. The value of
the scenes he placed before the reader was a value given them by the
capacity of his prose to render their precise register in his consciousness. The truth of what he described was subjective: it derived its significance from his imagination, as opposed to the objective truth offered
in travelers' descriptions of sites of historical or natural importance.
"One sees, after all, however, even among the most palpable realities,"
James wrote in 1873, "very much what one's capricious intellect projects there."[7] In 1909 he replaced "one's capricious intellect" with "the
play of one's imagination."[8]

But in his earliest sketches James did not yet display a confident
subjectivity. Together with an awareness of Hawthorne, he brought to
bear on the unfinished wonders of the America that he visited a sense of

the cultured sights he had passionately absorbed in his recent European pilgrimage, and did so with too great an air of the patronizing sophisticate.

Already in Hawthorne's day the subject of a multitude of written and pictorial representations, Niagara offered both an intimidating yet inescapable challenge to any writer who approached it. In 1846 Poe called the accumulated attempts to capture the falls in prose "desperate failures," reserving, however, praise for Margaret Fuller who had had the good sense, in his view, not to describe the falls at all but simply to express how she had felt when she saw them.[9] Hawthorne in 1835 claimed that "Never did a pilgrim approach Niagara with deeper enthusiasm than mine,"[10] yet once he arrived in the vicinity of the falls, he admitted, his ardor cooled and instead of rushing to see them he went to his hotel and dressed for dinner. The fear of failure—the falls' failure to meet expectations, his own failure to be able to see through his own eyes rather than the eyes of those who had written the descriptions he had read—held him back. Eventually he did view the cataract, only to exclaim: "Oh, that I had never heard of Niagara till I beheld it! Blessed were the wanderers of old, who heard its deep roar, sounding through the woods, as the summons to an unknown wonder, and approached its awful brink, in all the freshness of native feeling. . . . But I had come thither, haunted with a vision of foam and fury, and dizzy cliffs, and an ocean tumbling down out of the sky—a scene, in short, which nature had too much good taste and calm simplicity to realize" (Niagara, p. 58). He could not, he said, adjust his false conceptions to the reality, although after a period of disappointment he did return for hours at a time, came to terms with his inability to receive a direct impression, and finally managed to produce a description and admit that Niagara was indeed a wonder. Still, he remarked, "I will not pretend to the all-absorbing enthusiasm of some more fortunate spectators, nor deny, that very trifling causes would draw my eyes and thoughts from the cataract" (p. 59).

Aware of the history of despairing attempts to capture Niagara such as Hawthorne's, James, with a bit too much of the smugness of one fresh from the man-made marvels of the Old World, reduced the earthshaking spectacle to the dimensions of a framed and pretty picture. Picking up Hawthorne's suggestion as to the tastefulness of nature—as opposed to claims for its sublimity—he carried it well-nigh to absurdity. There is a studied archness, ultimately a disagreeable condescension, in speaking of the falls in this fashion: "The perfect taste of it is the great characteristic. It is not in the least monstrous; it is thoroughly artistic and, as the phrase is, thought out. In the matter of line it beats Michael Angelo. One may seem at first to say the least, but the careful observer will admit that one says the most in saying that it *pleases*" (CTWAm, p. 781). "Nothing," he added, " was ever more successfully executed" (p. 792).

One is reminded of Emerson's characterization of what he called defacements in the rhetoric of Thoreau, a trick of substituting the opposite for the obvious: "He praised wild mountains and winter forests for their domestic air, in snow and ice he would find sultriness, and commended the wilderness for resembling Rome and Paris."[11] In James as in Thoreau it was, after all, a trick, one which he was quickly to leave behind when he began to write of European scenes for the American reader. His best travel writing would always evolve from the viewpoint of a foreign visitor to the scenes he depicted. Even his eventual masterpiece on the American scene came only after his long expatriation permitted him to return to his native land with his youthful memories structured by the viewpoint of one alien to the scene before his eyes.

Henry James had not yet begun to write travel sketches when in a May 1869 letter from Florence he told his brother William about the Americans to be seen there. "There is but one word to use in regard to them—vulgar, vulgar, vulgar. Their ignorance—their stingy, defiant, grudging attitude towards everything European—their perpetual reference of all things to some American standard or precedent which exists only in their own unscrupulous wind-bags—and then our unhappy poverty of voice, of speech, and of physiognomy—these things glare at you hideously" (Edel, 1:304). This, as Leon Edel reminds us, was written in the year of Twain's *Innocents Abroad*. But as Edel goes on to illustrate, the theme of the entire letter to William is not so much one of contempt for Americans abroad as it is of distress at their lack of culture; it is significant that James refers to "*our* unhappy poverty." Moreover, during the same tour of Italy that caused his outburst he himself reached a point of saturation that led him, if only fancifully, to wonder whether modern improvements were not, after all, preferable to the conditions that conserved culture: "I'm sick unto death of priests and churches. Their 'picturesqueness' ends by making me want to go strongly into political economy or the New England school system. I conceived at Naples a ten-fold deeper loathing than ever of the hideous heritage of the past, and felt for a moment as if I should like to devote my life to laying railroads and erecting blocks of stores on the most classic and romantic sites. The age has a long row to hoe" (Edel, 1:311).* In avoidance of supplying such an excess in his travel sketches, James focused on exercising discriminating taste rather than providing comprehensive views. His selective, confidently articulated responses to foreign life and art were encouragements to American readers to know more about, to appreciate, a world both older and more furnished than was theirs, yet finally to ground their notions of that world in the truth of their own needs. The education in culture he provided resided, finally, in the style of his responses. All great travel writing consists in making discoveries and James's are no exception. His discoveries, however, do not reside in what he sees but in the way that he sees; they are the products of his technique.[12]

Almost every place James wrote about in the series of sketches he sent back to American magazines during his 1872–74 travels in Europe was on the standard tourist itineraries. He himself carried and referred to guidebooks, most notably those of John Murray, and he occasionally quoted from them as well. His originality did not so much consist in his describing standard sites in novel ways—the coy perversity of his

---

*This momentary distress rather resembles that of Hawthorne's New England maiden Hilda who in *The Marble Faun* temporarily falls out of sympathy with the great religious art of the Italian masters and develops a fleeting preference for the solid realism of the Flemish masters.

approach to Niagara had disappeared—as it did in the assured manner with which he selected only what impressed him and built his sketches from his impressions. Subjective as his reactions were, they were, nevertheless, so projected onto the scene by the precision of his prose that they appeared as qualities inherent in it.

"We complain of hackneyed and cocknified Europe," James wrote at the outset of his 1872 visit to the Continent, "but wherever, in desperate quest of the untrodden, we carry our much-labelled luggage, our bad French, our demand for a sitz-bath and pale ale, we rub off the precious primal bloom of the picturesque and establish a precedent for unlimited intrusion" (TS, p. 63). James's French, of course, was excellent, he did not desperately seek the "untrodden" but returned time and again to well-visited places that appealed to him, never carried the kind of baggage he here parodied, and had no illusion about discovering a place no tourist had previously visited. Rather, at the heart of the originality of viewpoint in the 1870s pieces is what James called "picturesque accident." No matter how well trodden the track he followed, he was alert to sights that without warning composed themselves before his eye, stirring his imagination to represent their sensory truth. So, for example, as he arrives at the Italian side of the Alps after passing through Swiss scenes that excited his chiding wit but not his admiration,* he writes in 1873: "the deep yellow light . . . enchants you and tells you where you are. See it come filtering down through a vine-covered trellis on the red handkerchief with which a ragged contadina has bound her hair; and all the magic of Italy, to the eye, seems to make an aureole about the poor girl's head. Look at a brown-breasted reaper eating his chunk of black bread under a spreading chestnut; nowhere is shadow so charming, nowhere is color so changed, nowhere is accident so picturesque"

---

*"There is a limit to the satisfaction with which you can sit staring at a mountain—even the most beautiful—which you have neither ascended nor are likely to ascend; and I know of nothing to which I can better compare the effect on your nerves of what comes to seem to you, at last, its inhuman want of condescension than that of the back of certain persons whom you come as near detesting as your characteristic amiability permit." (TS, p. 58).

(TS, p. 251). Picturesque accident; whatever place can supply this, within or outside of celebrated sites, is a place of human appeal. It is what the literary traveler seeks to capture for himself and, accordingly, his reader.

Throughout the 1870s James characterized himself as a "sentimental tourist," or "passionate pilgrim," an American abroad speaking to fellow Americans. The European difference from America—its long history, its class societies, its works of art—was everywhere before him, but his principal theme was not what Europe had that America lacked. Rather it was learning how to see past the material details to the sensory impress of the whole; learning, that is, to see not just different objects but to see differently. For example, a row of houses in Florence:

> Anything more battered and befouled, more cracked and disjointed, dirtier, drearier, shabbier, it would be impossible to conceive. They look as if, fifty years ago, the muddy river had risen over their chimneys, and then subsided again and left them coated forever with its unsightly slime. And yet, forsooth, because the river is yellow, and here and there, elsewhere, some mellow, mouldering surface, some hint of color, some accident of atmosphere, takes up the foolish tale and repeats the note— because, in short, it is Florence, it is Italy, and you are a magnanimous Yankee, bred among the micaceous sparkle of brown-stone fronts and lavish enthusiasm, these miserable dwellings, instead of simply suggesting mental invocations to an enterprising board of health, bloom and glow all along the line in the perfect felicity of picturesqueness. (TS, pp. 272–73)

James was not unaware of the danger of seeming heartless in such praise of the attractiveness the conditions of the Italian poor presented to a foreign eye. Squalor, however picturesque, indicates human suffering and speaks to readers, especially American readers, of economic injustice and an oppressive political system. Well enough for the tourist to enjoy the aesthetic appeal of dilapidated dwellings, but, once thought of, the human price paid to provide the spectacle reverses the charm and turns it to revulsion. If the Mark Twain of *Innocents Abroad* deserves to be numbered among those American tourists about whom James wrote to his brother William, the "vulgar, vulgar, vulgar" tourists who bore a grudging attitude toward everything European, he nevertheless did bring more than mere American brag to bear in his democratic disapproval of the misery he saw on the streets of foreign cities.

James's awareness of the social price of picturesqueness is implicit in a number of his early Italian sketches even as he maintains a central focus on the aesthetic appeal of what he sees, but nowhere in the sketches does he consider the conflict between aesthetics and politics as one to be resolved in principle. Rather, early in his travel writing as later in his novels (most notably *The Princess Casamassima*) he renders the conflict as a personal rather than an intellectual issue. There is no universal moral answer to the dilemma, because it is, finally, experiential not abstract, and one's answer depends upon one's temperament.

In an 1873 piece James wrote of a friend who regarded it as monstrous to come to Rome to feed on human misery. "Isn't it an abomination that our enjoyment here directly implies their wretchedness," the friend is quoted as saying; and further, "I want to see people who look as if they knew how to read and write, and care for something else than flocking to the Pincio to suck the knobs on their canes and stare at fine ladies they'll never by any hazard speak to" (TS, p. 128). Characteristically, James does not answer these objections by offering an opposing view but after reporting his friend's objections describes how his friend did find satisfaction: "He travelled due north, and has been having a delightful winter at Munich, where the march of mind advances to the accompaniment of Wagner's music" (TS, p. 129). The very cadence of the final clause is comment enough. Rome has other delights. One man's dirt is another's chiaroscuro.

At Vincigliata, an English millionaire's imitation of a fourteenth-century castle, James was more explicit:

There are moods in which one feels the impulse to enter a tacit
protest against too generous a patronage of pure aesthetics, in
this starving and sinning world. One turns half away musingly
from certain beautiful useless things. But the healthier state of
mind, surely, is to lay no tax on any really intelligent manifestation of the curious and exquisite. . . . This elaborate piece of imitation has no superficial use; but even if it were less complete,
less successful, less brilliant, I should feel a reflective kindness
for it. So handsome a piece of work is its own justification; it belongs to the heroics of culture. (TS, pp. 287–88)

A preference for the heroics of culture implies a conservative temperament in sympathy with established social and political forms. Such
a disposition is not necessarily at odds with the democratic American
viewpoint James believed he brought with him. But in social as opposed
to political matters his conservatism did lead him to an exclusiveness at
some distance from democratic ideals, and the sometimes derisive tone
of his exhibitions of refinement can be just as objectionable as the sometimes puerile tone of Twain's assertions of his commonness. In England,
James wrote in 1872, "conservatism has all the charm and leaves dissent and democracy and other vulgar variations nothing but their bald
logic. Conservatism has the cathedrals, the colleges, the castles, the
gardens, the traditions, the associations, the first names, the better
manners, the poetry. Dissent has the dusky brick chapels in provincial
by-streets, the names out of Dickens, the uncertain tenure of the h" (TS,
p. 17). One may quarrel, of course, with the accuracy of this depiction—
more than bald logic provides the passion of Milton, Blake, and other
mighty dissenters, upper-class convention yields nastier behavior than
does the dignity of self-respecting plain folk, common speech keeps
literary language from decay—but that is not the issue. It is, rather, that
in his sanctioning of the heroics of culture James at times did not just
school his readers in good taste but invited them to acknowledge the
natural superiority of the class in which such taste historically reposed.
Bayard Taylor's travel writings contributed ultimately to a belief in the

racial superiority of the white race, while Mark Twain's earlier travel books contributed to a belief in the political, and therefore the moral, superiority of the American system. Unconcerned with race as such (although his cultural outlook had strong racial implications), and repelled by American chauvinism, James in his travels implicitly identified with a superior class of taste that crossed national boundaries. Although one need not have been well born to possess such taste, historically its stewards were the members of the upper class. When the demands of culture are made to outweigh the logic of social justice the superiority of this class is being justified.

To note this, however, is not to overlook James's conscientious sense throughout his travel writings—even in the lamentations of *The American Scene*—that he was an American, nor the impatience he felt at times in the face of the reactionary intransigence of those autocracies in Europe that resisted the spread of human freedom and the opening of the minds of the underclass. Sitting in the Rheims cathedral, for instance, during the French political crisis of 1877 when a conservative ministry attempted to bypass the will of the republican majority, James found himself

> picturing to myself that conflict which must often occur at such a moment as the present—which is actually going on, doubtless, in many thousands of minds—between the actively, practically liberal instinct, and what one may call the historic, aesthetic sense, the sense upon which old cathedrals lay a certain palpable obligation. How far should a lover of old cathedrals let his hands be tied by the sanctity of their traditions? How far should he let his imagination bribe him, as it were, from action? This of course is a question for each man to answer for himself; but as I sat listening to the drowsy old canons of Rheims, I was visited, I scarcely knew why, by a kind of revelation of the anti-catholic passion, as it must burn to-day in the breast of certain radicals. I felt that such persons must be intent upon war to the death; how that must seem the most sacred of all duties. Can anything in the line

of action, for a votary of the radical creed, be more sacred? I asked myself; and can any instruments be too trenchant? I raised my eyes again in the dusky splendor of the upper aisles and measured their enchanting perspective, and it was with a sense of doing them full justice that I gave my fictive liberal my good wishes. (CTWCon, pp. 741–42)

Most notable in this eminently notable passage is the source of the power that enables a respecter of "the historic, aesthetic sense" finally to side against the sanctity of tradition. For James, what is sacred about the liberal is not his creed but the passion in which he holds it, a passion that transcends considerations of the self. For what, after all, is James's own passion for art but such a sacred commitment? The droning chanting of the canons, on the other hand, represents the departure of passion from a site that sacred passion built.

A sense of the past is crucial for the cultivation of character but a sense of the past is different from a knowledge of the past and is not to be gained from books but must be acquired in places where its presence is still felt. For James this meant Europe. He was, however, far from valuing Europe as a museum in which a past distinctly different from the present was preserved. Rather, the force of the European education was that there the present could be experienced as continuous with the past whereas in America such continuity was broken by three thousand miles of ocean, and museums that displayed the past as separate were the best that could be hoped for. "At least half the merit of everything you enjoy must be that it suits you absolutely," James wrote in Rome in 1873, "but the larger half here is generally that it has suited some one else, and that you can never flatter yourself you have discovered it. It is historic, literary, suggestive; it has played some other part than it is just then playing to your eyes" (TS, p. 153). The true sense of the past is not the sense of experiencing at a site the historical or poetic associations connected with an event that occurred long ago. It is, rather, the sense that the scenes in which you move and feel are scenes in which others have moved and felt. You are, that is, sharing the past with those of the past. Just as you feel, so

I felt, said Whitman looking forward to those who would come after him;* where I feel so you felt, says James looking back at the hosts that came before. That is the way a sense of the past civilizes one.

When describing the Carnival he saw while in Florence in 1874—disappointingly dull compared with written descriptions of what it once was—James wrote, "Meanwhile it occurs to me that by a remote New England fireside an unsophisticated young person" is reading in romance or old travel books how Carnival was celebrated in Catholic lands. He then developed a picture of this imagined reader: "Into the quiet room, quenching the rhythm of the Yankee pendulum, there floats an uproar of delighted voices, a medley of stirring foreign sounds." The young reader pensively turns from her book and stares out the window to the reality of dusk falling on beaten snow. "Down the road is a white wooden meeting-house, looking grey among the drifts"; she looks at it, then stares at the fire, and thinking of the color, the costume, the rapture of the Carnival in Florence, "discerns at last the glowing phantasm of opportunity and determines with a heart-beat, to go and see it all—twenty years hence!" (TS. pp. 282–83).**

In this tiny drama, the rhythm of the Yankee pendulum is momentarily quenched by the imagined sounds of revelry, but its more potent rival is the beat of the aroused heart. There may be a trace of rue in James's recognition that even in his day the Carnival of lore had become a shabby affair so that twenty years hence an even drearier scene will greet the yearning visitor. But his poignant picture of the wistful reader in the dusky grey of a New England winter is an endorsement of the passionate pilgrimage.

In 1878, two years after he had become a London resident, Henry James considered the literary consequences of being an expatriate. "It is hard to say exactly," he reflected, "what is the profit of comparing one

---

*The expression is in "Crossing Brooklyn Ferry," but the idea permeates much of Whitman's greatest verse.
**This passage foreshadows James's description in *Hawthorne* of the austere cultural environment of provincial New England.

race with another, and weighing in opposed groups the manners and customs of neighbouring countries; but it is certain that as we move about the world we constantly indulge in this exercise." Perhaps such is not an ideal situation and it is better to be a concentrated patriot than a traveling expatriate. There are a great many *patriæ* in the world, countries "filled with excellent people for whom the local idiosyncrasies are the only thing that is not rather barbarous." But "when one set of customs, wherever it may be found, grows to seem to you about as provincial as another . . . then I suppose it may be said of you that you have become a cosmopolite" (CTWCon, p. 721). While cosmopolitanism is, perhaps, a poor position for the exercise of citizenship, for James it was an ideal vantage for the practice of his art. In the first years of his expatriation he wrote the greatest of his travel sketches.

So striking were the pieces sent back to magazines in the 1872–74 period that when James returned to Europe a year later Whitelaw Reid, editor of the *New York Tribune,* commissioned him to furnish letters of political and social gossip from France. In those pieces James's sense that he was writing for newspaper rather than magazine readers did not much alter his literary style, but for his subject matter he did concentrate far more on descriptive surfaces and simple pleasures than on aesthetic analyses and social criticism.

One rides the train to Chartres and the walk from the station past "labour-stricken" grandams and the small children they have in tow, "little red-cheeked girls, in the close black caps and black pinafores of French infancy—a costume which makes French children always look like orphans" (CTWCon, p. 682) is as important and more vivid than a visit to the cathedral. In Paris in hot weather you take the penny steamer down the Seine to Auteuil and dine at a *guignette* on the banks of the stream, where "Your table is spread under a trellis—spread chiefly with fried fish—and an old man who looks like a political exile comes and stands before it and sings a doleful ditty on the respect due to white hairs" (p. 685). Etretat, not the most fashionable of seaside resorts, "may be primitive, but Etretat is French, and therefore Etretat is 'administered' " (p. 692). There the bathing is excellently managed

Henry James, cosmopolite, photographed by Alice Boughton during a visit to her New York studio in 1905 (Reprinted by permission of the National Portrait Gallery, Smithsonian Institution).

and you feel the firm hand of a paternal and overlooking government the moment you issue from your hut. The Government will
on no consideration consent to your being rash. There are six or
eight worthy old sons of Neptune on the beach—perfect amphibi-
ous creatures—who, if you are a newcomer, immediately accost
you and demand pledges that you know how to swim. . . . At a
short distance from the shore there are two boats, freighted with
sundry other marine divinities, who remain there perpetually,
taking it as a personal offence if you venture out too far. (pp.
693–94)

Such pictures in the *Tribune* letters are vivid and the tone is knowledgeable and amusing. But although James thus moved away from
analysis and reflection, since he did not correspondingly move toward
current events nor provide social gossip Reid wrote telling him that his
letters were not the right sort for a newspaper. James replied, agreeing:
"I know the sort of letter you mean—it is doubtless the proper sort of
thing for the *Tribune* to have. But I can't produce it." It would be poor
economy for him to attempt to be "newsy" and "gossipy"; he knew he
would always be too literary. In short, if his letters were, as Reid said,
"too good" for the newspaper, they were, as James rather tartly replied,
"the poorest I can do," and the arrangement ended.[13]

Thus released James again wrote for magazines and his essays of the
later 70s were the best he had yet published. Still writing for his fellow
Americans he now accepted that he did so as a cosmopolitan, just as
aware of the provincialism of the Europeans he observed as he was of
the Americans for whom he wrote. He maintained his evident delight in
depicting social scenes but now moved with seamless ease from the
surface to the structure of beliefs that produced it. His visit to Etretat, for
example, the basis for the *Tribune* letter on the bathing beach in 1876,
figured also in an essay he published in the magazine, *The Galaxy*, in the
following year, but now physical description led to social observation.
He began with a lightly comic picture of the women who resorted there:
"A majestic plumpness flourished all around me—the plumpness of tri-

ple chins and deeply dimpled hands. . . . It was the corpulence of ladies who are thoroughly well fed, and who never walk a step that they can spare" which led to an equally light yet telling contrast: "The assiduity with which the women of America measure the length of our democratic pavements is doubtless a factor in their frequent absence of redundancy of outline." Turning again to the spectacle at Etretat he described the way the young women moved in phalanxes, strictly guarded by their plump matrons. But he cautioned his readers against believing that the lot of the shielded maidens was as hard as it might seem to their American eyes: "if a *jeune fille* is for three or four years tied with a very short rope and compelled to browse exclusively upon the meagre herbiage which sprouts in the maternal shadow, she has at least the comfort of reflecting that . . . measures are being carefully taken to promote her to a condition of liberty." Almost imperceptibly, the picture he presented glides into a lesson in comparative sociology. To the French maiden:

> marriage does not mean, as it so often means in America, being
> socially shielded—and it is not too much to say, in certain circles,
> degraded; it means being socially launched and consecrated. . . .
> To be a *mère de famille* is to occupy not simply (as is mostly the
> case with us) a sentimental, but really an official position. The
> consideration, the authority, the domestic pomp and circum-
> stance alloted to a French mamma are in striking contrast with
> the amiable tolerance which in our own social order is so often
> the most liberal measure that the female parent may venture to
> expect at her children's hands.[14]

Daisy Miller, who enjoyed a freedom that, to her ruin, was incomprehensible in the world of the *jeune fille,* was a year or two away, but the observation that made her possible was recorded at Etretat and the theme was to continue to vibrate as long as twenty years later in *What Maisie Knew.*

To see the connection between the social analyses of the travel sketches and the themes of the fiction that followed, however, should not be to reduce those sketches to the status of preparatory studies. They, too, are works of literary art that shape their readers' attitudes and yield pleasure in ways that the fiction does not. In them readers, especially American readers, see foreign habits to be reactions to the same problems of leading the daily life that they face and in so doing understand that their own familiar patterns of behavior are no less arbitrary.

To travel with James in the late 1870s is to be in the presence of an open-eyed companion eager to gather experience wherever it may occur and in whatever shape it may present itself. He is especially adept at depicting the small details that accumulate into a sense of national difference and his presentation of them provides a series of small discoveries for the reader. Immediately after stepping from the Folkestone ferry on the quay at Boulogne the Frenchness of France comes upon one: "among the blue and red douaniers and soldiers, the small ugly men in cerulean blouses, the charming fishwives, with their crisp cap-frills, their short striped petticoats, their tightly-drawn stockings, and their little clicking sabots—when you look about you at the smokeless air, at the pink and yellow houses, at the white-fronted café, close at hand, with its bright blue letters, its mirrors, and marble-topped tables, its white-aproned, alert, undignified waiter, grasping a huge coffee-pot by a long handle, you are amused" (CTWCon, p. 726). But then, there also is "the injurious effect upon the genial French nature of the possession of an administrative uniform," and once on board a train over-administered by an official conscious "of brass buttons on his coat and stripes on his trousers" (p. 727) one feels in jail. In England when you arrive at your inn too late for the dinner hour you are served cold meat, bread, and cheese by a waiter in an old evening suit. In France, served by the host you eat *pot-au-feu* in the kitchen with commercial travelers while the staff sits eating at another table. "In England, certainly, one is treated more as a gentleman. It is too often forgotten, however, that even a gentleman partakes of nourishment" (p. 748). There are, to be sure, cathedrals and galleries to be visited on one's travels, but it is with such deft strokes addressed to the different quality of everyday sights and doings that James conveys the expansive sense of being abroad. Travel writers show or tell us what they have seen but James in the 1870s succeeds in taking us with him.

At Biarritz, an altogether disagreeable resort, the Casino "has quite the air of an establishment frequented by gentlemen who look at ladies' windows with telescopes" (p. 715). The distinctive white shoes worn by Basque men make them look like "honorary members of base-ball clubs" (p. 716) and "with their smooth chins and childish caps, they may be taken, in the distance, for a lot of very naughty little boys; for they have always a cigarette in their teeth" (p. 717).

Crossing over into Spain at San Sebastian James attended a bullfight, but he doubted that there was room in literature for yet another chapter on the subject: "It is extremely disgusting, and one should not describe disgusting things—except (according to the new school)* in novels, where they have not really occurred, and are invented on purpose" (p. 719). Still, he owed it to himself and to his readers to attend, as he studiously did. The blooming matron in a white lace mantilla who sat next to him with her three young daughters sometimes yawned but never shuddered; James sometimes shuddered but never yawned: "I thought the bull, in any case, a finer fellow than any of his tormentors, and I thought his tormentors finer fellows than the spectators. In truth, we were all, for the time, rather sorry fellows together. A bull-fight will, to a certain extent, bear looking at, but it will not bear thinking of" (p. 720).

James's decision to become a resident of England, however, imparted a more troubled tone to the English sketches written after he had settled in London than what one hears in the continental sketches. Prior to 1876 his English portraits were those of an observer out to amuse himself, and in *Transatlantic Sketches* he called himself "our old friend the sentimental tourist," a stock figure of travel literature from at least the time of Sterne. He was a kind of up-to-date Washington Irving as he

*Most obviously, of Zola.

visited rural villages and felt that he was in Old England where he might at any moment see Sir Roger de Coverly marching up the aisle of the local church. But once he committed himself to making his home in London his English essays, and especially those on London, while still aimed at the American reader were powerfully inflected by his struggle to realize just why it was he had made that decision.

Writing of Americans who chose to live abroad James said that they were willing to forego the social advantages one enjoyed in one's own country for the shops, the theatres, and the restaurants unavailable to them at home: "The average European mind can never understand that for many enriched American life at home has never been strikingly agreeable, and that public amusement in a European capital may not unfairly be held to outweigh the human advantages relinquished" (CTWAm, p. 789). But he was not describing himself. On the contrary, he had acquired rather than lost social advantages by settling in London and was so highly valued in the leading artistic and political circles of that city and so frequently invited to dinners that he had made a conquest of London. Moreover, although he enjoyed the public amusements there, he did not consider them the equal of those in Paris. Unlike the towns and villages he had described in his earlier English travel pieces, London did not compose itself into the picturesque, and what the pieces written after 1876 reveal is that London bewitched him precisely because it sprawled rather than delineated itself, teemed with life and defied design.

What is most striking in the dialogue with himself that is discernible in James's English essays[15] is the attractive force exerted by the physical ugliness and social squalor of London. His fiction is so centered in the city mansions and country homes of the affluent, so lit by the sun of Italy, and so enriched by the graces of France, that the personal attraction for him of ceaselessly damp, perpetually cold, indelibly grimy London seems anomalous,* until, that is, one looks at the London sketches

---

*Alone among his novels *The Princess Casamassima* is concerned with the way of life of the underclass, but this can accurately be called the exception that proves the rule.

and there sees how vital to him was his sense of what he called "the tremendous human mill." The subject-matter of his fictions arrived from a number of sources—the germs were frequently anecdotes heard on social occasions—but the surrounding sense of a larger, unruly life always pressing at the margins of his selected subjects, this came from his daily perception of the ungraspable London that encircled him.

As you walk along the London streets, James wrote, you are struck by the ugliness of the houses, the architecture of which makes not the least concession to beauty. Yet the spectacle appeals to one's feelings through its "agglomerated intensity. At any given point London looks huge; even in narrow corners you have a sense of its hugeness, and petty places acquire a certain interest from their being parts of so mighty a whole. Nowhere else is so much human life gathered together, and nowhere does it press upon you with so many suggestions. These are not all of an exhilarating kind; far from it. But they are of every possible kind, and that is the interest of London" (p. 114).

In so responding to the immensity of the nineteenth-century city James was following his favorite novelist, Balzac, but whereas it is Balzac's characters who experience, in Raymond Williams's phrase, the "enlargement of identity" that the city produces, it is not his characters but James himself who is so affected. The enlargement of identity afforded by the vast metropolis was a condition of authorship for him. Like the continental writers whom Williams cites (Balzac, Baudelaire, Dostoyevsky), James saw the city "as the reality of all human life."[16]

As he seeks to comprehend a city that contains so much that does not, as he says, exhilarate, James in his sketches speaks time and again of the poor he encounters in his walks about London with an aesthetic detachment that frames them as features in a civic landscape rather than as individuals deserving of sympathy. For example, with the comfortable classes all out of town in midsummer "one's social studies must at the least be studies of low life, for wherever one may go for a stroll to spend the summer afternoon the comparatively sordid side of things is uppermost. There is no one in the parks save the rough characters who are lying on their faces in the sheep-polluted grass" (p. 114). With

DARK MYSTERIOUS LONDON

Near Queen Anne's Gate, Westminster

Illustration by Joseph Pennell for *English Hours*
(Special Collections, Milton S. Eisenhower Library of The Johns Hopkins University).

a disinterested eye he observes "the elder people shuffling about the walks and the poor little smutty-faced children sprawling over the dark damp turf" (p. 116). "Certain it is," James wrote of the manifest poverty that confronted him in London, "that the impression of suffering is a part of the general vibration; it is one of the things that mingle with all the others to make the sound that is supremely dear to the consistent London-lover—the rumble of the tremendous human mill" (p. 35).

The notion that the poor are necessary to complete the attraction of London may be callous as a social commentary but is not necessarily heartless as an aesthetic observation. The artist's obligation is to render as best he can the complex city that interests him, and the poor are an indispensable part of the aesthetic whole.

In his 1879 piece, "An English New Year," however, James spoke autobiographically about his London life at a specific historical moment of large human suffering and by placing himself personally in the scene became accountable for his attitude toward the distressed classes. While the immunity of aesthetic detachment might be claimed for the author of the sketch insofar as he can be separated from the "I" who is its subject, the reaction of that "I" to the desperate plight of the under-class reveals him to be unfeelingly concerned for his own comforts.

The winter of 1878–79 was a season of particular misery in England: cold, harsh weather and a financial depression led to severe distress among the working class and necessitated both public and private poor relief. In some parts of the country workers were on strike, with regard to which James with an uncharacteristic lapse in sensibility remarked, "When the labouring classes rise to the recreation of a strike I suppose the situation may be said to have its cheerful side" (p. 219). The heavy snow in London was dirty with city grime, and a pervasive smoke-filled fog so irritated eyes and throat that:

> For recovery of one's nervous balance the only course was
> flight—flight to the country and the confinement of one's vision to
> the large area of one of those admirable homes which at this
> season overflow with hospitality and good cheer. By this means

the readjustment is effectually brought out—these are conditions that you cordially appreciate. Of all the great things that the English have invented and made a part of the credit of the national character, the most perfect, the most characteristic, the one they have mastered most completely in all its details, so that it has become a compendious illustration of their social genius and their manners, is the well-appointed, well-administered, well-filled country-house. (p. 222)

His flight to the country may be an understandable personal decision; the cold, the unbreathable air, the condition of the poor will not be alleviated by James's remaining in London. But what is only potentially heartless actualizes itself when he chooses that season of widespread distress as the occasion for a paean to the country house. The sought after "confinement of one's vision," seems ungenerous, to say the least, and no aspect of James's willed limitation of his vision—and so of sympathy—is more ignoble than his restricting true national character to the class that had the "social genius" to fill its large and well-staffed houses with agreeable guests at a time when those guests had they remained in the city would have been inconvenienced by the sight of the suffering poor. This is James at his least gracious. One is reminded of Poe's "Masque of the Red Death," in which the palace of the noble revelers who have quarantined themselves from the plague that ravages their country is nevertheless penetrated by the plague, and tempted to long for a parallel intrusion of the excluded into the country house at which James spends his holiday season away from those who lack the "social genius" to dwell in country houses.

Perhaps some such reaction is anticipated by James because with an impeccable critical instinct he closes his sketch by joining the social distress he has left with the hospitality to which he has fled. On Christmas Eve his hostess takes him along to the workhouse where she distributes presents to the children. James searches to find a face such as Oliver Twist's that looks cut out for romantic adventures. But those he saw "were made of very common clay indeed, and a certain number of them were idiotic. . . . The scene was a picture I shall not forget, with its curious mixture of poetry and sordid prose—the dying wintry light in the big bare, stale room; the beautiful Lady Bountiful, standing in the twinkling glory of the Christmas-tree; the little multitude of staring and wondering, yet perfectly expressionless faces" (p. 224). This picture with Christmas lights illuminating the benefactress while the children stand in the dimness of the dying light of winter, necessary but inarticulate participants in the scene, may be taken as a microcosm of English society as James perceived and, it is difficult not to conclude, approved of it.

The physical ugliness of vast stretches of London and the mean condition of large segments of the English population spoke to James of the superb force that organized the mighty British whole and assigned each part its role. This theme emerged explicitly in his description of a midsummer journey down to Greenwich on a sixpenny steamer. "Few European cities," he remarks, "have a finer river than the Thames, but none certainly has expended more ingenuity in producing a sordid river front. . . . A damp-looking dirty blackness is the universal tone" (p. 140). Within the vista that he depicts the social seamlessly merges with the physical as the poor, those who belong "to the classes bereft of lustre," assume a greyness that harmonizes with the sooty backs of warehouses and the opacity of the turbid stream. Far from depressing, however, the murky scene, this time lit not from a physical source such as the twinkling Christmas tree but from a mental illumination, exhilarates James:

Like so many of the aspects of English civilisation that are untouched by elegance or grace, it [the river vista] has the merit of expressing something very serious. Viewed in this intellectual light the polluted river, the sprawling barges, the dead-faced warehouses, the frowsy people, the atmospheric impurities become richly suggestive. It sounds rather absurd, but all this smudgy detail may remind you of nothing less than the wealth and power of the British Empire at large; so that a kind of metaphysical magnificence hovers over the scene, and supplies what may be literally wanting. (p. 141)

Unlike his visit to the country house, on the river journey James is a detached observer not a participant in the scene he observes, responding with an "imaginative thrill" to the essential reality—the "metaphysical magnificence"—he discerns behind the sordid facade.

Wealth, power, and empire do not appear as explicit themes in James's great fictions but they are the conditions that enable his characters to engage in the personal relationships that constitute his plots. His own wealth, such as it was, depended on his daily labors as a writer, his power was that of expression, and his empire consisted of an always uncertain readership. But like his characters he, too, required the surroundings of wealth, power, and empire for the realization of what he regarded as his best self. *English Hours* demands of the reader that the criticism which can be justly aimed at James's personal attitude toward the poor and powerless be put in the balance against the commanding impersonal authority exerted by his images of the social whole.

English Hours contained sixteen sketches, twelve of which had been written in the 1870s and then published in either *Transatlantic Sketches* or *Portraits of Places*. The remaining four sketches, dating from 1888, 1890, 1897, and 1905 possess neither the open-eyed touristic sprightliness of the sightseeing pieces written prior to James's settlement in London nor the self-reflexive analytic strength of the pieces written immediately after. James no longer needed the genre to supply a significant portion of his income and he had manifestly lost interest in it.

The same difference between early and late marks the twenty-two sketches in *Italian Hours* (1909). The eighteen that had appeared in periodicals before 1875, reappeared in *Transatlantic Sketches,* or in periodicals in the next nine years, and reappeared yet again in *Portraits of Places,* are superior in content and spirit to the four composed somewhat dutifully in later years.

Italy beyond all lands had early charmed James and called forth almost unqualified enthusiasms. As Morton Dauwen Zabel noted in his discussion of James the traveler, James personally was most deeply involved in the life and culture of France, England, and America: "He wrote about all three of them as a traveler: they obliged him to be critic, analyst, and moralist." But he found "the deepest spiritual and aesthetic affinity of his life" in Italy.[17] The sketches in *Italian Hours* that were composed in the early 1870s radiate a vivacity of spirit, an intelligent interest in people as well as monuments, and a passion for the very air of Italy. Everything pleases, and James gracefully takes the reader with him to experience the pleasures. Since he travels alone and knows no one in Italy, at least so far as the sketches are concerned, he is ready to talk to whoever seems willing to talk to him—a peasant on the road, a waiter at an inn—and his genuine interest in them and appreciation of their conversation nicely harmonizes with the urbanity of his style, grounding it in a world before words. "The gossip of an inn-waiter ought, perhaps, to be beneath the dignity of even such meagre history as this," James writes, "but I confess that when I have come in from my strolls with a kind of irritated sense of the dumbness of stones and mortar, I have listened with a certain avidity, over my dinner, to the proferred confidence of the worthy man who stands by with a napkin" (TS, p. 262).* For James the discreet conversation of the waiter serves to illustrate the natural grace and tact of the Italians of his class, socially far beneath the all but illiterate nobility yet possessed of a solid sense of self and a confidence in their relation to the world.

And since he travels alone, James is always alert to the passing details of the everyday life that surrounds him. His response to the Ducal Palace in Venice and the paintings of Tintoretto and Veronese is memorable, but no more so than his observation of a child eating an ice in a café in Siena. The latter speaks to him of the theatricality of Italian conversation, the manner in which gesture dominates words, and to describe it is to locate his reader in the living reality of Italy. Enjoying his *demi-tasse* at the Caffé Greco James sees "a little Sienese of I hardly know what exact age—the age of inarticulate sounds and the experimental use of spoon." The boy is sitting on his father's knee and eating a

---

*Those pieces in *Italian Hours* that first appeared in *Transatlantic Sketches* are quoted from the latter work in order to stay closer to James's early impressions.

strawberry ice with a spoon but when all that remains is a crimson liquid his mother confiscates the spoon, expecting the child to drink the remainder. The child's eloquent protest engages James. He does not cry but with "exquisitely modulated gestures" pleads his case. "He did everything that a man of forty would have done if he had been pouring out a flood of sonorous eloquence. He shrugged his shoulders and wrinkled his eyebrows, tossed out his hands and folded his arms, obtruded his chin and bobbed about his head—and at last, I am happy to say, recovered his spoon" (TS, pp. 260–61). As we follow the details of the child's pantomime, in addition to experiencing James's sense of the vivacity of Italian conversation we become aware of the companionless condition that led the observer to pay such close attention to so small an incident, and this awareness attaches us to him. Reading, too, is an act of solitary observation.

In later years James was to have a network of affluent friends, some Italian but most English or American, who resided in Italy, yet the sketches written in those years are somber—even rather disagreeable. No longer a tourist himself, when he goes to Italy to stay with friends and revisit familiar sites he is disturbed by the tourists who have made of cities such as Venice a "peep-show." Now invited into the interiors that exist behind the facades that fascinated his younger self he withdraws from his earlier enthusiasms as if to have them would be to participate in the barbarity of the tourists he deplores. He is inside, they outside, and in parallel with this condition his sketches are concerned with his interior, how he feels, rather than with any Italian exteriors, sights that are shared by the philistines.

The Venice of the earlier pieces is well-lit and described with excitement in an elegantly appealing prose. In the later pieces on Venice the light dims down to shadows and the darkness encourages James to indulge associations that are exclusively his in a prose of hovering abstractions. There is nothing pictured outside his mind to which the reader can attach his ruminations. "Dear old Venice," James writes in 1899, "has lost her complexion, her figure, her reputation, her self-respect; and yet with it all, has so puzzlingly not lost a shred of her distinction . . . one clings, even in the face of the colder stare, to one's prized Venetian privilege of making the sense of doom and decay a part of every impression." What sights in Venice, one may ask, induce this sense of loss? But sights are precisely what are to be avoided. James arrives by gondola at night, because it is "the real time," when you don't see but feel. "These are the moments," he says, "when you are most daringly Venetian, most content to leave cheap trippers and other aliens the high light of the mid-lagoon and the pursuit of pink and gold.* The splendid day is good enough for *them;* what is best for you is to stop at last, as you are now stopping, among clustered *pali* and softly-shifting poops and prows, at a great flight of water-steps that play their admirable part in the general effect of a great entrance" (IH, pp. 61–62). Thus saying he moves in the darkness from his gondola onto the water steps and through the great entrance into the palazzo. But the door closes behind him and the reader is left outside with the cheap trippers. In marked contrast to the inclusive spirit of his early travels James's Italy has become one of exclusion.

A good deal may be said for this and the few other late pieces on Italy insofar as they speak to us of Henry James in his maturity and the efflorescence of his late style. In a piece written some thirty years later, for example, the 1873 Siena of the inn-waiter and the experimental user of spoons fades into an impression that overwhelms its physical referent as James now visits with a nameless companion and their carriage enters "the great cloistered square, lonely, bleak, and stricken in the almost aching vision, more frequent in the Italy of to-day than anywhere in the world of the uncalculated waste of myriad forms of piety, forces of labour, beautiful fruits of genius" (IH, p. 236). All of the late pieces on Italy speak of this pain, the ache of one who no longer seeing with the eyes of his earlier years transfers his tragic sense of the changes time wrought in himself to an outside world he no longer cares to depict.

---

*How marvelously these colors had burst upon his sight years before when he landed on the Continent from England!

At a psychological midpoint between his youthful enthusiasms and the weary sadness of his maturity, however, James wrote the greatest of his Italian sketches, one that retains his avid passion for all things Italian yet recognizes not just the inevitability but the rightness of the changes that are pushing Italy into the modern world and eroding many of its charms. Indeed, "Italy Revisited," first published in two parts in the *Atlantic Monthly* in 1878, republished in *Portraits of Places* and finally again in *Italian Hours,* is among the finest appreciations of nineteenth-century Italy by any foreign traveler.

James had arrived in Italy fresh from witnessing the French elections of October, 1877 in which the republicans overwhelmed the reactionary party then in power. He had identified with the liberal cause, as his meditations in the Rheims cathedral revealed, and he found the winds of change were also blowing in Italy, with cultural as well as political consequences. "That the people who but three hundred years ago had the best taste in the world should now have the worst; that having produced the noblest, liveliest, costliest works, they should now be given up to the manufacture of objects at once ugly and paltry . . . all this is a perplexity to the observer of actual Italian life" (IH, p. 102). But a visitor should contemplate the matter further: "After thinking of Italy as historical and artistic it will do him no harm to think of her for a while as panting both for a future and for a balance at the bank" (p. 102). Such aspirations, James recognized, might not sit well with a foreigner who arrives wishing to experience what Byron and Ruskin (and perhaps the Henry James of 1873?) have led him to desire, but young Italians were heartily tired of being admired for their eyelashes and of preserving for the world a museum that existed in the new day but bore no relation to it. One evening in Florence, James said by way of illustration, he had strolled in the hills on which olives and villas mingled and breathing in the very ambience of the unchanged Italy that was so precious to him arrived at a wayside shrine

in which, before some pious daub of an old-time Madonna, a little votive lamp glimmered through the evening air. The hour, the atmosphere, the place, the twinkling taper, the sentiment of the observer, the thought that some one had been rescued from an assassin, or from some other peril and had set up a little grateful altar in consequence against the yellow-plastered wall of a tangled *podere;* all this led me to approach the shrine with a reverent, an emotional step. I drew near it, but after a few steps I paused. I became aware of an incongruous odour; it seemed to me that the evening air was charged with a perfume which, although to a certain extent familiar, had not hitherto associated itself with rustic frescoes and wayside altars. I wondered, I gently sniffed, and the question so put left me no doubt. The odour was that of petroleum; the votive taper was nourished with the essence of Pennsylvania. I confess that I burst out laughing . . . to me the thing served as a symbol of Italy of the future. (pp. 104–5)

James's acceptance of Young Italy is in keeping with his sense that the past that is valuable is the past that is continuous with the present rather than a past that is locked in place for the modern gazer. As a consequence, at the age of thirty-five he is far more willing to do battle with the Ruskin who informed a good many of his early impressions, especially with Ruskin's irritation (in *Mornings in Florence*) at the way in which the new Italy was wrecking the old that he cherished. "It seems to me," wrote James, "that it savours of arrogance to demand of any people as a right of one's own, that they shall be artistic." The natural reply Young Italy makes is that if you want the artistic be artistic yourself. "When a people produces beautiful statues and pictures," James continued, "it gives us something more than is set down in the bond, and we must thank it for its generosity; and when it stops producing them or caring for them we may cease thanking but we hardly have a right to begin and rail" (p. 114). The sentiment, as indeed the entire piece in which it appears, is admirable: Henry James the traveler at his best, recognizing the aspiration of the land he visits as well as the aspiration that brought him there and accepting his responsibility for the changes

that aesthetically he might deplore because it is, after all, as a bene-
ficiary of the new that he is able to visit the old.

In "Italy Revisited" James also attacks anew the dilemma that in an
earlier year had sent his friend to Munich while he remained at Rome.

> A traveller is often moved to ask himself whether it has been
> worth while to leave his home—whatever his home may have
> been—only to encounter new forms of human suffering, only to
> be reminded that toil and privation, hunger and sorrow and sor-
> did effort, are the portion of the mass of mankind. To travel is, as
> it were, to go to the play, to attend a spectacle; and there is some-
> thing heartless in stepping forth to foreign streets to feast on
> "character" when character consists of the slightly different cos-
> tume in which labour and want present themselves. (p. 106)

The travel writer, moreover, not only attends the play but writes it,
presenting the spectacle to others. Is not his heartlessness thereby increased by his inviting others to participate in it?

Characteristically, James responds to the perplexity by offering an
anecdote. On one of his mountain strolls he had encountered a young
man sauntering along with his coat slung over his shoulders and his hat
slanted over his ear like a cavalier in an opera, and the young man,
indeed, was singing with operatic flourishes. It seemed a picturesque
accident, just what the travel writer required, a romantic figure to set
off the landscape in his composition. But the young man approached
him to ask for a match for his cigar and in the ensuing exchange James
learned he was a communist who longed for a bloody revolution in Italy
like that of 1789 in France—he would gladly, he said, behead the royal
family. This colorful complement to the landscape was in reality an
unhappy, underfed, and unemployed human being: "This made it very
absurd to me to have looked at him simply as a graceful ornament to the
prospect" (p. 107).

If the circumstance of the young man's wanting a light for the remains of his cigar put an end to that romantic composition, how did the

event leave James's other Italian sketches which were composed from picturesque accidents and uninformed by knowledge of the lives of their human subjects? James's answer is tentative. Finally, he tells himself, "the sum of Italian misery is, on the whole, less than the sum of the Italian knowledge of life," (p. 106) and it is the latter that as a travel writer he celebrates. But the contention, he recognizes, is shaky and he consoles himself with the thought that even if his observations of foreign lands are superficial and easily crushed by an inhabitant those observations are not addressed to the inhabitant and so what he calls his "fancy-pictures" may still serve the ends of his readers. This contention, however, seems even shakier than that about Italian misery and with his fine intelligence James could not but perceive this. He was at an impasse, honestly arrived at and squarely faced. "Italy Revisited," 1878, tells us more about his withdrawal from the genre of the travel sketch than does a consideration of his financial situation. From that date he wrote relatively few short pieces and in them focused on his feelings rather than the scene before his eyes, and the two full-length travel books he subsequently wrote reflected his awareness of the likely superficiality and potential heartlessness of the travel sketch.

   A Little Tour in France (1885) and *The American Scene* (1907) faced the issue in contrasting ways. A narrative of a journey he had undertaken in order to write the book, the *Little Tour* is, in effect, a guidebook to the château country and the towns of the Midi, in which, as James stated, he was primarily concerned with delineating the "superficial aspects of things" (*France,* p. 156)—by which he meant the pictorial rather than the analytical. Proclaiming himself a "sentimental traveler," he described the places on his route and selected major sites, occasionally supplying archaeological and historical details as his casual narrative moved from place to place. Conversely, in *The American Scene* superficiality was disdained. Characterizing himself both as an "inquiring stranger" and an "initiated native" James used the loose travelogue structure to conduct an all but relentless analysis of American society as it manifested itself in the structures that it built (and tore down), the cultural institutions it supported, and the social behavior it displayed.

When an editor at Harper's suggested to James that he write a travel book about France, Leon Edel said, "this seemed to him a profitable thing to do" (3:51), and in October 1882 he set off from Paris on a tour the route of which took the shape of an oval severely dented at the top: southwest to the Atlantic at La Rochelle, southeast to the Mediterranean at Narbonne, then easterly along the coast, turning northeasterly inland toward Nimes and then due north to Dijon for a northwesterly return to Paris. He visited châteaux, Roman ruins, the celebrated cities of the wine markets, those with names that resonate in the history of Europe and the literature of travel, such as Montpellier, Arles, and Avignon, and those with literary associations, such as authors' birthplaces or scenes in their writings. Once back in England he rather swiftly composed his manuscript from the journal he had kept and although Harper's had since rescinded its interest Osgood took the book and published it in 1884, although it bore an 1885 date. It has been in print ever since, a discriminating guide for tourists who would undertake the journey, encouraging selectivity and a guiltless dismissal of what does not interest even if the dauntingly detailed guidebooks star it, and a lively, informative narrative for the armchair traveler, or, indeed, all thoughtful readers. Throughout his *Little Tour* James's aim was to provide pictures, and while these of necessity included descriptions of eminent sites such as the walls of Carcassonne or the Maison Carree at Nimes the charm of the book derives in greater part from his manner of paying as great attention to the bearing and business of persons in a town square or to the content and color of a field seen from a railway window as to the interior furnishings of a castle.

When a revised edition of the book appeared in 1900 it was illustrated with ninety-four drawings by Joseph Pennell, and in his brief preface to that edition James said that from the start his expectation had been that the work would be accompanied by illustrations although for reasons that he claimed were lost to him the first edition was not. He regretted this, he said, because he felt his verbal pictures were designed to "cling" to accompanying drawings. He thus raises an interesting issue for the critical reader because so far as the fiction of his day was concerned James was strongly opposed to the publishing fashion of accompanying the text with pictures, as was the case with, for example, Mark Twain's works: "I hate the hurried little subordinate part that one plays in the catchpenny picture-book—and the negation of all literature that the insolence of the picture-book imposes" (Edel, 4:95). Presumably, a travel book was not "literature" in this sense and so there was no contradiction in writing a text that would attach itself to illustrations. But only presumably because James insisted that his focus was on "perception of surface" rather than "perception of very complex underlying matters" (CTWCon, pp. 3–4) and that he dealt with the very same details that an illustrator would picture. As a result, if his text was not vulnerable to negation by an artist's drawings of the selfsame subject, it was at least put into competition with them—which picture, the verbal or the spatial, was subordinate to the other? Did pictures illustrate text or text serve as an explanation of the pictures?

In 1884, the same year as the publication of his *Little Tour,* in his essay, "The Art of Fiction," James said that exactness, the truth of detail, was the supreme virtue of the novel. Here it is, he said, that the novelist "competes with his brother the painter in *his* attempt to render the look of things."[18] Further in the essay he spoke against the notion that narrative and description were separate literary procedures with separate effects, insisting that the two fused, serving one another: description, he said, had a narrative intent and narrative was descriptive. Verbal pictures were thus assigned a function distinctly different from those drawn by the painter because they were carriers of narrative as well as descriptive. Although James was, to be sure, talking of the novel, since he did so in the same year that he was seeing his *Little Tour* through the press it is difficult not to imagine his remarks applying also to a travel book that was organized as a narrative and that he initially believed would be illustrated. In this context, the most striking characteristic of the verbal pictures James drew is that unlike the artist's pictures which did eventually accompany the text his functioned as incidents in his travel as well as descriptions of sights seen. Physical movement from one locale to the next and mental movement from impression to reflection situated his descriptions as continuations of his narrative. When Pennell's drawings finally did accompany the text, they formed their own separate account of the sites James described rather than picturing what James had been putting into words.

James's and Pennell's respective treatments of the Pont Du Gard may be taken as an example of this distinctness and a demonstration of the particular effect James achieves. Arrived at the site as the afternoon was fading, James sat for a soundless hour facing the monumental structure in order to receive, he said, a complete impression: "there was a fascination in the object I had come to see. It came to pass that at the same time I discovered in it a certain stupidity, a vague brutality. That element is rarely absent from great Roman work, which is wanting in the nice adaptation of the means to the end. The means are always exaggerated; the end is so much more than attained. The Roman rigidity was apt to overshoot the mark, and I suppose a race which could do nothing small is as defective as a race that can do nothing great" (pp. 161–62). This remark is followed by an insistence upon the "manly beauty" of the structure achieved by the number of arches in each tier growing "smaller and more numerous as they ascend" (p. 162).

Pennell's full-page drawing contrasts with rather than illustrates James's description. The artist does not face the structure so as to see the tiers of its ascension as did James but views it lengthwise as if starting to walk down the path running parallel to it. The Pont stretches straight on along the viewer's left and from that angle one sees only the well-lit lowest rank of arches which as they proceed down the shrinking distance achieve their effortless task of upholding whatever is in the grey above. Although far from airy, it is also far less brutal than the structure James sees face on, is more brightly lit, and affords no evidence for James's striking observation about the Roman inability to do anything in moderation.

Of all European countries, France offered James an example of the highest civilization. It was in the French language that he was educated during his crucial boyhood years and as a group the French writers whom he had met in Flaubert's circle in Paris at the outset of his own literary career together with Turgenev, who lived in exile in Paris, were for him the most accomplished and admirable of his literary contemporaries in any country. Yet, strikingly, unlike the Italy for which he had a profound aesthetic affinity or the imperial England which for all its ugliness magnetized him, France drew from him a conflicted response. The very mastery of the language that gained him access to the circle of French writers and the nuances of French culture served all the more to remind him of his being an outsider. For him, as Morton Dauwen Zabel observed, France "remained from first to last a test of his critical acumen: invaluable, imaginatively bracing, but never a home for himself or his art" (Zabel, p. 37).

James's somewhat uneasy relationship with France informs his critical essays and finds some reflection in his fiction. It may also in less profound fashion be detected in his *Little Tour*. Since he there wished to keep his impressions, as he said in his 1900 preface, "immediate, easy and consciously limited," he mentioned his discontentments lightly, even amusingly. Nevertheless, it is noticeable that as his tour progresses so he becomes increasingly vexed by the circumstances of his journey and the nature of the places he visits. At the outset he had cheerfully announced that there was more to the *doux pays de France* than Paris and he intended "to look it well in the face" (p. 1). In the event, what he looked at did not altogether please. The irksome seems in part to stem from his gathering discomfort with the genre of the tour book and its demand for surface impressions—he was never again to write such a book. But his repeated reports of annoyances, albeit amusingly expressed, speak also of an inability or unwillingness to come to terms with France as he had in differing ways formed defined relationships with Italy and England.

At the great wine exposition in Bordeaux: "I drank a most vulgar fluid" (pp. 121–22).

Of Toulouse: "The oddity is that the place should be both animated and dull" (p. 126).

At Villeneuve: the situation of the nuns is "most provincial," their residence a "doleful establishment," and the small shabby houses are "almost hovels." Looking at the remains of the Middle Ages one comes to the conclusion that "The theory that this was a period of general insanity was not altogether indefensible" (p. 209).

"It is a melancholy fact that the walls of Avignon had never impressed me at all, and I had never taken the trouble to make the circuit. They are continuous and complete, but for some mysterious reason they fail of their effect" (p. 210).

"I had a prejudice against Vaucluse, against Petrarch, even against the incomparable Laura" (p. 213).

The French railways are miserable: the "despotic *gare;* the deadly *salle d'attente,* the insufferable delays over one's luggage, the porter-less platform, the overcrowded and illiberal train" (p. 225).

Macon "struck me, somehow, as suffering from a chronic numbness." The house in which Alphonse de Lamartine was born, described by him as a lofty structure with a large portal, has, in fact, two meager stories and an air of extreme shabbiness. "Lamartine was accused of writing history incorrectly, and apparently he started wrong at first: it had never become clear to him where he was born" (p. 227).

"If Dijon was a good deal of a disappointment, I felt, therefore, that I could afford it. It was a time for me to reflect, also, that for my disappointments, as a general thing, I had only myself to thank. . . . At any rate, I will say plumply that the ancient capital of Burgundy is wanting in character; it is not up to the mark" (p. 240).

And yet, remarkably, the effect of the *Little Tour* as a whole is to make such a journey seem inviting, its itinerary well worth following with the book in hand as a guide. A number of sites, such as Chenonceaux or Carcassonne, seem all the more appealing because of the favorable impression they make on an eye that dares be critical about what does not attract it regardless of guidebook fame. Additionally, the easy-flowing narrative encourages the would-be traveler to form sensory impres-

sions in advance of consulting printed information and to fit the latter to
the former: "However late in the evening I may arrive at a place, I
cannot go to bed without an impression" (p. 72). Traveling that way
seems appealing. And most importantly, the emphasis on subjective
impressions collapses the distinction between travel and the written
report of it. Untoward incidents and tedious sights converted into literature become experiences well worth having.

The sensitive tourist travels, finally, in order to add to his own capacity to experience life fully. For James this meant visiting other civilized
peoples whose ways of life addressed the same questions that the tourist's native patterns of behavior did but answered them in ways that
amplified the tourist's sense of life's possibilities. Unlike travelers such
as Taylor, or Twain in his last long journey, James was unconcerned to
question the principles of civilization as the western world understood
them. He sought rather to advance them. The refinement to which he
was committed valued the legacy of the past as manifested in monuments of paint, of stone, of words. But he located the ultimate value of a
sense of the past in the societies, high or low, that lived life more fully because they were the inheritors of the experience of generations of predecessors and adhered to the pattern of behavior that had been conveyed to them. James does not mention history or custom or tradition in
speaking of a satisfying moment in Le Mans, yet without their ambient
presence he could not have received the impression he described:

> I sat before dinner at the door of one of the cafés in the market-
> place with a *bitter-et-curaçao* (invaluable pretext at such an
> hour!) to keep me company. I remember that in this situation
> there came over me an impression which both included and ex-
> cluded all possible disappointments. The afternoon was warm
> and still; the air was admirably soft. The good Manceaux, in little
> groups and pairs, were seated near me. My ear was soothed by
> the fine shades of French enunciation, by the detached syllables
> of that perfect tongue. There was nothing particular in the pros-
> pect to charm; it was an average French view. Yet I felt a charm,

a kind of sympathy, a sense of the completeness of French life. (pp. 90–91)

A comparable American moment did not seem possible.

In December 1883, shortly after writing *A Little Tour in France,* Henry James returned to the United States in response to news of his father's illness. He arrived too late to see his father and the succeeding nine months of his American visit were taken up with his duties as executor of Henry James, Sr.'s estate. He was back in London in September.

Nineteen years later, while seeing American friends off on their voyage back to America on a ship called the *Minnehaha*—an echo of the Longfellow of his Cambridge youth—James, who had not been back to his native land since his father's death, had a sudden urge to join them. "Now or never is my chance; stay and sail—borrow clothes, borrow a toothbrush, borrow a bunk, borrow $100; you will never be so near to it again" (Edel, 5:230). Although he did not give in to the impulse, the idea of going "home," as he put it, took an increasingly strong hold on him and he began to plan a book of American impressions as a means of financing his visit. When he boarded the North German Lloyd's *Kaiser Wilhelm II,* bound from Southampton to Hoboken, he had already made both magazine and book arrangements with Colonel George Harvey, head of the house of Harper's, and it was Harvey who first entertained him after he docked on August 30th, 1904, after a twenty-year absence.

James spent the first 36 hours of his American return at Harvey's summer home in Deal Beach, New Jersey, where his host had gathered a company of the prosperous and prominent to meet his honored guest. Mark Twain was of the party, and it was among this group of affable, business-minded, and thinly cultured Americans that, according to Edel, "the note of affluence and advertising, of impermanence, of a civilization created wholly for commerce" (5:247) was struck for James, a note that grew into a crescendo of antipathies as he progressed on his American travels, passing back and forth between New England and New York, journeying as far south as Florida and as far west as Seattle.

James's entrance upon the American scene as caricatured by F. Opper in *American Weekly,* the Sunday supplement of Hearst's *New York Journal,* January 21, 1906 (from the Collections of the Library of Congress).

After eight months of railroads and hotels, of giving lectures, being interviewed, and attending fêtes in his honor, James sailed for Liverpool on July 5th, 1905.

The American Scene (1907) is loosely organized along a route from New England to Florida. Each chapter takes its rise in a specific city or locale that James had visited, but the sequence of chapters does not correspond to any one actual journey. Rather, James had stopped at some of the cities discussed, especially New York, more than once, but in his book impressions based on multiple visits were synthesized into single units as he arranged his travelogue down the Atlantic seaboard

from New Hampshire to Florida. Although he omitted his western jour-
ney from the geographical spine of his chapters, his critical analysis of
America and Americans derived in some part from his sense of the
West, especially of its unshorn spaces.

The dominant picture painted in *The American Scene* is one of a
crassly materialistic society that young as it may be is nevertheless committed to the systematic elimination of whatever is not new rather than
the nurturing of continuity, so that a sense of the past—of tradition,
shared manners, inherited values—is ruthlessly obstructed. Personal
histories have no objects to which to attach themselves as buildings that
once were family homes are torn down to make room for newer structures. A skyline once defined by church steeples is now dominated by
skyscrapers that in their rise symbolize commerce's eclipse of older
public values. The landed class descended from the original settlers,
whose sense of history should have shaped national identity, has abandoned this responsibility with the consequence that for the waves of
immigrants breaking on the American shore being an American means
only getting more materially than they once had. Otherwise they, Italians, Jews, Irish, exist in a cultural limbo with nothing of the beauty,
order, or restraint that they had left behind in Europe.

Once upon a time, James reflected when he visited Newport, there
was a society that did not just resort there in the summer, fleeing to the
city in the winter, but lived there year-round. They were cosmopolites,
"united by three common circumstances, that of their having for the
most part more or less lived in Europe, that of their sacrificing openly to
the ivory idol whose name is leisure, and that, not least, of a formed
critical habit."[19] Such a society offered promise for American civilization. But the cosmopolites now live in Europe, or, remaining in America,
reside in the city and participate in the national devotion to commerce,
avoiding as shamefully unpatriotic the improvement of leisure that enables the cultivation of critical habits. "James," as Edel summarized his
reaction, "found America terribly wanting. It was founded on violence,
plunder, loot, commerce; its monuments were built neither for beauty,
nor for glory, but for obsolescence" (5:324).

Yet as persistent as James's dismayed assault on American values is, the scenes in his book are so varied in content, his analyses so penetrating, and the intricacy of his style so commands attention that his discontents never become a litany. As Mark Twain seized upon the serial nature of the travel narrative—one place follows another without the causal linkage required of fictional narrative—to indulge his wandering memory, so James seized upon it to indulge his thoughts, traveling in and out of the scenes that ostensibly lay before him with so intense an intellection that his narrative calls into question whether he reacts in thought to what he sees or constructs what he sees from what he thinks.[20]

The American Scene was written after James had completed his American visit—it is not a revised series of journal entries. But prior to book publication most of its parts did appear in magazines and the early chapters, especially, reflect James's having formed his governing sense of the whole very early on in his travels. Although his authorial self-characterization was that of the "inquiring stranger" or "restless analyst" there is something revealingly overwrought when at the outset of his journey he calls himself the "victim" of his subject, as if the subject of his book had already been settled in his mind prior to travel and he was journeying through America to serve it rather than receiving the unrehearsed impressions that would form it.

"Yes; it was all actually going to be drama, and *that* drama; than which nothing could be more to the occult purpose of the confirmed, the systematic story-seeker, or to that even of the mere ancient contemplative person curious of character" (p. 12), he insisted at the start. After this there follows a remarkable, extraordinarily abstruse even for James, representation of the task that lies before him as a traveling writer. The given of the task is a society that is "reaching out into the apparent void for the amenities, the consummations, after having earnestly gathered in so many of the preparations and necessities." The chore for the narrator is to "gouge an interest *out* of the vacancy." As a consequence, what is in operation at the start and throughout *The American Scene* is not the American scene itself, which is designated a "void," a "vacancy," so much as it is the consciousness that will fill it in. As Sharon Cameron points out, in so positioning his consciousness against a void James, in effect, eliminates other people from his design. In his Italian ramblings as in his English and his French, other people had entered James's frame to temper his impressions. But in America they are absent except as unresisting aggregates with which he fills in the blank that he has predicated. One is reminded that thirty years before *The American Scene* in *Transatlantic Sketches* James had written that one sees very much what one's capricious intellect projects there. In *The American Scene* the operation of the intellect is far from capricious and determines all that is seen or, put another way, James's analyzing mind precedes every scene so that the scene appears as a projection of his consciousness rather than an impression made upon it.

At a few points in the book James uncharacteristically but revealingly constructed images that conflict with the picture they were meant to serve, and at these extrusive points one senses an authorial agitation in excess of any represented object. His detestation of the skyscraper, for example, is articulated splendidly at some length in more than one place. Yet in the vehemence of his distaste he can never quite find an apt image, and his insistence on the wrong, or inept, image suggests a prejudice that precedes judgment. In New York the skyscrapers that overshadow older buildings crush them "quite as violent children stamp on snails and caterpillars" (p. 81). The brusque motion of the children works against the immobile verticality of the skyscraper and the violence of the squashing vulgarizes the idea that the rise of the skyscraper is representative of an uncultured commercial civilization that overshadows all other aspects of the society. In Boston, the high-rise buildings that swallow the Athenaeum are like "School-bullies who hustle and pummel some studious little boy" (p. 233). Again violent motion is conflictingly assigned to objects whose distinguishing feature is their fixedness. In both cases brutal children are invoked and no further comment is required, it would seem, than to recognize that James after a twenty-year absence is both in New York and Boston revisiting scenes of his own childhood and assigning to the dominant architectural feature of the civic terrain aversions that have their origins in a private landscape.

A revealing extrusiveness again appears when James turns his attention to the massed communities of immigrants. When he approached Rutgers Street in lower Manhattan and first saw a Jewry that appeared to have burst all bounds in its swarming he received the impression of a human horde increasing like a flood of rising waters that reaches even above the housetops: "It was as if we had been thus, in the crowded, hustled roadways, where multiplication, multiplication of everything, was the dominant note, at the bottom of some vast sallow aquarium in which innumerable fish, of over-developed proboscis, were to bump together, for ever, amid heaped spoils of the sea" (p. 131). The image of the sea is rather mixed—it is both the rising tide of proliferating Jewry and yet the water in which that Jewry swims—but is effective in conveying James's consciousness of the New York Jews as not just massed but proliferating uncontrollably. America is being drowned.

He does not, however, rest with the image of the sea but is driven to construct another, and both the fervor with which he proceeds to exceed what is already sufficient as well as the content of the image itself indicate a prejudicial outlook that determines what will be seen: "There are small strange animals, known to natural history, snakes or worms, I believe, who, when cut into pieces, wriggle away contentedly and live in the snippet as completely as in the whole. So the denizens of the New York Ghetto, heaped as thick as the splinters on the table of a glassblower, had each, like the fine glass particle, his or her individual share of the whole hard glitter of Israel" (p. 132). The fish have descended to the status of snakes or worms and the proliferation that threatens to drown America is not a matter of multiplication through immigration and procreation. Rather, even if severed, or precisely *because* they have been severed, they will continue to double in number. Then, curiously, the image contradicts itself, and glass splinters, in their brittle fragility the very opposite of wriggling sensate creatures, are made to stand for the same subjects in order to emblematize the Jews' essential resistance to assimilation into the American scene. Despite the "over-

The kind of street scene on New York's Lower East Side that so appalled James it led to an uncharacteristic barrage of mixed images (from a photo spread across two pages in E. Idell Zeisloft, *The New Metropolis,* 1899).

developed proboscis," of the earlier passage, Leon Edel has insisted against others that James's attitude toward the New York Jewry he visited is not anti-Semitic but consistent with his active interest in "the study of racial traits and national characteristics."[21] And certainly James had been sharply critical in his anatomy of certain English classes and his description of typical French behavior. But the derangement of images as he proceeded from fish to worms to glass splinters suggests an abhorrence in excess of representable causes.

In his preface James wrote, "I would take my stand on my gathered impressions, since it was all for them, for them only, that I returned; I would in fact go to the stake for them—which is a sign of the value that I both in particular and in general attach to them and that I have endeavoured to preserve for them in this transcription" (pp. xxv-xxvi). This attitude contrasts strongly with the manner in which with a seeming diffidence—a flexibility even in certainty—he had offered his impressions in earlier travel narratives. Like particular figures of speech that will follow in the book, "go to the stake" seems excessive, a manifestation of the conversion of the passionate pilgrim into a victim. In *English Hours* James had spoken of London as "the capitol of our race" (p. 38) and of himself traveling there as an "American who remounts the stream to the headwaters of his own loyalties" (p. 145). Return to America after a twenty-year absence was a return down the remounted stream, but "our race" had disappeared and the stream had been diverted from its headwaters.

If *The American Scene* is the one of James's travel books in which all images are shaped by preceding persuasions, however, it is also the most profound of his travel books, eliciting from him a consistently high level of analysis in justification of his convictions. Unlike the agitated images that overshoot their ostensible subjects to indicate unarticulated biases, the explicit analyses brilliantly uncover the meaning beneath one social scene after another. In his earlier travel sketches James had frequently conveyed ideas through anecdote or emblem. In the far more ambitious and profounder *American Scene* the figures sometimes go awry but the ideas are brilliantly prescient.

On a Saturday afternoon James paid a visit to the Windsor Theater in New York's Bowery and was instantly fascinated by the vast amount of confectionery being purchased and consumed by the audience. This led him to recall the presence of confectionery shops in other places of public congregation such as railway stations, and he felt that this told him more about the "economic and even the social situation of the masses" he had been observing "than many a circumstance honoured with more attention." At first he wondered what this indicated about wages—how working people could afford so widespread an indulgence—and about manners—the extent to which this was indicative of larger patterns of behavior. But then he broke through to a remarkable conclusion: "Wages, in this country at large, *are* largely manners, the only manners, I think it fair to say, one mostly encounters; the market and the home therefore look alike" (p. 197). Put in other terms, James saw in America the collapse of the distinction between the private (domestic) and public (marketplace) sphere, a separation that for him marked the European cultures he admired, a division that, in his opinion, made civilization possible.

Accordingly, when he turned his attention from the audience to the play on the stage James saw in its predictable compliance with the conventions of popular drama—clichés far from "truth and the facts of life"—a psychological process of Americanizing the immigrant population that paralleled the material process of the fusing of wages and manners:

Nothing (in the texture of that occasion) could have had a sharper interest than this demonstration that, since what we most pretend to do with them is thoroughly to school them, the schooling by our system, cannot begin too soon nor pervade their experience too much. Were they going to rise to it, or rather to fall to it—to *our* instinct, as distinguished from their own, for picturing life? Were they to take our lesson, submissively, in order to get with it our smarter traps and tricks, our superior Yankee machinery (illustrated in the case before them, for instance, by a wonderful folding bed in which the villain of the piece, pursuing the virtuous heroine round and round the room and trying to leap over it after her, is, at the young lady's touch of a hidden spring, engulfed as in the jaws of a crocodile?) Or would it be their dim intellectual resistance, a vague stir in them of some unwitting heritage—of the finer irony, that I should make out, on the contrary, as withstanding the effort to corrupt them, and thus perhaps really promising to react, over the head of our offered, mechanic bribes, on our ingrained intellectual platitude? (pp. 198–99)

The separation of high culture from popular—of highbrow from lowbrow—had accelerated in the second half of the nineteenth century. Very often those who deplored what came to be called the lowbrow did so in a manner that barely disguised the fact that the real object of their contempt was the masses themselves. James's criticism of mass entertainment markedly proceeded from an opposite view, one that respected the cultural values the immigrants brought with them from Europe but deplored the manipulative fantasies for which they were being exchanged. In so doing he also contested the view of those who believe they serve the human dignity of the classes that consume lowbrow entertainment by insisting upon its aesthetic equality with highbrow art. They are, in James's analysis, betraying the capacity of those classes to experience a fuller life than is provided them by methods of artistic production no different than those that produce the candy they consume.

In the social criticism of succeeding chapters James, as in his visit to the Bowery theater, put imagery to the service of thought. The fervor that led in his earlier chapters to a manner in excess of the material it presented disappeared and a series of astute analyses resulted. At the Confederate Museum in Richmond he spoke tellingly of a Southern community now disinherited of art and letters by its compulsive reversion to "the heroic age, the four epic years" of the war (p. 386). At Charleston he weighed the undeniable aesthetic appeal of an antebellum mansion and the almost Venetian promise the city's relation to the sea once had against the aesthetic poverty that had prevailed since the War to remark "Had the *only* focus of life then been Slavery? . . . so that with the extinction of that interest no other of any sort was left" (p. 418). This led, in turn, to a consideration of what he termed the "monomania" of the South and his judgment that the only "Southern" book of any distinction published for many a year was *The Souls of Black Folk* by W. E. B. Du Bois. And in Florida he sketched a prescient profile of what he called "the hotel-spirit": "The jealous cultivation of the common mean, the common mean only, the reduction of everything to an average of decent suitability, the gospel of precaution against the dangerous tendency latent in many things to become too good for their context, so that persons partaking of them may become too good for their company" (p. 442).

James did not write about his western journey, but his American visit took place during the presidency of Theodore Roosevelt, a period in which, thanks in good part to the writings and consciously theatrical exploits of that public figure, the American West came in the public imagination to stand for the virtues that had made America great and were now being threatened in the effete cities of the East. The theme was sounded in Owen Wister's immensely popular novel, *The Virginian* (1902), the book that in effect invented the genre of the Western. It was dedicated to Roosevelt who had read parts in manuscript and made suggestions that were incorporated into it. For Roosevelt, Wister's view of the cowboy as the exact modern equivalent of the chivalric knight of Arthurian lore, and of the West as the continuing scene of the elemental struggle between good and evil that shaped what was best in the American character, was a needed antidote to what he called the "overcivilization" that had led to the effeminacy of Eastern manners. In *The Virginian* the immediate villains are those who would enclose the ranges that in their openness breed manly self-sufficiency free from external regulation, while a remoter threat looming on the near side of the horizon is the advent of commercial society, personified by the fast-talking Jewish traveling salesman.

Both Roosevelt and Wister were scions of the patrician families of the East. When he was in his early twenties, Wister, with his grandmother, Fanny Kemble, and mother, Sarah Butler Wister, had accompanied their close acquaintance Henry James on the initial leg of the journey he described in *A Little Tour in France,* and when James arrived in Charleston on his American tour, Wister, then resident in that city, had been his guide.

Although unstated as such, implicit in *The American Scene* is James's awareness that the new gospel of muscular America had not emerged from the West but was actually the creation of members of the patrician class to which he himself was most closely connected by birth and breeding. They it was who promulgated the message that the authentic America was located in the rough-riding, straight-shooting West where the savage land awakened the atavistic superiority of the Anglo-Saxon male who knew book learning to be woman's business. This model American expressed himself in deeds rather than words. As James saw the matter, it had been the duty of the patrician class to have evolved from its connection to the past a sense of America to which immigrants could be assimilated—this was, as it were, the project he had observed being pursued by men such as Longfellow and Lowell when he as a young man lived in Cambridge. It was the duty of those who had had the advantages of university study and European travel to provide a critical stance with which to counter the meretriciousness of political demagogues and the distortions of mass entertainment, providing a vision of social cohesion that opened American culture to the European stream that flowed into it. But he returned to an America in which the patrician response to the problems raised by the unlicensed sway of commercial interest and the vast influx of immigrants was to glorify the habits of the least civilized region of the nation as the splendid standard of American character. The cultural condition of the deracinated aliens who swarmed into the city with no coherent America to which to attach themselves was not, James believed, the responsibility of the aliens themselves but rather of the members of his own class.

At the conclusion of *The American Scene* in a passage omitted by his publisher from the first American edition because of its potential offensiveness to American readers, James on his return northward from Florida looked from his train window at a landscape without "the honour, the decency or dignity of a road—that most exemplary of all civil creations, and greater even as a note of morality, one often thinks than as a note of facility" (p. 464), and raised the question: "Is the germ of anything finely human, of anything agreeably or successfully social, supposably planted in conditions of such endless stretching and such boundless spreading as shall appear finally to minister but to the triumph of the superficial and the apotheosis of the raw?" (p. 465). It is not difficult to conclude that although he professed to be looking at the landscape south of Washington he was thinking of the myth of the West, the "apotheosis of the raw," promulgated by men who should have known better but were instead arresting, indeed reversing, the promise of American civilization.

The advertisement opposite the title page of Henry James's *Transatlantic Sketches* began with a quotation taken from the *New York Tribune*. "Few men," Bayard Taylor had written there, "have ever been so brilliantly equipped for literary performance. Carefully trained taste, large acquirement of knowledge, experience of lands and races, and association with the best minds, have combined to supply him with all the purely intellectual requisites which an author could desire." No one could have supplied a more authoritative and commercially useful endorsement for a book of travels than Bayard Taylor, "The American Traveler." Since he was a friend of Longfellow's, was a prolific contributor to the *New York Tribune,* and a member of New York literary circles, it is probable that he and James met, yet no such meeting is on record.

James and Twain, however, did know one another. At the outset of his travel-writing career James could not but have been acutely conscious of the way Twain had revolutionized the genre. *Innocents Abroad* was published in 1869, the same year that James had written his brother William about the "vulgar, vulgar, vulgar" American tourists he was encountering in Europe. And in 1875 while living in New York and seeing *Transatlantic Sketches* through the press he was reading the installments of Twain's *Old Times on the Mississippi,* then appearing in the *Atlantic Monthly,* a magazine to which he had contributed some of the sketches he was now putting into his book. "In the day of Mark

Twain," he observed at that time, "there is no harm in being reminded that the absence of drollery may, in a sketch, be compensated by the presence of sublimity" (Edel, 2:185). His remark was possibly a criticism of Twain and a defense of his own approach to Europe's cultural treasures, far different in tone and content from Twain's boisterous debunking. Still, eight years later when *Life on the Mississippi* was published, incorporating into it the *Old Times* chapters that had appeared in the *Atlantic,* James found in that book what he called the "presence of sublimity" (Edel, 5:34). By then he had been in Twain's company on a number of occasions.

For his part, Twain had famously claimed that he would rather be condemned to John Bunyan's heaven than to have to read James's novel, *The Bostonians* (published by Osgood in 1886 after its serialization in the *Century*). Yet as early as 1879 Twain had also referred to James by the title that was in future decades to become synonymous with his authorial presence, calling him a "master."

Twain and James were accomplished men of letters and each could recognize artistry of a high order in the other despite literary differences so fundamental as to seem organic. As celebrities they met and continued to meet at dinners or as guests at the great houses of their common acquaintances when both happened to be in either London or New York at the same time. Each enjoyed a close friendship with William Dean Howells, who was also for each a literary confidant and editor, and when the 250-member National Institute of Arts and Letters decided in December 1904 to elect a much smaller number from its membership to an American Academy of Arts and Letters as a mark of highest distinction, they together with Howells were among the initial fifteen persons chosen as founding members.

It is probable that when Twain and James did meet and have a private moment together they, as fellow professionals, talked about the marketplace for their wares. It is certain that they also talked about the mechanics of writing. In 1896 at the conclusion of his global tour, Twain had settled in London to complete the writing of *Following the Equator,* and there James who was plagued with a wrist made painful by writing learned that Twain composed his works by dictating to a stenographer. He hired a stenographer himself, experimented with the same procedure, and found it so agreeable to both his prose and his carpus that he continued the practice for the remainder of his life. Indeed, the conservative James went the Mark Twain who was addicted to mechanical improvement and its attendant gadgetry one better by dictating to a stenographer who sat at a typewriter and by its means transmitted the spoken words directly onto a typed page. "I was amused when I was in London," Twain wrote Howells, "to have James tell me that he had taken to dictating all his fiction, because he had heard that I always dictated. He makes it go, but if there could be anything worse for me, than a typewriter, it would be a human typewriter" (Edel, 5:34).*

The American writer, James said, "*must* deal, more or less, even if only by implication, with Europe; whereas no European is obliged to deal in the least with America. No one dreams of calling him less complete for not doing so" (Edel, 3:21). Even if one believed that the American Revolution and the consequent founding of the nation started history over again by erasing the relevance of the British institutions that preceded it, freeing men to build their political world anew, American culture unlike American politics did not start over again with the lowering of one flag and the raising of another. English was still the common tongue of the new nation and it carried in its diction and syntax the way of life of the civilization that had shaped it. Europe was, in Hawthorne's phrase, "our old home," and so an ineradicable part of the national memory, regardless of how preferable the American present might be to the European past. Indeed, those who believed in American superiority were all the more dependent upon a sense of Europe.

But if Twain and James were both, in James's term, more complete for dealing with Europe, they also aimed to make America itself more complete because of what they wrote. For the Twain of the earlier travel books this meant ridding Americans of their feeling of inferiority in the

*In the period stenographers who operated typewriters were themselves called "typewriters."

face of Old World culture through a boisterous critique of its shrines and a punishing satire on the tourists who mindlessly worshipped at them. In his last travel book, however, moved by the peoples of color whose lands he visited, Twain recognized that the completion of America could only reside in a recognition of the humanity of its nonwhite populations and an appreciation of the alternatives these populations offered to the avaricious commercialization of American life. Seeing an America that was so far from awareness of this national need that it was bent on the imperial expansion of its racial pretensions he grew bitter. America was less complete than ever.

For James the completion of America resided in an augmented sense of the European past flowing into the American present, and a conservation of those local landmarks that would in time accumulate into a distinctively American heritage that was crucial for the formation of a national civility. All of his travel writings were directly addressed to an American audience and in all save *The American Scene* he sought to recover for his fellow Americans a fresh feeling for the manners and art of Europe that were worthy of respect and even emulation although her political institutions were rejected. He brought the play of imagination to what he saw as he traveled and his resulting impressions worked to civilize not just by their content but by their manner; the very style of his reactions exemplified what it meant to be cultured. But in *The American Scene,* James like Twain, although for quite different reasons, found America to be less complete than ever, as it made a shambles of those vestiges of its past needed to anchor a society in danger of being dashed into fragments by the flood of immigration.

After more than twenty years of London living, Henry James in 1898 moved to the ancient Sussex town of Rye. Fifteen years later, however, then 70 years of age and in ill health, he once again took up residence in London in order to spend his remaining days within earshot of the human mill from which he had drawn his greatest literary energies. He died there on February 28, 1916. Funeral services were held at a church in the neighborhood of his London flat, after which he took yet another transatlantic journey. His body was cremated and the ashes were transported to the family plot in Cambridge where they were buried. A memorial to him has since been erected in Westminster Abbey.

In life James assumed what he called the "terrible burden" and chose England rather than America. But in death both England and America have chosen him.

Afterword

———⟫•◦•⟪———

Henry James's momentous visit to the United States took place in 1904–05, a time when national interest in the West, strong though it had always been, intensified dramatically. In those years the original journals of the Lewis and Clark expedition of one hundred years before were published for the first time and in the same period, Reuben Gold Thwaites, the editor of the eight Lewis and Clark volumes, also edited and published a thirty-two volume set of *Early Western Travels 1748–1846*. Rough-riding Teddy Roosevelt was in the White House, the Pacific cable had just been completed, the digging of the Panama Canal had commenced. The history of the United States seemed, in effect, to be a travel narrative, the story of a people accomplishing the great journey from the Atlantic seaboard to the Pacific and then beyond.

Given this master narrative, it is tempting also to see the main tradition in American travel literature as the story of the venture into the West. And certainly in addition to the multitude of explorers' and early settlers' accounts such as Thwaites edited, there are a number of more distinguished, consciously literary works that carry this theme. Even so sophisticated a cosmopolite as Washington Irving took it up. In 1832, after seventeen years abroad during which he had exploited to the full the poetic associations of England, Germany, and especially Spain, he returned to America and with a shrewd sense of how to rehabilitate his reputation as a great American author made a journey west out of St. Louis. The result was *A Tour of the Prairies* (1835), a work that has never since been out of print. In the next decade two other classics of American travel in the West joined that book, Richard Henry Dana's *Two Years Before the Mast* (1840) and Francis Parkman's *The California and Oregon Trail* (1849). And to the same list of western travel narratives of high literary merit as well as historical interest can be added the lesser known *Commerce of the Prairies* (1844) by Josiah Gregg and the far lesser known *Narrative of an Expedition across the Great Southwestern Prairies* (1844) by George W. Kendall, both of which deserve reclamation.

Yet as the works that formed the substance of this book indicate, a tradition of greater literary quality and at least equal cultural importance is formed by those American travelers who wrote of other societies, primitive and civilized, reported on their everyday activities, social beliefs, political systems, and works of imagination, and described the texture of landscapes domesticated by centuries of human settlement and those that defied a human presence.

The literature of western travel celebrated America's unique features and in so doing encouraged provincial self-satisfaction in the face of a wider world. The literature of travel abroad, however, attached America to that world. It pointed up the many advantages Americans enjoyed under the democratic system peculiar to them. But it also revealed that a great deal of what they regarded as the American and therefore the natural way of meeting the demands of daily life was arbitrary, in some cases not so rewarding as the way other peoples met those demands, and in other cases downright deleterious. In this literature America's remarkable material progress was not measured as

Americans looking in the mirror measured it, in terms of the breathtaking speed with which other nations had been overtaken and left behind, but was weighed comparatively against cultures such as that Taylor experienced in family life in Frankfurt, Twain in the thronging streets of Ceylon, James at twilight in the marketplace of Le Mans; in terms, that is, of the contentments within daily living that eluded the American scramble for success. Great works of art might eventually be brought to America by the profits from its astonishing material progress, but travel writers although they reported upon pyramids and pictures also rendered what it meant to inhabit a culture.

In *Letters of An American Farmer,* written on the eve of the American Revolution, Hector St. John de Crèvecoeur defined "this new man," the American, by dramatizing the unlimited social and material opportunities open to those immigrants who in Europe had been confined by birth to lives of labor, with no prospect of owning property or possessing political rights. In America, however, they achieved a new identity. "*Ubi panis, ibi patria,*" said Crèvecoeur, and after the bread earned through hard work, the model American he depicted soon acquired property, social standing, the franchise, and local political office.

But geographical distance and a radical change in social and material conditions do not annihilate cultural continuity although they may repress it. In the same period that Crèvecoeur was farming in New York, one John Jones farming on the nearby Pennsylvania frontier wrote a letter in Welsh to a kinsman in Wales. He began by saying, "I have heard my father speak much about old Wales, but I was born in this woody region, this new world," after which he rolled out a string of Welsh place names—Llanuchllyn, Hafodfadog, Cwm Tir y Manach—"because it affords me great delight even to think of them, although I do not know what kind of places they are; and indeed I much long to see them."[1] For Jones, as for a measureless host of the children of immigrants who constituted the nation, to be American was to be at a distance from their profoundest sense of origin.

The American experience at large was the experience of a movement away from the Old World and into a series of frontiers that shaped the composite nationality of the American people. But whatever the shape given to the visible American character by the American experience, for each individual a fundamental, invisible sense of self was incomplete without attachment to a deeper source. A tree is known to observers by its leaves, but a tree knows itself by its roots.

F. Scott Fitzgerald splendidly concluded *The Great Gatsby* by characterizing the "fresh green breast of the new world" that flowered once for the Dutch sailors who in 1609 sailed past Long Island to the mouth of the Hudson. Man, he said, was then "face to face for the last time in history with something commensurate to his capacity for wonder." The eloquence of the passage compels assent. Yet as wave after wave of immigrants arrived in the new world a psychological undertow of return set in and if the capacity for wonder was diminished with each wave that broke upon the shore the undertow of a desired return of the spirit to a world of origins was increased. For a European, African, Asian, travel abroad is travel away from home, but for an American it is also travel toward it.

Varied as their declared motives were, at a level beneath articulation the undertow of return drew Ledyard, Stephens, Taylor, Twain, and James forth on their travels. The books they constructed from those travels beguiled American readers with their depictions of the old and the exotic, everything that America was not. Yet their hold on the imagination finally derives from the unfolding sense that the venerable and the foreign do not contrast with the raw and the familiar but are, rather, their buried halves.

Notes

⟶»◦«⟵

INTRODUCTION

1. The Memorial is printed in Hellmut Lehman-Haupt, *The Book in America* (New York: R. R. Bowker Company, 1939), p. 88.

2. Ibid, p. 90.

3. The edition of Ledyard's *Journal* cited throughout the following pages is *John Ledyard's Journal of Captain Cook's Last Voyage,* ed. James Kenneth Munford with an introduction by Sinclair H. Hitchings (Corvallis: Oregon State University Press, 1963). The excellent introduction serves as the chief secondary source for the biographical information in these pages. Also important is Jared Sparks, *Life of John Ledyard, The American Traveler* (Boston: Little, Brown and Company, 1864), which Sparks compiled in 1827.

4. John Rickman, *Journal of Captain Cook's Last Voyage to the Pacific Ocean* (Readex Microprint, 1966), p. 382. This is a facsimile of the 1781 edition.

5. See the foreword to the facsimile of the Rickman *Journal.*

6. The spirit but not the letter; international copyright legislation would not arrive for more than another hundred years. Further amusement, irony may be too heavy a term, attaches to the fact that Rickman's data was not

always accurate so that a portion of what Ledyard copied verbatim is in error.

7. Christine Holmes, ed., *Captain Cook's Final Voyage, The Journal of Midshipman George Gilbert* (Honolulu: University Press of Hawaii, 1982).

8. Marshall Sahlins, *How "Natives" Think: About Captain Cook For Example* (Chicago: University of Chicago Press, 1995), p. 45.

9. Most notably Sarah Kemble Knight's journal of her travel in 1704, first published in 1825, and Dr. Alexander Hamilton's "itinerarium" of his 1744 journey, first published in 1948.

10. Of travelers in general, Michel Butor observed, "They travel in order to write, they travel while writing, because for them travel *is* writing," in "Travel and Writing," *Mosaic,* VIII/1 (1974), p. 14.

11. This idea is set forth in Eric J. Leed, *The Mind of the Traveler: From Gilgamesh to Global Tourism* (New York: Basic Books, 1991), p. 10.

12. Quoted from Thomas Law Nichols, *Forty Years of American Life, 1820–1861* by Wolfgang Von Hagen in *Maya Explorer, John Lloyd Stephens and the Lost Cities of Central America and Yucatán* (Norman: University of Oklahoma Press, 1947), p. 67n.

13. Claude Lévi-Strauss, *Tristes Tropiques,* trans. John and Doreen Weightman (New York: Viking Penguin, 1992), pp. 17–18.

14. Charles L. Batten, Jr., *Pleasurable Instruction, Form and Convention in Eighteenth-Century Literature* (Berkeley: University of California Press, 1978), p. 29.

CHAPTER ONE: JOHN LEDYARD

1. *John Ledyard's Journal,* p. xxiii.

2. Ibid, pp. xxii–xxiii.

3. David Samwell, surgeon's mate, quoted in Richard Hough, *Captain James Cook* (New York: W. W. Norton & Company, 1955), p. 280.

4. *John Ledyard's Journal,* p. xl.

5. Rickman, *Journal,* p. 148.

6. As pointed out by Hitchings in *John Ledyard's Journal,* p. xliii.

7. The word "discover" is consciously used despite the fussy claim that its use is insulting because it implies that the natives of the discovered lands did not exist until they were discovered. To discover means to expose to view and this the discoverers certainly did.

8. Rickman, *Journal,* p. 114.

9. Holmes, *Gilbert,* p. 33.

10. The details in this paragraph are drawn from the introduction to Stephen D. Watrous, ed., *John Ledyard's Journey Through Russia and Siberia,*

1787–1788: The Journal and Selected Letters (Madison: University of Wisconsin Press, 1966).

11. *The Papers of Thomas Jefferson,* ed. Julian P. Boyd, et. al. (Princeton: Princeton University Press, 1950–58), 9:273.

12. Watrous, ed., *John Ledyard's Journey,* p. 102. Unless otherwise indicated all page references to Ledyard's writing that follow are to this edition.

13. *Proceedings of the Association for Promoting the Discovery of the Interior Parts of Africa* (London: W. Bulmer and Co., 1810), 1:17.

14. Harold B. Carter, *Sir Joseph Banks, 1743–1820* (London: British Museum, 1988), p. 242.

15. *Proceedings,* p. 18.

16. John Barrell, "Death on the Nile: Fantasy and the Literature of Tourism 1840–1860," *Essays in Criticism,* Vol. XLI, No. 2 (April 1991), p. 99.

17. Mary Louise Pratt, "Scratches on the Face of the Country; or, What Mr. Barrow Saw in the Land of the Bushmen," *Critical Inquiry* 12 (Autumn, 1985), p. 127.

CHAPTER TWO: JOHN LLOYD STEPHENS

1. All four Stephens titles begin with the phrase *Incidents of Travel* and the latter two titles both include the word *Yucatan*. In the interest of clarity and concision, each work will be referred to by the first place name mentioned in the title; viz, *Egypt, Greece, Central America,* and *Yucatan.* Stephens himself used the Spanish accent when talking of the "Yucatán" but his modern editors have not and the accent will be omitted except when it appears in quoted material.

2. Jeremy A. Sabloff, foreword to John Lloyd Stephens, *Incidents of Travel in Central America, Chiapas, and Yucatan,* ed. Karl Ackerman (Washington: Smithsonian Institution Press, 1993), p. xiii.

3. Norman Hammond, *Ancient Maya Civilization* (New Brunswick: Rutgers University Press, 1982), p. 15.

4. The factual details of Stephens's life are taken from Victor Wolfgang Von Hagen, *Maya Explorer, John Lloyd Stephens and the Lost Cities of Central America and Yucatán* (Norman: University of Oklahoma Press, 1947).

5. Michael Davit Bell, "Conditions of Literary Vocation," in Sacvan Bercovitch, ed., *Cambridge History of American Literature, Volume Two: Prose Writings 1820–1865* (New York: Cambridge University Press, 1995), p. 18.

6. Von Hagen is here quoting from Thomas Law Nichols, *Forty Years of American Life, 1820–1861* (1937).

7. *The Works of Edgar Allan Poe* (Philadelphia: John D. Morris & Company, 1902), 7:108.

8. *Incidents of Travel in Egypt, Arabia Petraea, and the Holy Land* (New York: Harper & Brothers, 1838) 1:vi.

9. Daniel J. Boorstin, *The Image: A Guide to Pseudo-Events in America* (New York: Vintage Books, 1992), p. 275. First edition, 1961.

10. On this topic see Lawrence W. Levine, *Highbrow/Lowbrow* (Cambridge, Mass.: Harvard University Press, 1988).

11. See Eric J. Leed, *The Mind of the Traveler: From Gilgamesh to Global Tourism* (New York: Basic Books, 1991), p. 145.

12. *Incidents of Travel in Greece, Turkey, Russia, and Poland* (New York: Harper & Brothers, 1838). This too went into numerous editions within a year of its appearance.

13. See E. S. Bates, *Touring in 1600: A Study of the Development of Travel as a Means of Education* (Boston: Houghton Mifflin Company, 1912).

14. On this subject see the excellent book by Dennis Porter, *Haunted Journeys: Desire and Transgression in European Travel Writing* (Princeton: Princeton University Press, 1991). As he writes, "at one level, most forms of travel at least cater to desire: they seem to promise or allow us to fantasize the satisfaction of drives that for one reason or another is denied us at home. As a result, not only is travel fueled by desire, it also embodies powerful transgressive impulses" (p. 9).

15. N. P. Willis, *Pencillings by the Way* (Philadelphia: Carey, Lea, and Blanchard, 1836), 2:123.

16. Victor Wolfgang Von Hagen, *Frederick Catherwood Archt.* (New York: Oxford University Press, 1950), p. 50. Details of the life of Catherwood are based on this book and on Norman Hammond, *Ancient Maya Civilization*.

17. Introduction to Von Hagen's *Catherwood,* p. xv.

18. The edition cited in the following pages is that edited by Victor Wolfgang Von Hagen (Norman: University of Oklahoma Press, 1962), 2 vols.

19. John Lloyd Stephens, "An Hour with Alexander von Humboldt," *Literary World* (1847), p. 152.

20. Facts and conjectures about the railroad are based on David McCullough, *The Path Between the Seas* (New York: Simon and Schuster, 1977) and Joseph L. Schott, *Rails Across Panama* (Indianapolis: Bobbs-Merrill, 1967).

CHAPTER THREE: BAYARD TAYLOR

1. *Life and Letters of Bayard Taylor,* ed. Marie Hansen-Taylor and Horace E. Scudder (Boston: Houghton, Mifflin and Company, 1884), 1:227.

2. John Richie Schultz, ed., *The Unpublished Letters of Bayard Taylor in the Huntington Library* (San Marino: Huntington Library Publications, 1937), p. v. With such an outlook as their organizing principle, Taylor's two major

biographers each produced useful studies in the sociology of a literary career: Albert H. Smyth, *Bayard Taylor,* in the "American Men of Letters" series (Boston: Houghton Mifflin and Company, 1896), and Richard Croom Beatty, *Bayard Taylor: Laureate of the Gilded Age* (Norman: University of Oklahoma Press, 1936). I have drawn details of Taylor's life and times from these works as well as from Paul C. Wermuth's sketchier *Bayard Taylor* (New York: Twayne Publishers, 1973).

3. James Clifford, "Traveling Cultures," in Lawrence Grossberg et al., eds., *Cultural Studies* (New York: Routledge, 1992), p. 108.

4. Bayard Taylor, *Life and Landscapes from Egypt to the Negro Kingdoms of the White Nile* (London: Sampson Low, Son, & Co., 1854), p. 307.

5. This applies especially to Taylor's fascination with Muslim societies and in considering this I follow the lead of Edward W. Said's *Orientalism* (New York: Vintage Books, 1979). What he says (p. 160) in analysis of the book of the Orientalist Edward William Lane informs my view of Taylor's books on the Orient.

6. Bayard Taylor, *John Godfrey's Fortunes* (New York: G. P. Putnam, Hurd and Houghton, 1864), p. 38.

7. Bayard Taylor, *Views A-Foot; or Europe Seen with Knapsack and Staff* (New York: G. P. Putnam's Sons, 1890), p. 147. This is the "Revised Household Edition."

8. Bayard Taylor, *Eldorado, or Adventures in the Path of Empire* (G. P. Putnam, 1862), p. 444.

9. Bayard Taylor, *Life and Landscapes from Egypt to the Negro Kingdoms of the White Nile, Being a Journey to Central Africa* (London: Sampson Low, Son, & Co., 1854), p. 2. This London edition reverses the American title and subtitle. The Putnam edition's title begins *A Journey to Central Africa* but the texts are the same.

10. Bayard Taylor, *Lands of the Saracen* (New York: G. P. Putnam, 1862), p. vi. This is the 20th edition. The first edition was published in 1855 and the letters that make up the book are dated 1852.

11. My account of the Perry expedition is based on the official version: Francis L. Hawks, ed., *Narrative of the Expedition of the American Squadron to the China Seas and Japan, Performed in the Years 1852, 1853, and 1854, Under the Command of Commodore M. C. Perry, United States Navy, By Order of the Government of the United States* (Washington: A. O. P. Nicholson, 1856), 3 vols., parenthetically cited as "Hawks." I also draw upon the notes by Sidney Wallach in his abridged edition of the *Narrative* (New York: Coward McCann, Inc., 1952).

12. Bayard Taylor, *A Visit to India, China and Japan in the Year 1853* (New York: G. P. Putnam, 1862), p. 281.
13. Bayard Taylor, *By-Ways of Europe* (New York: G. P. Putnam's Sons, 1889), p. 11. This is a volume in the "Household Edition"; the first edition appeared in 1869. Taylor's prefatory "Familiar Letter to the Reader," running twelve pages, is the longest reflection on travel writing he ever offered.
14. Bayard Taylor, *Northern Travel* (New York: G. P. Putnam & Sons, 1871), p. 26.
15. Bayard Taylor, *The Poetical Works* (Boston: Houghton Mifflin and Company, 1894), p. 214.

CHAPTER FOUR: MARK TWAIN

1. Bayard Taylor, *Egypt and Iceland in the Year 1874* (New York: G. P. Putnam's Sons, 1874), pp. 51–52.
2. Justin Kaplan, *Mr. Clemens and Mark Twain* (New York: Simon and Schuster, 1966), p. 228.
3. *Mark Twain's Autobiography* (New York: Harper & Brothers, 1924), 2 vols., 1:245.
4. Mark Twain, *A Tramp Abroad* (New York: Oxford University Press, 1996), p. 31. This and all other works by Twain in the "Oxford Mark Twain" are facsimiles of the first editions.
5. In his excellent study, *Traveling in Mark Twain* (Berkeley: University of California Press, 1987), Richard Bridgman suggests that the mind's associative wandering is analogous to travel. Speaking of his study, Bridgman writes, "As the looseness of the travel account provided a particularly receptive vehicle for such materials, this essay is obliged to think as much about psychological patterns as geographical ones" (p. 4).
6. Mark Twain, *Roughing It* (New York: Oxford University Press, 1996), p. 294.
7. Ade is quoted by Beverly R. David and Roy Sapirstein on p. 22 of their essay on illustrations appended to the Oxford *Roughing It.*
8. *Mark Twain's Travels with Mr. Brown,* ed. Franklin Walker & G. Ezra Dane (New York: Alfred A. Knopf, 1940), p. 136.
9. Mark Twain, *The Innocents Abroad* (New York: Oxford University Press, 1996), p. 93.
10. *Mark Twain's Letters from Hawaii,* ed. A. Grove Day (New York: Appleton-Century, 1966), p. 215.
11. In his introduction to *A Tramp Abroad,* p. xxxiii.
12. *Traveling with the Innocents Abroad,* ed. Daniel Morley McKeithan (Norman: University of Oklahoma Press, 1958), p. xi.
13. Mark Twain, *Life on the Mississippi* (New York: Oxford University Press, 1966), p. 66.

14. In *The Beaten Track, European Tourism, Literature, and the Ways to Culture, 1800–1918* (Oxford: Clarendon Press, 1993), James Buzzard has argued that travelers such as Twain describes himself to be, and tourists such as he observes, travel in order to convert the " 'culture' encountered through travel into exchangeable items, tokens of cultural accomplishment that are legal tender in the sign-market of personal acculturation at home. . . . Symbols of Europe become commodities that tourists exchange by displaying them to an audience, which responds (or is imagined to respond) by recognizing the tourist as a person of culture" (p. 225). This is persuasive; Twain abroad with the innocents admits as much when he talks of showing off back home. Moreover, as a writer of travel letters he does not even await the return home but "shows off" from the start.

15. *The Adams-Jefferson Letters,* ed. Lester J. Cappon (Chapel Hill: University of North Carolina Press, 1959), 2:502.

16. Beverly R. David & Ray Sapirstein, "Reading the Illustrations in *Roughing It,*" p. 28, appended to the Oxford edition, op. cit.

17. Quoted by James S. Leonard in his afterword to the Oxford edition of *A Tramp Abroad,* p. 6.

18. The definitive treatment of the sacralizing of art in America is Lawrence Levine, *Highbrow/Lowbrow* (Cambridge, Mass.: Harvard University Press, 1988).

19. Mark Twain, *Life on the Mississippi* (New York: Oxford University Press, 1996), p. 247.

20. Mark Twain, *Following the Equator* (New York: Cambridge University Press, 1996), p. 125.

21. Fred Kaplan, "Afterword" to *Following the Equator,* p. 1.

22. In New Zealand Twain is shown a lignified caterpillar with a plant growing out of the back of its neck, "a ghastly curiosity," and this kindles an invective that begins, "No caterpillar can deceive Nature. If this one couldn't suffer Nature would have known it, and would have hunted up another caterpillar. Not that she would have let this one go, merely because it was defective. No. She would have waited and let him turn into a night-moth; and then fried him in the candle" (p. 288).

CHAPTER FIVE: HENRY JAMES

1. Henry James, *A Small Boy and Others,* in *Henry James Autobiography,* ed. Frederick W. Dupee (New York: Criterion Books, 1956), pp. 32–33.

2. Leon Edel, *Henry James, The Conquest of London: 1870–1881* (Philadelphia: H. B. Lippincott Company, 1962), p. 70. This is the second of the five volumes of Edel's magisterial biography each of which bears a separate

descriptive title. Future references to this work, however, will be by author's name, volume number, and page number; the present citation in this format, for example, would be "Edel, 2:70."

3. I am greatly indebted to Richard Howard's excellent "Notes on the Text" appended to each of the two volumes he edited for the Library of America: *Henry James, Collected Travel Writings: Great Britain and America,* and *Henry James, Collected Travel Writings: The Continent,* both 1993. Hereafter these works will be referred to parenthetically as (CTWAm) and (CTWCon).

4. Henry James, *Hawthorne* (New York: St. Martin's Press, 1967), p. 76.

5. The sketch, "Old Ticonderoga, A Picture of the Past" appeared in the *American Monthly Magazine* in 1836 and was reprinted, with revisions, in the collection, *The Snow-Image and Other Tales* (1851).

6. Henry James, *A Little Tour in France,* ed. Leon Edel (New York: Farrar, Straus and Giroux, 1963), p. 116.

7. Henry James, *Transatlantic Sketches* (Boston: Houghton, Mifflin and Company, 1888), p. 126. Hereafter this book is referred to parenthetically as (TS).

8. Henry James, *Italian Hours,* ed. John Auchard (University Park: Pennsylvania State University Press, 1992), p. 133. Hereafter parenthetically referred to as (IH).

9. Edgar Allan Poe, "Sarah Margaret Fuller," in Edmund Wilson, *The Shock of Recognition* (New York: Farrar, Straus and Cudahy, 1955), p. 148.

10. "My Visit to Niagara" in Alfred Weber, Beth L. Lueck, and Dennis Berthold, *Hawthorne's American Travel Sketches* (Hanover, N.H.: University Press of New England, 1989), p. 55.

11. "Thoreau," *Selected Essays of Ralph Waldo Emerson.* ed. Larzer Ziff (New York: Penguin Books, 1982), p. 411.

12. Mark Schorer's fine essay, "Technique as Discovery," is too little read. It may be found in his book, *The World We Imagine* (New York: Farrar Straus and Giroux, 1968).

13. *The Selected Letters of Henry James,* ed. Leon Edel (New York: Farrar, Straus and Cudahy, 1955), pp. 67–68.

14. "From Normandy to the Pyrenees," first printed in *The Galaxy,* was reprinted in *Portraits of Places* and is here quoted from CTWCon, pp. 705 through 708.

15. Quotations from the English essays that follow are taken from *English Hours* (1905) as published in CTWAm and the page references are to that volume. But the dates assigned the essays are those of their original journal

publication even though the *English Hours* version may be slightly revised. Moreover, those essays written before 1883 had also appeared in book form that year in *Portraits of Places*.

16. Raymond Williams, *The Country and the City* (New York: Oxford University Press, 1973), p. 234.

17. Morton Dauwen Zabel, *The Art of Travel, Scenes and Journeys in America, England, France and Italy from the Travel Writings of Henry James* (Garden City: Doubleday Anchor, 1958), p. 37.

18. Henry James, "The Art of Fiction," *The Portable Henry James,* ed. Morton Dauwen Zabel (New York: Viking Press Inc., 1951), p. 403.

19. Henry James, *The American Scene,* ed. Leon Edel (Bloomington: Indiana University Press, 1968), p. 222.

20. See the introductory chapter of Sharon Cameron, *Thinking in Henry James* (Chicago: University of Chicago Press, 1989) for an acute analysis of this aspect of *The American Scene*.

21. In the Introduction to *The American Scene,* p. xvi.

AFTERWORD

1. The letter is reprinted in Albert Cook Myers, ed., *Narratives of Early Pennsylvania, West New Jersey, and Delaware* (New York: Charles Scribner's Sons, 1912).

Index

James, Henry, travel writing (continued)
dents," 233–34; selective approach
to, 232, 233; sense of past, 238–39;
social observation in, 242–45, 273–
76; on standard tourist itineraries,
232–33; subjectivity of, 228–29; publications: *The American Scene*, 224,
225, 237, 259–60, 266–78, 281; *English Hours*, 225, 246–52, 273; *Italian
Hours*, 225, 226, 252–59; *A Little Tour
in France*, 225, 259–66, 276; *Portraits
of Places*, 225, 252, 256; *Transatlantic
Sketches*, 224, 225, 245, 252, 270,
278

James, William, 222, 231
Japan, Perry's expedition to, 121, 132,
141–48
Jay, John, 38
Jefferson, Thomas, 19, 114, 191; correspondence with Ledyard, 37, 39, 44,
52; and death of Ledyard, 52–53; on
Ledyard, 36, 38–39; measuring
scheme of, 50; race theory of, 47; and
transcontinental crossing, 10, 33–34,
35–36
*John Ledyard's Journey Through Russia
and Siberia* (Watrous), 41
Johnson, Samuel, 21
Jones, John, 285
Jones, John Paul, 19, 34
*Journal of Captain Cook's Last Voyage to
the Pacific Ocean on Discovery Per-
formed in the Years 1776, 1777, 1778,
1779*, 4
*Journal of Captain Cook's Last Voyage to
the Pacific Ocean and in Quest of a
North-West Passage* (Ledyard), 4–6,
20–21, 26, 28–29
*Journal and Letters from France and
Great Britain* (Willard), 60
*Journey to Central Africa, or Life and
Landscapes from Egypt to the Negro

Kingdoms of the White Nile (Taylor),
132

Kaplan, Fred, 213
Kaplan, Justin, 176, 221
Kemble, Fanny, 276
Kendall, George W., 284
Kennedy, John Pendleton, 142, 143
King, James, 4, 26
"King Leopold's Soliloquy" (Twain), 219
Knickerbocker's History of New York
(Irving), 62

Laborde, Leon, 72
Lafayette, Marquis de, 19, 36
*Lands of the Saracen: or Pictures of Pal-
estine, Asia Minor, Sicily, and Spain*
(Taylor), 132, 136–37
Ledyard, John, 119, 134, 145, 157; African journey of, 49–52; American identity of, 2–3, 9–10, 45, 46; in British
army, 1, 10, 18; characterized, 19;
connection with Melville, 30, 40; on
Cook's voyage (*See* Cook's third voyage); and copyright protection, 3–4, 5,
6; at Dartmouth, 17–18; death of, 52–
54; democratic ideals of, 15, 45; desertion from British frigate, 3; financial backers of, 34, 36–37, 39, 55; fur
trade scheme of, 31–34, 55; Jefferson
on, 36, 38–39; lack of scientific training, 47–48; among Native Americans,
18, 27–30, 56; on native cultures, 23–
26, 28–30, 44, 55–56; on polygenetic
race theory, 47; publication of Journal, 4–5; Russian journey of, 36–45,
46, 165; at slave market, 51; transcontinental travel plan of, 34–36; as
travel writer, 5–6, 9, 20, 47, 48, 56–
57; on women, 45
Leed, Eric J., 116
Leggett, William, 86